POLITICAL LIBELS

Political Libels:
A Comparative Study

IAN LOVELAND
Professor of Law, City University

·H A R T·
PUBLISHING
OXFORD – PORTLAND OREGON
2000

Hart Publishing
Oxford and Portland, Oregon

Published in North America (US and Canada) by
Hart Publishing c/o
International Specialized Book Services
5804 NE Hassalo Street
Portland, Oregon
97213-3644
USA

Distributed in the Netherlands, Belgium and Luxembourg by
Intersentia, Churchillaan 108
B2900 Schoten
Antwerpen
Belgium

Hart Publishing Ltd is a specialist legal publisher based in Oxford, England.
To order further copies of this book or to request a list of other
publications please write to:

Hart Publishing Ltd, Salter's Boatyard,
Folly Bridge, Abingdon Road, Oxford OX1 4LB
Telephone: +44 (0)1865 245533 or Fax: +44 (0)1865 794882
e-mail: mail@hartpub.co.uk
www.hartpub.co.uk

British Library Cataloguing in Publication Data
Data Available
ISBN 1 84113–115–6 (cloth)

Typeset by Hope Services (Abingdon) Ltd.
Printed in Great Britain on acid-free paper
by Bookcraft (Bath) Ltd., Midsomer Norton

Contents

Preface	ix
List of Cases	xi
List of Statutes	xvi
1. Introduction	1
The Basics of English Libel Law	3
The Nature and Proof of the Loss	3
Defences	7
Justification	7
Absolute and Qualified Privilege	8
Qualified Privilege	8
Absolute Privilege	11
Fair Comment	12
Damages	13
Criminal Libel	14
Slander	15
Malicious Falsehood	15
Conclusion	16
2. The Common Law and Political Libels in Nineteenth- and Early Twentieth-Century Britain	19
The *Stockdale* v. *Hansard* Controversy	21
'Political Information'—a Narrower Perspective	22
The English Common Law in the Early Democratic Era	24
Campbell v. *Spottiswoode*	24
Wason v. *Walter*	26
Purcell v. *Sowler*	30
Davis v. *Shepstone* and *Alexander* v. *Jenkins*	32
Manchester Corp. v. *Williams*	34
An Absolute Protection for Libellous Statements and Publications Made during 'Debates or Proceedings in Parliament'	36
Conclusion	36
3. American Perspectives on Political Libels in the Early Democratic Era	37
Kansas—*Coleman* v. *Maclennan*	37
Illinois	41
Pennsylvania	43

Iowa	45
An Absolute and Constitutional Protection for Libels of Government Bodies	46
Conclusion	48
4. The English Common Law in the Early Years of the Modern Democratic Era	51
Braddock v. *Bevins*	52
Trades Unions as Non-political Actors	54
A Commonwealth Innovation?	55
The Defamation Act 1952	56
Against Informed Consent?	58
A Radical Reform to the Common Law? *Webb* v. *Times Publishing*	59
Truth (NZ) v. *Holloway*	61
Conclusion	63
5. *Sullivan* v. *The New York Times*	65
The Appeal to the US Supreme Court	66
The Judgment	67
A Balancing Test, Not an Absolute Principle	70
Conclusion	71
Extending the Doctrine	72
Remedial Considerations	72
From Elected to Appointed Officials . . .	73
. . . to Matters of Interest to the Public . . .	74
. . . to Political and Public Figures . . .	76
. . . to Candidates for Office	77
Recklessness—a Subjective or Objective Test?	78
Narrowing the Reach and Effect of the *Sullivan* Defence	80
Conclusion	83
6. The *Sullivan* Principle in 'English' Law	87
On Damages	87
Political Libels in the 1970s and 1980s—Dynamic and Static Conceptions of the Common Law	92
Bognor Regis UDC v. *Campion*	93
Horrocks v. *Lowe*	95
Blackshaw v. *Lord*	96
Templeton v. *Jones*	99
The Report of the Faulks Committee	100
Conclusion	101
The Requirements of the European Convention on Human Rights	101
Political Libels and Article 10 ECHR	102
The First Wave of Convention Case Law	104

Political Defamation and Article 10 ECHR—The Second Wave of   107
  Cases
  Lingens v. *Austria*   108
  Barfod v. *Denmark*   110
  Oberschlick v. *Austria*   111
  Castells v. *Spain*   112
  Thorgeirson v. *Iceland*   113
Conclusion   114

7. English Law—the First Phase of Reform   115
The Identity of the Plaintiff—*Derbyshire County Council* v. *Times*   117
  Newspapers
  The High Court   117
  The Court of Appeal   118
  The House of Lords   120
  The Weaknesses of the Judgment   121
Extending the *Derbyshire* Principle—Political Parties   123
The Heads of Damage and Quantum of Damages   125
  Rantzen v. *Mirror Group Newspapers*   126
  Tolstoy v. *United Kingdom*   128
  Elton John v. *Mirror Group Newspapers*   129
Conclusion—Making a Mess of Libel Law Reform?   132

8. *Sullivan* v. *The New York Times* in Australia   133
Reducing the Chilling Effect   134
A Constitutional Obstacle to Political Libel Actions   136
  Theophanous v. *The Herald and Weekly Times*   138
  In Dissent   142
  Stephens v. *West Australia Newspapers Ltd*   144
From Constitutional to Common Law Protection—*Lange* v. *ABC*   147
  The judgment   147
Conclusion   150

9. English Law—the Second Phase of Reform?   153
Further Developments before the ECHR   153
The Defamation Act 1996   156
  The Terms of the Act   157
Lange in New Zealand   159
  The High Court   160
  The Court of Appeal   162
Reynolds v. *Times Newspapers*   163
  The High Court   164
  The Court of Appeal   165
  The House of Lords   169

viii   *Contents*

10. Conclusion   177

Bibliography   185
Index   189

Preface

This book expands upon and lends a more coherent character to a series of journal articles and essays I have written since 1994 on the issue of political libels. Much of that work has been comparative in nature, and has been written primarily to critique the way in which Parliament and the English courts have addressed this issue over the past 100 years. This version of that critique is written in the style of an extended essay, and attempts to revisit some of those articles in the light of a more sophisticated analytical perspective which I have developed as I have become more familiar with the areas of law concerned.

The thesis advanced in the book is a simple one—namely that English law has in the main been too jealous of defending the reputations of politicians and insufficently alert to the legitimate interest of the electorate in consuming political information about those who govern us. It will be suggested that a strong case can be made for reforming the law substantially; a case which rests both on experience that may be drawn from other jurisdictions and on a rather unorthodox re-reading of a handful of English libel decisions from the mid-to-late nineteeth century whose significance has been downplayed by lawyers in subsequent years.

I owe thanks to Anthony Lester QC and Emma Dixon, of Blackstone Chambers, for providing me with counsel's skeleton arguments in *Reynolds*, and to John Lowry—a colleague at Brunel—for alerting me to some aspects of tort law with which I was unfamiliar. Once again, I must also thank Richard Hart for his enthusiastic and efficient support for the project. Any errors which remain in the text are of course my responsibilty.

IAN LOVELAND

London, June 1999

Table of Cases

Abrams v United States (1919) 250 US 616..47, 67
Alexander v Jenkins [1892] 1 QB 797 32–4
Ambrosious v O'Farrell (1905) 199 Ill App 265......................41, 42, 48, 80, 123
Arrowsmith v UK (1981) 3 EHRR 218 106
Associated Newspapers Group Ltd v Wade [1979] 1 WLR 697 1076
Associated Press v US 326 US 1..68
Attorney-General v BBC [1981] AC 303 106
Attorney-General v Guardian Newspapers Ltd (No 2) (*Spycatcher* No 2)
    [1988] 3 All ER 545..115, 126
Australian Capital Television v Commonwealth of Australia (1991–2) 177
    CLR 106 ....136, 137, 139, 142, 144

Balch case *see* State v Balch
Barfod v Denmark (1989) 11 EHRR 493 ....110–11, 114, 153, 155, 178
Bays v Hunt (1882) 60 Iowa 251; 14 NW 785 45
Beauharnais v Illinios (1952) 343 US 250 103
Blackshaw v Lord [1984] 1 QB 9 (CA)................96–99, 100, 101, 105, 106, 108,
                                                              123, 154, 166, 173, 179
Bognor Regis UDC v Campion [1972] 2 QB 169..............93, 94, 95, 96, 98, 101,
                                                              104, 114, 118, 121, 123, 161
Braddock v Bevins [1948] 1 All ER 450 ....52–4, 56, 58, 61, 98, 99,
                                                              100, 161, 162
Brandenburg v Ohio (1969) 395 US 444 ....67, 103
Bridges v California 314 US 252..68
Brind [1991] 1 All ER 720 126
Briggs v Garrett (1886) 11 PA 406; 2 ATL 513......................43, 44, 45, 119, 169
Broadway Approvals v Odhams Press [1965] 2 All ER 523 90
Broome v Casels & Co [1971] 2 All ER 187..90, 91, 104
Brown v Board of Education (1954) 347 US 483 ....65, 66, 77

Campbell v Spottiswoode (1863) 3 B & S 769..............13, 24–26, 29, 30, 31, 32,
                                                              36, 49, 60, 61, 95, 97, 100, 160, 163, 169
Campion case *see* Bognor Regis UDC v Campion Capital and
    Counties Bank v Henry (1880) 5 CPD 514..11, 40
Carson v John Fairfax & Sons Ltd (1992) 178 CLR 44...........134, 135, 136, 153
Castells v Spain (1992) 14 EHRR 445..............................112–13, 114, 119, 129
Chalmers v Payne (1835) 2 CM & R 156 10
Cheney v Conn [1968] 1 WLR 242..102

Chicago *v* Tribune Co (1923) 139 NE 87 ....46, 49, 66, 67, 70, 94, 113, 117,
                                                118, 119, 120, 122, 123, 140, 181
Church of Scientology *v* Johnson-Smith [1972] 1 All ER 379 157
Clarke *v* Taylor (1836) 3 Scott 95 7
Coleman *v* McClennan (1908) 98 Pac 281 ....37, 38, 50, 62, 64, 66, 67, 69, 70,
                                71, 72, 75, 76, 84, 85, 100, 112, 114, 117, 119,
                                    120, 146, 148, 154, 162, 165, 174, 178, 183
Cook *v* Alexander [1973] 3 All ER 1037 ....92, 93
Coyne *v* Citizen Foinance Ltd (1991) 172 CLR 211................................135
Curtis *v* Butts, Associated Press *v* Walker (1967) 388 US 130.......76, 77, 78, 80, 156
Curry *v* Walter (1796) 1 Esp 456..5, 6, 10

Davis *v* Shepstone (1886) 11 App Cas 187................................32–4, 39, 62
Davison *v* Duncan (1857) 7 E & B 229..22, 30, 31, 55
De Buse *v* McCarthy [1942] 1 KB 156 ....51, 52, 53
De Crespigny *v* Wellesley (1829) 5 Bing 392..4
De Haes and Gisjels *v* Belgium (1997) 25 EHRR 1 ....153, 154, 155, 156, 163
Derbyshire County Council *v* Times Newspapers [1992] 4 All ER 795;
    [1992] 3 All ER 65 (CA); [1993] 1 All ER 1011 (HL)............117–23, 124, 126,
                                    128, 131, 132, 143, 151, 161, 165, 182
Desmond *v* Thorne [1983] 1 WLR 163..106
Die Spoorbond *v* South African Railways [1946] AD 999 121
Dillon *v* Balfour 20 LR Ire 600 ....36, 156
Dingle *v* Associated Newspapers [1960] 1 All ER 294...................................157
Dingle *v* Foot [1960] 1 All ER 294..157
Duncan *v* Thwaites (1824) 3 B & C 577 ....10, 27
Duncombe *v* Daniel (1837) 8 Car & P 222 ....20, 26, 53, 98

Edwards *v* Bell (1824) 1 Bing 403..7
Express Printing Co *v* Copeland (1895) 64 Tex 354......................................48

Friedell *v* Blakely Printing Co (1925) 203 NW 974..48

Garrison *v* Louisiana (1965) 379 US 64 ....70, 72, 73, 111, 178
Gay News *v* United Kingdom (1982) 4 EHRR 123......................................106
Gertz *v* Robert Welch Inc (1974) 418 US 323............80, 81, 82, 83, 85, 101, 110,
                                                116, 125, 131, 161
Gillian case *see* National Union of General and Municipal
    Workers *v* Gillian
Gitlow *v* New York (1925) 268 US 652..37, 67, 103
Gleaves *v* Deakin [1979] 2 All ER 497 106
Goldsmith *v* Bhoyrul [1997] 4 All ER 268 ....123, 125, 182
Greenlands Ltd *v* Wilmshurst and London Association for the Protection of
    Trade [1913] 3 KB 507..87

Handyside *v* UK 1 EHRR 737 ....106, 107, 109

Harman *v* Secretary of State for the Home Department [1983] 1 AC 280 106

Hector *v* Attorney-General of Antigua and Barbuda [1990]
    2 All ER 103 ....116, 117, 118, 121

Hill case see Time Inc *v* Hill

Horrocks *v* Lowe [1975] AC 135....................95–96, 97, 101, 104, 161, 163, 167

Hulton *v* Jones [1910] AC 20...57

Jackson *v* Pittsburgh Times (1893) 152 PA 406; 25 ATL 613..........................45

John (Elton) *v* Mirror Group Newspapers Ltd [1996]
    2 All ER 35 (CA)..129–32, 153

King *v* Root (1829) 4 Wend (NY) 114 40

Klos *v* Zahorik (1900) 84 NW 1046 45

Lake *v* King (1680) 1 Saund 131..12

Lange *v* ABC (1997) 71 ALJR 818.....................147–50, 153, 160, 163, 164, 165,
                                        166, 167, 168, 170, 172, 180, 183

Lange *v* Atkinson [1997] 2 NZLR 22 (HC); [1998] 3 NZLR 424 (CA) ....
                                        159–63, 164, 165, 166, 182

Lewis *v* Daily Telegraph Ltd [1962] 3 All ER 698..88

Lingens *v* Austria (No 1) App No 8303/79, 26 D & R 171;
    (1986) 8 EHRR 407..........105, 106, 107, 108–10, 111, 112, 114, 116, 118, 119,
                                        120, 129, 155, 156, 162, 166, 168, 174, 178, 183

Lingens v Austria (No 2) (1991) 19 EHRR 389 111

McCarey *v* Associated Newspapers Ltd [1964]
    3 All ER 947 ....89, 90, 91, 115, 128, 130, 184

MacIntosh *v* Dunn [1908] AC 390..62, 97

Manchester Corporation *v* Williams [1891] 1 QB 94 ....34–5, 47, 54, 92,
                                        93, 114, 118

Manson *v* Associated Newspapers [1965] 2 All ER 954 90

Marks *v* Baker (1881) 9 NW 678...48

Merivale *v* Carson (1887) 20 QBD 275..13

Metropolitan Saloon Omnibus Co Ltd *v* Hawkins (1859) 4 H & N 87;
    [1843–60] All ER Rep 430...34

Miami Herald *v* Tornillo (1974) 418 US 241 ....150, 183

Monitor Patriot *v* Roy (1971) 401 US 265 ....78, 156, 178

Morse *v* Times Republican Printing Co (1904) 124 Iowa 707; 100 NW 867....45

Mortenson *v* Peters (1906) 14 SLT 227...102

Myers *v* Longstaff (1900) 84 NW 233 48

National Union of General and Municipal Workers *v* Gillian [1945]
    2 All ER 593..54, 55, 94

Nationwide News *v* Wills (1991–2) 177 CLR 1 ....136, 139, 142, 144
Newstead *v* London Express Newspapers [1940] 1 KB 377 ....57, 88

O'Rourke *v* Publishing Co (1896) 36 Atl 398...48
Oberschlick *v* Austria (No 1) (1991) 19 EHRR 389...........111–12, 114, 155, 162
Oberschlick *v* Austria (No 2) (1997) 25 EHRR 357 ....155, 156, 162
Ogren *v* Rockford Star (1925) 237 Ill App 349...................................12, 42, 80
Otto-Preminger Institut *v* Austria (1995) 23 EHR 34 155

Palko *v* Conecticut (1908) 302 US 319 103
Palmer *v* Concord (1881) 48 NH 211 48
Parmiter *v* Coupland (1840) 6 M & W 105 3
Pepper *v* Hart [1993] 1 All ER 42..29
Perera *v* Peiris [1949] AC 1 ....55, 56, 57, 61, 64
Phillips *v* London and South Western Railway Co (1879) 5 QBD 78 ....87, 88
Plummer *v* Charman [1962] 3 All ER 823..63
Posnett *v* Marble (1890) 20 Atl 813..48
Post Publishing Co *v* Hallam (1893) 59 Fed 530 40
Praed *v* Graham (1889) 24 QBD 53..87
Prebble *v* Television New Zealand Ltd [1994] 3 NZLR 1 ....156, 157, 158
Press Co Ltd *v* Stewart (1888) 119 Pa 584; 14 ATL 51....................................44
Purcell *v* Sowler (1876) 1 CPD 781; (1877) 2 CPD 215 (CA) 30–2, 33, 34,
                                                         59, 92, 93, 97, 98, 99, 173

R *v* Lee (1804) 5 Esp 123..6, 10, 23, 31, 45
R *v* Wright (1799) 8 TR 292.......................5, 6, 10, 19, 21, 22, 23, 27, 28, 30, 55
Rantzen *v* Mirror Group Newspapers [1993] 4 All ER 975 ....125, 126–8,
                                                                 129, 130, 134, 135
Reynolds *v* Times Newspapers [1998] 3 All ER 961 ....163–74, 177
Rookes *v* Barnard [1964] 1 All ER 367 ....88, 89, 90, 91, 115, 130, 131
Rosenblatt *v* Baer (1966) 383 US 75 ....73, 74, 77, 78
Roth *v* United States 354 US 476...68

St Amant *v* Thompson (1968) 390 US 727; 88 S Ct 1323 79
Salinger *v* Cowles (1922) 191 NW 167 ....46, 48, 111, 119, 178
Schenk *v* United States (1919) 249 US 47 ....47, 67, 103
Schering Chemicals Ltd *v* Falkman Ltd [1982] QB 1...................................106
Scott *v* Musial [1959] 3 All ER 429 88
Shurtleff *v* Stevens (1888) 31 Am Rep 698 48
Silkin *v* Beaverbrook Newspapers [1958] 1 WLR 743 ....58, 59, 63, 95, 166
Sim *v* Stretch [1936] 2 All ER 1237 3
South Hetton Coal *v* North Eastern News Association Ltd [1894]
    1 QB 133..35, 54, 94, 118
State *v* Balch (1884) 31 Kan 465; 2 Pac 609................................37, 38, 41, 66

State *v* Burnham (1842) 9 NH 34 48

State *v* Hoskins (1899) 109 Iowa 656; 80 NW 1063..................................45, 111

Stephens *v* West Australia Newspapers Ltd [1994] 68 ACJR 713 ....12, 144–6, 147, 148, 149, 168

Sullivan *v* New York Times (1964) 376 US 254.................64, 65–85, 87, 94, 100, 101, 103, 104, 105, 108, 112, 113, 114, 116, 117, 118, 119, 120, 122, 123, 131, 132, 133–51, 154, 156, 159, 160, 161, 163, 164, 165, 166, 173, 174, 177, 178, 180, 181, 182, 183

Sunday Times *v* United Kingdom 2 EHRR 245 ....103, 106, 126

Sutcliffe *v* Pressdram [1990] 1 All ER 269...115

Templeton *v* Jones [1984] 1 NZLR 448......................99–100, 159, 161, 163, 169

Theophanous *v* The Herald and Weekly Times (1994) 182 CLR 1094; (1994) 68 AJLR 713 ....138–44, 145, 147, 148, 149, 150, 151, 153, 160, 181

Thorgeirson *v* Iceland (1992) 14 EHRR 843................................113–14, 154

Thorley *v* Lord Kerry (1812) 4 Taunt 355 14

Time Inc *v* Firestone (1976) 424 US 448 82

Time Inc *v* Hill (1967) 385 US 374 ....74, 75, 76, 77, 78, 80, 82, 83, 84, 156, 177, 178

Tolstoy *v* United Kingdom (1995) 20 EHRR 442.................128–9, 130, 136, 153

Toogood *v* Spryng (1834) 1 C M & R 181...............................8, 9, 43, 146, 160

Truth (NZ) Ltd *v* Holloway [1960] NZLR 69 ....61–3, 97, 99, 159, 161

Wakley *v* Cooke (1849) 4 Exch 511 7

Wason *v* Walter (1868) LR 4 QB 73...................26–30, 31, 32, 34, 36, 37, 38, 39, 52, 53, 54, 55, 56, 58, 59, 60, 63, 67, 72, 84, 92, 93, 98, 99, 100, 102, 139, 146, 148, 157, 160, 162, 173, 174

Webb *v* Times Publishing [1960] 2 QB 535.............59–61, 62, 63, 64, 67, 69, 87, 90, 92, 94, 96, 97, 98, 99, 104, 114, 154, 173

Willis *v* Brooks [1947] 1 All ER 191...55

Wingrove *v* United Kingdom (1996) 24 EHRR 1 155

Wright *v* Woodgate (1835) 2 C M & R 573...10

X *v* Germany App No 6988/75, 3 D & R 159..................104, 106, 107, 110, 166

Zoernesch *v* Waldock [1964] 1 WLR 675 (CA)...102

Table of Statutes

Australia

Constitution 133, 144
  s 51(xxxv) 137
Industrial Relations Act 1988
  s 299 136
  s 299(1) 136, 137
Political Broadcasts and Political Disclosures Act 1991
  s 95 138
  ss 95B–D 137
  ss 95F–R 138
New South Wales: Defamation Act 1974 134
Western Australia: Constitution 145

Austria

Criminal Code
  Art 111 ....105, 108, 109, 110, 111
  Art 115 155

Belgium

Penal Code 154
  Arts 275–276 153

Iceland

Penal Code
  Art 108 113

New Zealand

Bill of Rights Act 1990 ....160, 162
Electoral Act 1993 ....160, 162
Legislature Act 1908 156
Official Information Act 1982
  s 4 162

Spain

Criminal Code
  Art 161 112
  Art 162 112

United Kingdom
Bill of Rights 1689
   Art 9 ....12, 21, 26, 27, 59, 64, 156, 157, 158
Courts and Legal Services Act 1990
   s 8(1)..125, 126
   s 8(2)..125
Defamation Act 1952 ....56–8, 59, 64, 65
   ss 2–3 57
   ss 5–6 57
   s 5...57
   s 6...57
   s 7...57
   s 10 ....56, 57, 63
   Sch 1 ....57, 95
Defamation Act 1996..156–9
   s 13 ....158, 159
Great Reform Act 1832 19
Human Rights Act 1998..101, 177, 179
Libel Act 1792 4
Libel Act 1843
   s 6..14
Parliament Act 1911...51
Parliamentary Papers Act 1840...27, 29, 59, 64
   s 3...22, 157
Public Bodies Corrupt Practices Act 1889 34
Reform Act 1867..26, 29, 52

Rules of the Supreme Court
   Order 59, r 11(4)..125

United States of America
Constitution 103
   First Amendment 37, 102, 138, 165, 174, 183
   Fourteenth Amendment..174
Sedition Act 1798..47, 67

Illinois: Constitution
   Art 1, s 7 43
   Art 2, s 4 46
Kansas: Constitution, Bill of Rights
   Art 11 38
   Art 18 38
Pennsylvania: Constitution 43

European Community

European Convention on Human Rights (ECHR) 101, 102
    Art 6 104
    Art 10...102–104, 105, 106, 107–14, 115, 116, 119,
                           126, 127, 130, 131, 153, 154, 155, 177
    Art 10(2) 103, 104, 105, 106, 107, 109, 111, 154

1

Introduction

Few political careers have come so abruptly and spectacularly to grief as that of Jonathan Aitken. By the mid-1990s, after having spent many years on the Conservative backbenches, Aitken had progressed up the ministerial ladder with dazzling speed and served in the Major cabinet as Chief Secretary to the Treasury. He then resigned from the Cabinet in order to pursue a libel action against *The Guardian* newspaper, which had run several stories accusing him of unethical financial dealings. The case suddenly collapsed shortly after the trial began when *The Guardian* fortuitously (and—at least to Aitken—wholly unexpectedly) uncovered proof that Aitken was prepared to give perjured evidence in court, and had persuaded his co-plaintiff and his daughter to corroborate his lies on oath. Aitken lost his Commons seat at the 1997 general election. He subsequently pleaded guilty to charges of perjury and conspiracy to pervert the course of justice, and was sentenced to eighteen months' imprisonment.

Aitken's fall from grace was almost matched by that suffered by Neil Hamilton, the Conservative MP for Tatton and formerly a junior Minister in the Department of Trade and Industry. He too had been accused by *The Guardian* of financial malpractice by taking large, undeclared sums of money from the multi-millionaire businessman Mohammed Al-Fayed in return for political favours. He too began libel proceedings against *The Guardian*. These too were halted when Hamilton's co-plaintiff indicated that he could not support Hamilton's version of the facts. Hamilton's unwillingness to proceed cast obvious doubt on his honesty. Hamilton then lost his seat at the 1997 general election to the independent candidate, Martin Bell, who ran on an anti-corruption ticket.

One obvious question which arises from the Aitken and Hamilton episodes is how on earth Aitken and Hamilton thought they could get away with giving untrue evidence in court, or that they could win their libel cases, thereby vindicating their (evidently undeserved) reputation for political integrity and financial probity, and perhaps pocket a substantial sum in damages as well. The answer to the question is a simple one. The English law of libel in the mid-1990s made it extremely easy for a wealthy politician plaintiff to succeed in an action against a newspaper which cast aspersions on his/her honesty or integrity, even if the plaintiff knew full well that the attacks on his/her character were entirely accurate.

Many other sitting and former MPs had also initiated libel actions against media bodies in the late 1980s and early 1990s.[1] John Major had won a

---

[1] There is nothing to indicate that the MPs mentioned below were anything other than entirely honest in beginning such proceedings.

settlement against the *New Statesman* that threatened to bankrupt the magazine: the story concerned had reiterated rumours that he might be having an extra-marital affair. Michael Foot had extracted a similarly substantial settlement from *The Sunday Times* over a story accusing him of being a Soviet spy. Peter Bottomley recovered some £40,000 against *The Sunday Express* for an article accusing him of 'fraternising' with Sinn Fein. Paddy Ashdown was quick to act against a local West Country paper which aired allegations about his personal life. On the Labour benches, Keith Vaz announced he would sue both *The Sun* and *The Guardian* for repeating television programme allegations that he favoured segregationist housing policies. His colleague George Howarth accepted damages and an apology from *The Guardian* over an article falsely accusing him of drunken behaviour. Clare Short and Kevin McNamara received 'substantial damages' from *The Guardian* over a story suggesting they were sympathetic to the IRA. Even prospective MPs joined the litigation queue; the left-wing barrister Liz Davies, deselected by the NEC as a candidate for a Leeds seat, responded by commencing libel proceedings against a fellow Islington councillor for allegedly defamatory comments about her activities in local government; while John Kennedy, Conservative candidate in 1997 for Halesowen, sued the Labour Party's campaign co-ordinator over a story linking him with Radovan Karadzic. Not all such actions have been successful. David Ashby's ill-fated suit against *The Sunday Times* over allegations that he was homosexual may be the most readily remembered of such incidents, but the former Conservative MP Rupert Allason, perhaps the most assiduous of libel litigators in the Commons, also lost—very expensively—an action against *The Daily Mirror*. Local politicians also initiated sometimes lucrative actions. David Bookbinder, former leader of Derbyshire County Council, extracted an alleged £800,000 in damages and costs from *The Sunday Times* over a story accusing him of financial corruption. Throughout the 1980s and 1990s, there was—if not a torrent—then certainly a steady stream of political libel actions passing through the English courts. This was not an historical anachronism. The stream was not noticeably wider nor flowing more quickly than it had in any other period during the past 150 years.[2] British politicians have always displayed a propensity to sue for libel; a propensity which, given the basic features of the remedy, is readily understandable.

The rest of this chapter offers a brief and selective outline of those features. It makes no attempt to be comprehensive, indeed it is often rather simplistic, and is merely intended to acquaint readers unfamiliar with the fantastic intricacies of English[3] libel laws with those elements of the law which are particularly relevant to the issue of political libels. This book is largely concerned with tracing the development of a particular facet of defamation law from the mid-

---

[2] For comment on some of the more celebrated of such cases see Hooper D., *Public Scandal, Odium and Contempt* (London: Coronet 1986); Rubinstein M., *Wicked, Wicked Libels* (Harmondsworth: Penguin 1972).

[3] And Welsh. This book does not address Scots law.

nineteenth century up to the late 1990s. Consequently much of the initial description that follows is based on authorities of considerable vintage.[4] More recent authority is generally alluded to only when it articulates principles which were already discernibly nascent in older judgments.

THE BASICS OF ENGLISH LIBEL LAW

As with many common law remedies, the early origins of libel are obscure, but there appears to be a broad consensus that the law emerged as a means to dissuade citizens who felt their integrity had been unjustly impugned from resorting to violence as a means of revenging themselves upon their defamers.[5] Libel remedies developed in both the criminal and civil law. In its civil law form, libel has traditionally been regarded as a sub-division of the law of torts. Tort law covers a great many areas, and the details of its many remedies vary considerably. However, at the risk of some oversimplification, a successful action in tort will require that the following criteria be met. First, the plaintiff will have to demonstrate that he/she has suffered a loss. Secondly, the plaintiff will have to prove that the loss was caused by the defendant's behaviour. Thirdly, the plaintiff will have to prove that the defendant's behaviour failed to conform to the reasonable standard of care that might be expected of a person undertaking the activity in question. However, the remedy in libel shares little common ground with other facets of tort law.

The Nature and Proof of the Loss

The loss presumed to be in issue in a libel action is an injury to the plaintiff's reputation. The nature of the injury has been defined in various ways. A standard point of reference has been provided by Parke B's 1840 judgment in *Parmiter* v. *Coupland*, in which he suggested that a libel was a publication 'calculated to injure the reputation of another by exposing him to hatred, contempt, or ridicule'.[6] More recent judgments have suggested that this was perhaps too restrictive a definition. Lord Atkin's oft-quoted 1936 opinion in *Sim* v. *Stretch* offered a test that might be more easily satisfied: 'would the words tend to lower the plaintiff in the estimation of right-thinking members of society generally'.[7] These formulae are directed in large part towards attacks on a plaintiff's personal, moral character. That she was a liar, for example, or a hypocrite; that he had committed a crime, or abused a position of trust, or betrayed a confidence.

---

[4] With that purpose in mind, the most helpful academic guide to the basic ingredients of defamation law is perhaps Spencer Bower G., *The Law of Actionable Defamation*, (London: Sweet and Maxwell, 1908).

[5] See in particular Veeder, V., 'The History and Theory of the Law of Defamation' (1903) *Columbia LR* 546 and (1904) *Columbia LR* 33.

[6] (1840) 6 M & W 105 at 108.

[7] [1936] 2 All ER 1237 at 1240.

It is also clear that libel extends to publications which denigrate a person's competence in her chosen employment or occupation. In this respect, the loss might be seen as injury to the plaintiff's professional or commercial persona, such as would be caused by allegations that she was unqualified to practise her chosen profession, that she was a bankrupt, that she mistreated her employees or misled her customers.

At common law, the responsibility for determining whether a publication was libellous rested with the judge. The jury's fact-finding role was limited to deciding whether the defendant had published the information in issue and that the information concerned the plaintiff.[8] The rule was subjected to constant criticism by Whigs and political radicals in the late eighteenth century, with the eventual result that the Libel Act 1792 gave the jury the responsibility of deciding whether or not a given publication was libellous.[9]

The test of what is libellous is a flexible one, primarily because the law's concern is with the view that would be taken of a given publication by 'right-thinking members of society'. Neither statute nor the common law has ever required plaintiffs to engage in any sophisticated endeavours to establish what 'right-thinking members of society' actually believe; the matter has instead been left to the presumed good sense of the jury hearing the case, subject to the caveat that it is the opinion of society as a whole, and not a faction therein, that is to be considered.

It is for the plaintiff to prove that the publication complained of was libellous, and that it could be construed as referring to her.[10] Having discharged those burdens however, the plaintiff's evidentiary task is in most circumstances complete. In contrast to most other torts, libel does not require a plaintiff to prove he/she has suffered a loss. Rather, that loss is presumed to flow automatically from the mere publication of libellous material. In that respect, Parke B's suggestion in *Parmiter* that a publication was libellous if 'calculated' to injure the plaintiff's reputation can be misleading. It is not necessary that the defendant intended to injure the plaintiff's reputation. Nor is it even necessary that the loss was caused (as is required in most other torts) by negligence on the defendant's part. Liability in libel is strict.

Several cases decided at the turn of the nineteenth century seemed to indicate however that accurate reports of judicial and parliamentary proceedings simply could not be libellous, irrespective of the damage that their dissemination might

[8] 'Publication' includes the repetition of a libel, not just its original dissemination. See McEwen R. and Lewis P., *Gatley on Libel and Slander* (6th ed, London, Sweet & Maxwell, 1967) ch.7, and especially the quotation at 130 from *De Crespigny* v. *Wellesley* (1829) 5 Bing 392 at 404: 'Because one man does an unlawful act to any person, another is not to be permitted to do a similar act to the same person. Wrong is not to be justified or even excused by wrong'.

[9] Strictly construed, the Act applies only to criminal libel actions. It appears to have led however to an almost instantaneous change of the law in civil proceedings as well.

[10] This latter point can raise complex questions, but they need not be addressed here. The matter of identification of the plaintiff was not an issue of any significance in the cases discussed in detail in subsequent chapters. On the point generally see *Duncan and Neill on Defamation* (3rd ed, London, Butterworths, 1998) ch.6.

do the reputations of the individuals whose behaviour was being examined in the proceedings concerned.[11] The plaintiff in *Curry* v. *Walter*[12] was a magistrate, who had been prosecuted for misconduct in office. Walter was a proprietor of *The Times*, which had published what was accepted to be an accurate account of the court proceedings. The case was dismissed, for reasons which the report of the case explained in the following terms:

> An objection being taken whether the action was maintainable, Eyre, Chief Justice, held, that *bona fide* report of what passed in a court of justice was not actionable, but that he would hold the defendant to very strict proof that the report as published contained precisely the substance of that delivered in court. . . .[13]

The report is not a model of reliability, being both very brief and lacking any verbatim quotation of the judges' opinions. Nor is there anything in the report to explain the policy underlying the rule. Both of these shortcomings were addressed three years later in *R* v. *Wright*.[14]

The alleged libel in *Wright* was contained in a book published by Wright which reproduced verbatim a passage in a House of Commons' committee report which accused certain individuals of treason. The Court—in what appears to be a lengthy and verbatim report of the judgments given—unanimously concluded that an accurate report of such proceedings could not be libellous. Thus, per Lord Kenyon CJ: '[i]t is impossible for us to admit that the proceeding of either of the Houses of Parliament is a libel'.[15] Lord Kenyon CJ did not explain why this was the case, nor did Grose J, who concurred in the result. The most expansive judgment was given by Lawrence J. He reasoned by analogy with *Curry*, which he read as holding simply that an accurate report of court proceedings could not be libellous. If that was so, neither could accurate reports of parliamentary proceedings have that character. He then partially explained why the common law had adopted that rule:

> though the publication of such proceedings may be to the disadvantage of the particular individual concerned, yet it is of vast importance to the public that the proceedings of courts of justice should be universally known. The general advantage to the public of having these proceedings made public, more than counterbalances the inconvenience to the private persons whose conduct may be the subject of such proceedings.[16]

Lawrence J did not go on to identify just what this 'general advantage' actually was. The obvious inference is that the political or moral legitimacy of the courts and the two Houses of Parliament rested in large part on their activities

---

[11] The cases discussed in the following paras. are *stricto sensu* actions in criminal libel. However on the issue of whether a given statement could be defamatory, there is no distinction of substance to be drawn between civil and criminal libel laws.
[12] (1796) 1 Esp. 456.
[13] *Ibid.*, at 457.
[14] (1799) 8 TR 292.
[15] *Ibid.*, at 296.
[16] (1799) 8 TR 292 at 298.

being open to constant and unhampered discussion and evaluation among the public at large. In effect, these cases suggested that the legitimacy of courts and Parliament as institutions of government demanded not simply that citizens *consent* to the laws which each institution produced, but also that such *consent* be *informed*, premised on an accurate understanding of how the courts and legislators operated in practice. Since most citizens could not collect information on these subjects through their own efforts, individuals who published such accounts were performing a vital public service which merited extensive protection at common law. Put in more grandiloquent terms, the principle suggests the common law assumed that one important facet of the doctrines of parliamentary governance and the rule of law is that the administration of justice and the conduct of parliamentary proceedings is always a proper subject for public scrutiny, discussion and debate among the population as a whole.

In an 1804 case, *R. v. Lee*,[17] the defendant had tried to extend this principle much further, reaching beyond merely parliamentary and judicial proceedings to all matters of public interest. The defendant owned a newspaper which had published an admittedly accurate report of preliminary proceedings in a criminal trial which contained apparently defamatory allegations. His counsel argued that there was no case to answer, on the basis that:

> the publisher of a newspaper had a right to publish a fair account of all public transactions which occurred and which were matters of public notoriety, provided they were given fairly and impartially . . . a true narrative of public matter could not be deemed to be libellous.[18]

The argument was promptly rejected by the judge, Heath J, who held that even accurate reports of *preliminary* or *ex parte* judicial proceedings could be the subject of a libel action if they contained defamatory allegations. That conclusion is not formally inconsistent with *Curry*, since the former case was concerned with a report of a full trial. No currency was given to the full sweep of the defendant's claim; namely that dissemination of any information on matters of 'public notoriety' could not be libellous.

If *Curry* and *Wright* did indeed hold that accurate reportage of trials and parliamentary proceedings could not be libellous, the publishers of such material need not concern themselves about the adequacy of any defences that might be available to disseminators of defamatory information. The significance of this point becomes apparent when one considers how effective those defences seemed to be.

---

[17] (1804) 5 Esp. 123.
[18] *Ibid.*, at 125–6. The 'truth' at issue in the contention relates to the accuracy of the reporting, not to the substance of the allegations reported.

Defences

While liability is strict, the law does afford the defendant defences in several instances. These defences have emerged in part to ensure that a plaintiff cannot use the remedy in respect of a loss she/he has not actually suffered, and in part in recognition of the need to protect freedom of expression, particularly in relation to matters of legitimate interest to the audience being addressed by the defendant.

Justification

The defence of justification provides complete protection to the defendant who can prove the truth (to the usual civil law standard of the balance of probabilities) of any factual assertions she has made. The rationale for the defence would seem to be a simple one; namely that a plaintiff should not be able to claim a reputation that she/he does not possess. That an allegation is true does not mean it is not defamatory, but rather that it is a justified (hence the style of the defence) libel. The burden of proof of the truth or falsity lies on the defendant, a situation which reverses the normal presumption in civil law actions, which requires the plaintiff to prove culpability on the defendant's part.

The orthodox common law rule did not require that the defendant prove the truth of absolutely every detail of the allegations made, but rather that they were 'substantially true'.[19] A defence of justification would (probably) not have failed, for example, if the defendant had claimed that the plaintiff had engaged in a particular course of reprehensible conduct on twelve occasions, but could prove only that the plaintiff had done so eleven times. The common law did however require a very high degree of commonality between the allegation and the proof offered. A defendant could not justify the accusation that a plaintiff had stolen a car by proving that he had stolen a bicycle.[20] Similarly, to take an oft-quoted example,[21] a defence of justification would fail in respect of an allegation that the plaintiff was 'a libellous journalist' if the defendant could prove only that the plaintiff had on one occasion been held to have published libellous material. As will be seen in subsequent chapters, legislatures in different jurisdictions have modified this basic common law position in various ways. Clearly, the looser the commonality required between the allegation levied and the justification offered, the less effective the remedy would be for a plaintiff. In English law, the defence has proven a difficult one for publishers to establish.[22]

---

[19] Cf. *Edwards* v. *Bell* (1824) 1 Bing. 403; *Clarke* v. *Taylor* (1836) 3 Scott 95.

[20] Had the allegation been merely that the plaintiff was a thief, a justification defence would have succeeded on these facts.

[21] Offered by Parke B in *Wakley* v. *Cooke* (1849) 4 Exch. 511.

[22] In the context of political libels, the limited utility of the defence is best shown by the notorious case involving the senior Labour politicians Aneurin Bevan and Richard Crossman against *The Spectator* in 1957. *The Spectator* ran an article noting that Crossman and Bevan were frequently

Absolute and Qualified Privilege

A limited range of defences is also available in respect of presumptively *false* allegations of fact in some circumstances. The rationale underpinning the defences has no basis in preventing the plaintiff from recouping undeserved damages—as does the justification defence—for it is accepted that he/she has suffered an untruthful attack on her reputation. Rather the presumption is that there is a sufficient public interest in the dissemination of the libel concerned (or analogous libels) to absolve the publisher from legal liability entirely in some circumstances (absolute privilege), and to make it very difficult for the plaintiff to succeed in others (qualified privilege). The defences accept that the dissemi-nators of some types of false information should be protected (in varying degrees) against a libel action. If the only defence available in a libel action was justification, a person in possession of defamatory information might be deterred from publishing it unless she was certain that she could prove its truth in court. In the event that the information was indeed false, the deterrent effect against publication would serve a useful social purpose. However, if the infor-mation was true, its suppression would render a disservice to all those members of society who had a legitimate interest in receiving it. In effect, the absolute and qualified privilege defences accept that the common law has recognised that there are some types of information in respect of which it is better to run the risk that individuals be falsely defamed than that potentially true allegations be withheld.

Qualified Privilege

The more wide-ranging but less effective of the two defences is qualified privilege. This is primarily a common law principle, although it has on occasion been extended (and curtailed) by statute. The gist of the defence is that if a given pub-lication is made on a privileged 'occasion', the defendant is not liable for the pub-lication of false[23] information unless the plaintiff can prove that the publication was made with 'malice' on the defendant's part. Two questions therefore arise. Which 'occasions' are privileged? And what is meant by 'malice'? In terms of prin-ciple, the leading English authority on the question of 'occasion' is the 1834 deci-sion in *Toogood* v. *Spyring*.[24] In *Toogood*, the court held that qualified privilege would attach to factually false and defamatory statements if they were:

> fairly made by a person in the discharge of some public or private duty, whether legal or moral, or in the conduct of his own affairs, in matters where his interest is con-

drunk during a conference in Venice. Crossman and Bevan vehemently denied the accusations, and began proceedings. Both men (it later emerged) had lied on oath about their sobriety, and were suf-ficiently convincing to win a damages award of £20,000. For a fascinating account see Hooper, n. 2 above, ch. 10.

[23] There would of course be no need for such a defence in respect of allegations which could be justified.

[24] (1834) 1 C M & R 181.

cerned . . . [S]uch communications are protected for the common convenience and welfare of society; and the law has not restricted the right to make them within any narrow limits.[25]

The 'common convenience and welfare of society' is a principle of potentially very broad application, and one which could plausibly be applied to a great many types of information. The *Toogood* principle has traditionally, however, been confined within quite narrow bounds. The occasion in issue in *Toogood* itself was an allegation made by the defendant to the plaintiff's employer that the plaintiff had been negligent and dishonest when conducting work for the defendant. The court also indicated that the rather more general 'occasion' of 'a former master giving the character of a discharged servant'[26] would be protected by qualified privilege.

In formal terms, *Toogood* required only that the disseminator of the information was under a duty to pass it on. It did not specifically require in addition that the recipient had an interest in receiving it. However subsequent judgments appeared to read *Toogood* as holding that qualified privilege could only arise if there were a considerable degree of personal or professional intimacy between the subject matter of the information and the identities of its disseminator and recipient, requiring that the publisher's duty to provide the information was matched with a reciprocal duty or interest on the recipient's part to be made aware of it.[27] It is evident that (as in *Toogood*) a person's former and current employer have a legitimate, reciprocated interest in dissemination of information concerning the employee's professional competence. However no occasion of privilege would arise in respect of defamatory information about the employee passed between those two individuals that had no bearing on the employee's work performance. Nor would such an occasion arise if either employer communicated information about the employee's professional suitability to unconnected third parties, or to the general public or a section thereof.

The limits placed by English courts on the scope of the 'common convenience and welfare of society' principle are perhaps best illustrated by further examples. Privilege would attach to allegations made by the defendant to the police about possibly criminal behaviour by the plaintiff. The law-abiding citizen has a moral duty to bring criminal activity to the police's attention, and the police have a reciprocal duty to receive it. But privilege would not be available if the allegations to the police did not involve criminal behaviour, or if allegations of criminality were aired in a letter to a newspaper or in a public forum.[28] Similarly, an occasion of qualified privilege would arise if a mother made defamatory allegations to her daughter about her fiancé. The parties would share a reciprocal interest in the daughter being able to make an informed choice about

---

[25] *Ibid.*, at 193.
[26] *Ibid.*
[27] See Mitchell, P., 'Malice in Qualified Privilege' [1999] *Public Law* 328.
[28] For a nice illustration of the 'subtleties' of English libel law in relation to accusations of theft see McEwen and Lewis, n. 8 above, 218–22.

whether to continue the engagement. The occasion would not however be privileged if the mother repeated the allegations to her friends or acquaintances.

There is little indication in early nineteenth-century English case law that
qualified privilege could extend to an 'occasion' in which the audience was the
public in the country as a whole, or even to particular regions or communities.
The one obvious exception to this concerned verbatim reports or accurate summaries of judicial (and by analogy parliamentary) proceedings. This might seem
a surprising exception, given that it was suggested above that there was clear
early nineteenth-century authority for the proposition that such publications
simply could not be defamatory. However, some considerable doubt was cast
on Lawrence J's reading of *Curry* in *Wright* by Abbot CJ in the 1824 decision
Duncan v. *Thwaites*[29]:

> The case is of great authority in itself, and derives additional weight from the manner
> in which it is mentioned by Mr Justice Lawrence in *The King* v. *Wright*. It has not
> however received the sanction of subsequent judges . . .[30]

Having doubted the *Curry* principle *per se*, Abbot CJ observed—following *R.*
v. *Lee*—that it was in any event inapplicable to the present case, since the libel
concerned had been raised in a preliminary hearing. He then considered whether
a publication of this sort might, while libellous, benefit from qualified privilege.
He concluded it did not. The report of the case does not make his reasoning
entirely clear, but it suggests that the libel was not protected because it was
extracted from a preliminary hearing, an 'occasion' which did not raise any reciprocal right/duty in the dissemination of defamatory information between a
newspaper and its readers.

The full significance of the judgment does not become apparent until one considers the 1835 decision in *Chalmers* v. *Payne*.[31] In *Chalmers*, the court accepted
as beyond argument the proposition that accurate reports of an actual trial
attracted qualified privilege. The previous rule in *Curry* that such publications
were not libellous had rather mysteriously disappeared, and no pertinent
authority was cited for the new rule. That this rule is much less to the benefit of
publishers than the rule in *Curry* becomes apparent when one considers the
meaning attached to the concept of 'malice'.

The common law provided that malice on the defendant's part (which had to
be proven beyond reasonable doubt by the plaintiff) could arise on any one of
several grounds. The first was if the defendant was not motivated by a concern
to discharge the relevant moral/legal duty which created the privileged occasion,
but by a desire to inflict damage on the plaintiff.[32] The second again concerned
the defendant's motive: dissemination could be malicious if the defendant's
intention was to achieve an objective unconnected to the discharge of the duty,

---

[29] (1824) 3 B & C 577.
[30] *Ibid.*, at 583.
[31] (1835) 2 C M & R 156.
[32] See especially Parke B in *Wright* v. *Woodgate* (1835) 2 C M & R 573.

even if he/she harboured no personal animosity towards the plaintiff. The third ground addressed the defendant's state of mind *vis-à-vis* the accuracy of the information published: if she/he knew it to be false she/he has (generally[33]) acted maliciously in communicating it to another.[34] There is also some indication that malice might be inferred from overbroad dissemination of the libel. This is a rather ungainly idea, as it obviously overlaps with the preliminary question whether an occasion of privilege has arisen. Overbroad communication would be to an audience with no reciprocal interest in receiving the information, and is presumably intended to meet those situations where the defendant's actions have led to the defamatory information spilling over the channels of communication legitimately linking him/her to the disseminee.

Qualified privilege therefore provided an effective, but not insurmountable, defence to publishers of a limited range of libellous information. Malice is a difficult concept to prove, but by no means an impossible one. Much would no doubt turn in practice on the forensic skill brought to bear on the facts of a given case by the defendant and plaintiff's counsel.

Absolute Privilege

The law relating to absolute privilege was rather more straightforward. If an 'occasion' of absolute privilege arose, it was irrelevant that the publisher had acted with malice. He would enjoy an unassailable defence even if he knew the information published was false, and/or was motivated solely by a wish to injure the defendant, and/or disseminated the information to the world at large. *De facto*, if not strictly as a matter of law, the defence is closely analogous to a conclusion that the publication complained of is not libellous *per se*, the major difference being that while a plaintiff would have to prove that a publication could be libellous, it is for the defendant to prove that an occasion of absolute privilege is at issue.

The categories of absolute privilege initially embraced information receiving a very limited circulation. Information provided by participants (be they judges, counsel, parties or witnesses) in judicial proceedings were so protected. Communications between military officers and between civil servants made in the course of their official duties were also afforded absolute privilege against defamation actions, as were communications between a solicitor and her/his client in so far as they were relevant to matter in respect of which the solicitor had been engaged.

---

[33] There are a very narrow set of circumstances in which qualified privilege can attach to communication of a known falsehood; see McEwen and Lewis, n. 8 above, 258, 355–6.

[34] That she/he was negligent in failing to establish its truth, or was reckless in not doing so, was not generally regarded as malice *per se*, but might be invoked as evidence to support the contention that the defendant had no honest belief in the truth of the information; see *Capital and Counties Bank* v. *Henry* (1880) 5 CPD 514. The dividing line between matters of *definition* and *evidence* in relation to malice is far from clear-cut in much English case law, and is even more obscure—as will become evident in later chs.—when one considers the way in which English authority was later developed by courts in other common law jurisdictions. For a suggestion that English law is much more coherent on this point than I have allowed, see Mitchell, n. 27 above.

The above categories of absolute privilege were the creation of the common law. A statutory form of absolute privilege appeared to be contained in Article 9 of the Bill of Rights 1689, which provided that 'freedom of speech and debates or proceedings in Parliament shall not be impeached or questioned in any place out of Parliament'. Quite what amounts to a proceeding in Parliament is not made clear in the Bill of Rights itself, but there would seem little scope for doubt that it embraced conversations or documents produced by either House's members or officers in the conduct of their official business. A rather ancient common law authority, the 1680 case of *Lake* v. *King*,[35] suggests that the same protection is afforded at common law to petitions addressed to either House.

The rationale for the defences is similar to (albeit more compelling than) that underpinning qualified privilege. The courts (or the legislature) have recognised that sometimes there is so intense a public interest in keeping participants in certain channels of communication wholly unencumbered by the fear of legal action that they are willing to take the risk that some of those participants will publish defamatory and false information. The public interest underlying the defence is not, however, in the communicated information itself, for absolute privilege was not granted to repetition (whether by individuals or the press) of any libels aired in such situations to the public at large. As noted above, such repetition or reportage might attract qualified privilege, but this is a much less efficacious defence than its absolute counterpart.

Fair Comment

Absolute and qualified privilege are defences which apply in theory to inaccurate representations of fact. In contrast, the defence of fair comment is available not in respect of factual allegations, but of the expression of opinions or value judgements as to the conclusions which might legitimately be drawn from particular facts. The defence is manifestly a recognition of the high (but not absolute) importance that the common law attached even as long ago as 1850 to protecting the expression of opinion on certain matters.

The relationship between the fair comment and absolute/qualified privilege defences is, however, rather complicated in practice. The distinction between fact and opinion is not—as might readily be imagined—unproblematic. What to one bystander (or one judge) might appear as an allegation of fact could well be seen by another as a statement of opinion.[36] This difficulty is compounded by the tendency of some judges in pre-twentieth century cases (both in England and other common law jurisdictions) to refer to fair comment as a 'privilege' and to intertwine their analysis of the point with their discussion of qualified privi-

---

[35] (1680) 1 Saund. 131.
[36] See, for example, the divergence of judicial opinion on this question in *Ogren* v. *Rockford Star* (1925) 237 Ill App. 349 and *Stephens* v. *West Australia Newspapers Ltd* [1994] 68 ACJR 713, respectively discussed at 42 and 144–6 below.

lege.[37] This nomenclature has come to be seen as little more than stylistic affectation, which obscures a clear substantive dichotomy. As will be suggested in subsequent chapters, that view is perhaps overly simplistic.

Fair comment can be invoked only in respect of comments made in relation to factual allegations which can be proven by the defendant to be (substantially) true, or which—if they are not so proven—can be shown to have been made on an occasion attracting the defences of absolute or qualified privilege. The comment ('opinion' or 'criticism' might be a more accurate label) is not rendered 'unfair' simply because it is intemperate in tone, or premised on an exaggerated or unreasonable interpretation of the underlying facts. It becomes so only if it so far removed from any plausible factual base that it amounts to a view that could not feasibly be held by any fair-minded person. Lord Esher's formulation in *Merivale* v. *Carson* conveys this idea quite clearly: '[t]he question which the jury must consider is this—would any fair man, however prejudiced he may be, however exaggerated or obstinate his views, have said that which this criticism has said'.[38]

The defence may however only be used in respect of information raising a matter of 'public interest'. Even by the mid-nineteenth century, this concept had been afforded a wide meaning. The conduct of governmental business, at both central and local level, fell into this category, as did the administration of the legal system and the church. The defence also reached to criticism of published books and works of art, and to comment on any other matter published in response to information previously presented for public consumption by the plaintiff. A plaintiff could however overcome the fair comment defence if she/he could demonstrate malice on the defendant's part. For this purpose, malice bore the same meaning as it did in respect of qualified privilege.

Damages

There may be circumstances in which the plaintiff's primary concern is to gain injunctive relief to prevent a libel being repeated. It may even be that her sole wish is to have a court issue a declaration that the libel is an untrue and unwarranted attack on her reputation. The predominant remedy in civil libel cases is however damages. As in other tort actions, these fall under several nominally discrete heads. General, or compensatory, damages are available to recompense any injury the plaintiff has suffered to her reputation and feelings. Reputation and feelings are not objectively quantifiable phenomena, and the common law traditionally left the trial jury considerable discretion in assessing the quantum of such awards. Quantifiable pecuniary loss could also be recovered as part of general damages. The compensation award could also be increased by

[37] Duncan and Neill, n. 10 above, 160. See particularly *Campbell* v. *Spottiswoode* (1863) 3 B & S 769, discussed at 24–6 below.
[38] (1887) 20 QBD 275 at 280–1.

aggravated damages, payable primarily for actions undertaken by the defendant after publication of the libel. Matters such as a failure to apologise, or insistence on deploying (unsuccessfully) a justification defence, would fall within this head. As will be seen in later chapters, some problems are engendered by the obvious overlap between aggravated and punitive damages. The latter are awarded not to compensate the plaintiff *per se*, but to penalise the defendant for particularly reprehensible behaviour. They are thus analogous in a limited sense to a fine levied in criminal proceedings, and need have no obvious relationship to the intensity of the loss suffered by the plaintiff.

English juries have never been required to apportion the total sum of damages between the various heads, and judges have until very recently been notably reluctant to overturn awards which might appear either extravagantly large or inexplicably small. The size of damages awards is obviously a factor of considerable significance in the utility of the libel remedy from the plaintiff's perspective. The higher the award likely to be achieved, the more likely it is that a plaintiff will begin proceedings. It would also seem plausible to assume that the size of awards will have some appreciable impact on a putative defendant's willingness to publish defamatory material which he is not absolutely certain can either be justified or brought within the absolute/qualified privilege or fair comment defence.

CRIMINAL LIBEL

The criminal remedy was associated closely with the offences of sedition and blasphemy. However it could also be invoked against defamatory comments which did not involve criticism of the government or the church, but might be thought to have the tendency to trigger a breach of the peace.[39] There is also early nineteenth-century authority for the proposition that a possible or likely breach of the peace was not necessary for a criminal action to be launched and that a prosecution was tenable against *any* libellous publications.[40]

At that time, truth was not a defence to a criminal libel prosecution, although it would seem that absolute and qualified privilege and fair comment could be invoked as a defence. Legislation enacted in 1843 allowed truth to be pleaded as a defence, but this would be effective only if the defendant both proved the truth of the allegations and convinced the jury that publication was for the public benefit.[41] Publication of a known falsehood carried a gaol term of up to two years. A one-year sentence could be imposed on defendants who did not know the allegation made to be untrue.

---

[39] For a succinct outline see Duncan C. and Neill B., *The Law of Defamation*, (London, Butterworths, 1977) ch. 20.

[40] *Thorley* v. *Lord Kerry* (1812) 4 Taunt. 355.

[41] Libel Act 1843 s.6.

SLANDER

The tort of slander shares many of the characteristics of libel. There are however several important differences between the two actions. The first concerns the manner of communication of the defamatory material. Slander emerged traditionally in respect of spoken rather than written defamation. This historical dichotomy became blurred at the edges by the development of technologies which lent formerly ephemeral spoken words a permanent character, and Parliament has on occasion enacted legislation intended to clarify which type of defamation is occasioned by certain types of technological innovation.

The clarification is significant, because the two remedies differ in some important substantive respects. In slander, only a limited number of types of damage to reputation are presumed to flow automatically from defamatory allegations. At common law, the accusations regarded as slanderous *per se* have included those alleging that the plaintiff has committed a crime, that she is suffering from a contagious disease, or that are calculated to undermine her professional or commercial reputation. Parliament also enacted in 1891 a provision that it was slanderous *per se* to accuse a female of adultery or, if unmarried, of being sexually active.

In all other respects, the two torts are virtually identical, and much defamation case law is applied with equally alacrity to both remedies. There is no obviously compelling reason for retaining the distinction between libel and slander, but as yet neither Parliament nor the courts have taken steps to unify the two remedies. Slander is clearly a much less expansive and accommodating remedy from a plaintiff's perspective, and is a remedy of declining significance in the modern era.

MALICIOUS FALSEHOOD

There is some scope for arguing whether or not the tort of malicious (or injurious) falsehood should be bracketed alongside libel and slander. In a broad sense, malicious falsehood has obvious similarities with libel (and more particularly slander) in that it provides a remedy for plaintiffs whose reputations have been injured by the publication of false factual allegations, whether in permanent or transient form.

In contrast to the position in libel however, the recoverable loss in malicious falsehood is restricted to injury to the plaintiff's commercial persona. In that respect, malicious falsehood is more readily comparable to slander than libel, although at common law it was not assumed—as was the case in slander—that certain types of allegations were actionable *per se*.[42] Rather, the plaintiff is always required to prove that he/she has actually suffered a loss.

---

[42] That position has been modified somewhat by statute; see 57 below.

Malicious falsehood diverges markedly from both slander and libel in that the burden of proof of falsity falls on the plaintiff rather than the defendant. The plaintiff must also prove 'malice' on the defendant's part. This bears a rather different meaning from the same term deployed in libel and slander. In malicious falsehood, the plaintiff must prove that the statement was calculated to cause him/her a pecuniary loss, and that the defendant either knew the statement was false or was recklessly indifferent as to its falsity.

That the plaintiff must prove her loss, the falsity of the allegation and the defendant's malice clearly makes malicious falsehood a far less attractive remedy than libel (and, to a lesser extent, than slander) from the plaintiff's perspective. For the plaintiff, the remedy's utility would seem to lie in the rule that it is not necessary that the allegations made be defamatory. That they cause a commercial loss, are false and are made with malice is sufficient for an action to succeed. The obvious example is a lie about the quality of a trader's goods, an allegation which need not have any bearing on an individual's reputation for honesty, competence or integrity. It is more difficult—although not impossible—to imagine circumstances in which a non-defamatory allegation could undermine an individual's personal reputation in a way that causes him/her a financial loss. Much here might turn on the audience to which the false information was communicated. An example would be where one of two traders competing for the business of a known anti-Semitic falsely tells the putative customer that the other trader is Jewish. The accusation is not defamatory, but it is false and is calculated to cause the other trader a (quantifiable) economic loss. In the modern era, the relative substantive disadvantages of malicious falsehood as compared to slander and libel have been offset by the fact that legal aid is available for actions in malicious falsehood but not for the other two remedies.

Notwithstanding the proviso that a malicious falsehood need not be defamatory, the remedy has often been treated (particularly in legislation and textbooks, and to a lesser extent by the courts, especially in overseas common law jurisdictions) along with libel and slander as part and parcel of a broader umbrella category of speech torts. As will become evident in later chapters, this imprecision in the language used by counsel, judges and legal commentators can engender some uncertainty about the substantive meaning of particular judicial decisions. This is especially the case when judges in a jurisdiction which apparently draws a clear line between defamation and malicious falsehood invoke as authority judgments produced in jurisdictions where that distinction is much less clearly made.

CONCLUSION

The foundations of English libel law were securely laid long before Britain could defensibly have been described as a country possessing a democratic system of government. Even the most cursory reading of modern-day textbooks in the field reveals that many leading authorities date from the early to mid-nineteenth century; they were the product of a pre-democratic age. The primary concern of the remainder of this book is to chart the way in which the principles underlying the law of defamation, and the rules which those principles have produced, have been adapted by Parliament and the courts in the light of the increasing democratisation of the constitutional context in which they are located.

2

The Common Law and Political Libels in Nineteenth and Early Twentieth Century Britain

The Great Reform Act of 1832 has widely been accorded the status of the initiative which revolutionised Britain's electoral laws and instituted the beginnings of the democratic era in British constitutional history. The Act's initial impact was perhaps more symbolic than practical; its effect on the extent and nature of voting rights was very limited in terms of the number of citizens it enfranchised. The legislation nonetheless undoubtedly altered the political basis of the relationship between the citizenry and members of the House of Commons, and signalled a clear subordination of the House of Lords to the House of Commons within Parliament.[1] In combination, those factors pointed towards a growing societal recognition that the legitimacy of the governmental system rested on the active consent rather than mere deference of a broadening proportion of the population.

There was no immediate indication however that the extension of the franchise was to be accompanied by legislative reforms which would enhance the probability that such active consent was also *informed* consent. The press had no legally guaranteed entitlement even to report, still less to comment upon or criticise, the beliefs or behaviour of MPs. This was in part a consequence of defamation laws, but it was also rooted in the question of parliamentary privilege. The House of Commons had resolved in 1762 that:

> [I]t is an high Indignity to, and a notorious breach of the Privilege of this House . . . for any printer or Publisher of any printed Newspaper . . . to give therein any Account of the Debates or other Proceedings of this House . . . and this House will proceed with the utmost severity against such offenders.

The resolution had been vigorously enforced in the late eighteenth century in an attempt to curb the activities of political radicals, and although its use had markedly declined by the early 1830s the threat of action against an overly critical press remained.[2]

---

[1] See Loveland, I. *Constitutional Law* (London, Butterworths, 1996) ch. 7.

[2] *R. v. Wright* thus protected publishers of parliamentary proceedings from prosecution at common law; what it did not do was safeguard them against an action by either house for breaching parliamentary privilege. See Loveland, n. 1 above, ch.8 for a fuller account.

There was, in contrast, some indication that the courts regarded the 1832 Act as an invitation to reconsider the common law rules of defamation which structured the relationship between voters, unenfranchised citizens and their elected representatives when critical political information was published for public consumption. The plaintiff in *Duncombe* v. *Daniel*[3] was a former MP, who was standing for re-election in the Finsbury constituency in London. Daniel, a voter in Finsbury, had written letters, published in a London newspaper—*The Morning Post*—in the run-up to a general election, which accused Duncombe of fraud and sharp practice in his financial dealings, and invited him to rebut the charges at a public meeting.

In the ensuing trial, Daniel's counsel argued that the letters attracted qualified privilege, on the basis that:

> as Mr Duncombe was a candidate for the representation of the borough of Finsbury, and Mr Daniel was an elector, the defendant was justified in stating these imputations to the other electors, if he did so bona fide and without malice, believing the imputations to be true.[4]

The defence failed on the facts. Lord Denman CJ stated quite forcefully that:

> However large the privilege of electors may be, it is extravagant to suppose that it can justify the publication to all the world of facts injurious to a person who happens to stand in the situation of a candidate.[5]

It is perhaps curious that Lord Denman CJ felt a person could 'happen' to be a candidate for political office, as if that were a matter of chance rather than a conscious decision of the individual concerned. His statement is certainly authority for the proposition that the common law did not recognise any reciprocal right/duty between the press and the general public to consume political information. However, he also indicated, as did Coleridge J, that privilege would have arisen if the means of publication had been more narrowly tailored to minimise the likelihood that the defendant's claims were read by people other than local voters. Neither judge specified how this might be achieved, but an obvious device would have been the distribution of leaflets at public meetings or to homes in the constituency.[6] Given that there were then no national news media, and that local issues rather than abstract party political loyalties still played a substantial part in determining voter behaviour, the limited scope accorded to the defence seems reasonably well-suited to assisting voters to exercise informed consent to their choice of MP given the realities of the political culture within which it was located.

---

[3] (1837) 8 Car & P 222.
[4] *Ibid.*, at 226.
[5] *Ibid.*, at 229.
[6] Both judges also indicated that they saw the issue of overbroad publication as preventing an occasion of privilege arising, rather than going to the question of malice.

That Lord Denman was conscious of a need to distinguish between 'political' and 'private' libels was also made evident in the following year during the *Stockdale v. Hansard* controversy. A Commons inquiry into prison administration, published on the House's instructions, had made potentially libellous comments about a medical textbook found in a gaol. Stockdale, the book's publisher, commenced defamation proceedings against Hansard, the Commons' publisher. The House instructed Hansard not to contest the case, but merely to inform the court that it had resolved that the report was a proceeding in Parliament, and as such—under the terms of Article 9 of the Bill of Rights 1689—not subject to judicial jurisdiction.

The court, for which Lord Denman CJ gave the leading judgment, rejected the Commons' assertion. In a controversial opinion, Lord Denman CJ maintained that it was for the courts rather than the House of Commons to determine the meaning of Article 9. Lord Denman considered that 'proceedings in Parliament' could not form *the subject* of a defamation action. However he would not accept that the publishers of reports of Commons proceedings subsequently circulated outside the house enjoyed such protection; these reports were not 'proceedings in Parliament' unless their publication was 'necessary' for members of the House to perform their duties. Since he saw no 'necessity' for the publishers of parliamentary reports invariably to be immune from a libel action, Stockdale could proceed with his action and expect the court to deliver judgment in his favour if his case was well founded.

The judgment must therefore be regarded as discrediting (if not strictly overruling) *R. v. Wright*, a case which was—as we have already seen—of dubious authority by the mid-1830s. Lord Denman treated *Wright* at some length.[7] He was scathing in his criticism of Lord Kenyon CJ's assertion that any accurate republication of a parliamentary proceeding could not be libellous. The assertion 'bore the marks of haste' and was not strictly necessary to have resolved the point at issue in *Wright*, and so no more than obiter: it was thus 'open to investigation'.[8] He was rather kinder in his criticism of Lawrence J's opinion in *Wright*, which he described as displaying 'good sense and liberality'.[9] However Lawrence J's judgment was, he suggested, even if correct, limited only to criminal libel cases. It had no direct bearing on the civil action before the court in *Stockdale*.

Many of the various judgments delivered by Lord Denman and his colleagues were concerned with the narrow question of parliamentary privilege. But their opinions also alluded briefly to the more general matter of freedom of political expression. As well as rejecting the argument that republication of a parliamentary proceedings could not be libellous, Lord Denman dismissed the contention

[7] (1839) 9 Ad & E 1 at 121–3.
[8] *Ibid.*, at 122.
[9] *Ibid.*

raised by Hansard's counsel that the common law should recognise an absolute privilege for parliamentary papers because such papers were an essential means for MPs to communicate important issues to their electors. He did not dismiss the argument because he considered it intrinsically unattractive. Rather he rejected it because he perceived a clear distinction between 'political' and 'private' information. The libel in issue in *Stockdale* had no political dimension at all.[10] There was thus no necessity for it to be disseminated by the House. It could not therefore be protected by either absolute or qualified privilege.

The obvious inference to be drawn from this reasoning is that the common law may have recognised that some privilege, be it absolute or qualified, should attach to the wide publication of parliamentary reports if they addressed political issues, but not if they discussed matters of purely private interest.[11] Lord Denman considered that a court should be astute—as he felt Lord Kenyon CJ had failed to be in *Wright*—not to 'confound the nature of the composition with the occasion of publishing it'.[12] Lord Denman also suggested that the Commons' argument was intensely hypocritical, given that the House still claimed the power to punish anybody who had the temerity to reproduce verbatim accounts or summaries of its proceedings without its permission. The House could hardly plead the necessity of an informed consent principle if its own behaviour indicated that it accorded the principle no worth. The inference would seem to be that if Parliament enacted legislation to publicise House proceedings, or if the House published them itself, it would be more appropriate for the common law to offer those publications protection against the ordinary laws of libel. The current state of the law was, Lord Denman suggested, 'no doubt susceptible of improvement, but the improvement must be a legislative act'.[13]

Stockdale should therefore not be seen as a judgment which allowed libel laws to be used to restrain freedom of political expression. There was no 'political' information in issue in the case. And the court indicated that if there had been, the common law might have afforded it considerable protection in a defamation suit.

'POLITICAL' INFORMATION—A NARROW PERSPECTIVE

That the notion of 'political' bore a narrow meaning at common law at this time is well illustrated by the 1857 decision in *Davison* v. *Duncan*.[14] The case arose

---

[10] (1839) 9 Ad & E 146 at 149–50.

[11] Littledale J also indicated that he might be receptive to such an argument: *ibid.*, at 182–3.

[12] *Ibid.*, at 122.

[13] *Ibid.*, at 153. The judgment was subsequently reversed by the Parliamentary Papers Act 1840. The Act empowered the Speaker to issue a certificate staying any legal proceedings in respect of documents published by order of either house. S.3 of the Act provided that it would be permissible to refer to the text of the relevant parliamentary proceeding in subsequent court action for the purpose of establishing that the alleged libel was contained in an accurate report of parliamentary activity.

[14] (1857) 7 E and B 229.

following a meeting of the West Hartlepool Improvement Commission, a statutory body whose various powers included approving the grant of chaplaincies by Bishops. In the course of a public meeting of the Commission, it was claimed that Davison had secured a chaplaincy by lying to the Bishop of Durham. This allegation was then repeated in the *Durham County Advertiser*, whose proprietor was the defendant in the ensuing action. The defendant's plea in response to the suit was that he had produced a fair and accurate report of the Commission's public proceedings, and that, having done so without malice, he should be able to rely on the qualified privilege defence in respect of any false allegations contained in the report.

Lord Campbell CJ, who gave the leading judgment, rejected the defendant's argument in an opinion which drew a sharp distinction between judicial proceedings and public meetings:

> A fair account of what takes place in a court of justice is privileged. The reason is, that the balance of public benefit from publicity is great. It is of great consequence that the public should know what takes place in court. . . . The inconvenience, therefore, arising from the chance of injury to private character, is infinitesimally small as compared to the convenience of publicity.
>
> But it has never yet been contended[15] that such a privilege extends to a report of what takes place at all public meetings. Even if confined to a report of what was relevant to the object of the meeting, it would extend the privilege to an alarming extent.[16]

This substantially mischaracterised the defendant's plea, which was tailored explicitly to the meetings of the Commission, and not to *all* public meetings. To have accepted the plea would hardly have had the 'alarming' implications to which Lord Campbell referred, although it would obviously have raised an inference that accurate reports of the public proceedings of all *statutory* bodies should attract qualified privilege.[17]

In a passage which seemed to reject the notion that the common law had any legitimate constitutional role to play as the progenitor of innovative legal principles, Lord Campbell then suggested that any such extension of qualified privilege would be a matter for Parliament; '[w]e in a Court of law, can only say how the law now stands; and, according to that, it is clear that the action lies, and the plea is bad'.[18]

---

[15] An even wider contention had in effect been made in *R. v. Lee*, see p. 6 above.

[16] (1857) 7 E & B 229 at 231.

[17] Coleridge J also concluded, for the same reason, that no privilege attached to such a publication. He too misrepresented the pleading as applying to any public meeting. Wightman J, however, re-affirmed the *Wright/Curry* principle that an accurate report of judicial/parliamentary proceedings was not actionable, rather than merely being privileged. Crompton J appeared to approve this reasoning. Is it conceivable that these two judges meant the same thing by 'not actionable' and 'privileged'? If so, they had engaged in a very lax use of language. While *de facto* absolute privilege renders a libel non-actionable, qualified privilege—which was the defence invoked—has no such effect.

[18] (1857) 7 E & B 229 at 231.

Within barely a dozen years however, both the substance of the common law's rules on the nature of political libels and the methodological techniques through which those rules were created appeared to undergo a rapid and profound (albeit short-lived) evolutionary shift. Three cases seem to be of particular significance. The first, *Campbell* v. *Spottiswoode* in 1863, indicated that there might be some types of information possessing a 'public-interest' character that could be disseminated to 'all the world' while still attracting a dilute version of the qualified privilege defence.[19]

Campbell v. Spottiswoode

The plaintiff in *Campbell* was a religious activist, accused by the defendant's newspaper of exploiting the credulity of his followers to amass a substantial fortune for his own use. The defence rested primarily on fair comment, but it was also claimed that any factual assertions made in the story should attract qualified privilege on the basis that they were directed towards an issue of considerable public concern.

All four judges hearing the case rejected the suggestion that the orthodox version of qualified privilege should arise on these facts, even though the story might indeed be a matter of public interest. Three of the judges reached this conclusion on the basis that extending the defence to all such stories would lay too many reputations open to essentially irrebuttable attack. For the plaintiff to prove—as 'malice' required—that the defendant had no honest belief in the truth of his assertions was too onerous an obstacle to have to surmount.

The fourth—and apparently leading—judgment was given by Lord Cockburn CJ. He reached the same conclusion, but did so in terms which suggested that the purveyor of libels on matters of public interest to a general audience would have a defence if he could establish that he had taken reasonable care to establish the truth of any claims he made. Lord Cockburn began by setting out the policy objectives the common law was seeking to achieve in cases of this nature:

> It is said that it is for the interests of society that the public conduct of men should be criticised without any other limit than that the writer should have an honest belief that what he writes is true. But it seems to me that the public have an equal interest in the maintenance of the public character of public men; and public affairs could not be conducted by men of honour with a view to the welfare of the country, if we were to

---

[19] What follows is an unorthodox reading of the case. As will become evident in subsequent chapters, the force of the argument that this book makes is not noticeably undermined if this reading of *Campbell* is rejected.

sanction attacks upon them, destructive of their honour and character, and made without any foundation.[20]

Unlike his fellow judges, Cockburn CJ made repeated reference to the question whether or not the publisher's honest belief had a plausible foundation. Thus, in the passage quoted above, the public interest was not well served by criticism 'made without *any* foundation' (emphasis added). At other points in the judgment, Lord Cockburn observed that the publisher of this type of information would not be liable if 'a jury shall find, not only that he had an honest belief in the truth of his statements, but that his belief was not without foundation'[21]; and that an action could not succeed if a jury were to conclude that 'the criticism were not only honest, but also well founded'.[22]

That a belief has some foundation, or even that it has strong foundations, does not mean that it is true; rather it denotes that there is some objective support for the publisher's subjective belief. This is very much the language of negligence—a test which was the staple ingredient of most torts but which had not hitherto been accepted as playing any significant role in libel. Cockburn CJ actually decided the case in the plaintiff's favour because he could not discern any foundation at all for the defendant's belief; all the defendant had was a 'mere suspicion'.

The task of extracting a clear meaning from Lord Cockburn's judgment is complicated by an apparent elision in his opinion between the fair comment and qualified privilege defences.[23] But the tenor of his judgment, coupled with the nature of the defamatory publication, which mixed factual allegation and comment, indicates that he intended his 'well-founded' belief to apply to matters of fact as well as opinion. The obvious inference which then arises from the judgment is that Cockburn CJ sensed that there was an unhappy lacuna in the common law. On occasions when the qualified privilege defence was available, the law provided almost insurmountable protection to false information afforded only the narrowest of circulations and of legitimate interest to the smallest of audiences. On occasions when it was not, in respect of information circulated to and of legitimate interest to the public at large, the defendant could plead only the frequently useless defence of justification. Cockburn CJ's reasoning hinted at a middle way between these two extremes, which would accommodate information whose substance had a public interest dimension.

Campbell did not concern the activities of an elected politician, nor was the issue in question an explicitly governmental matter. It did however raise

---

[20] (1863) 3 B & S 769 at 777. That granting a defence of honest belief to disseminators of 'public interest' libels would undermine the honourable conduct of public affairs was a theoretical surmise on the Chief Justice's part. He offered no empirical support for the proposition.

[21] *Ibid.*, at 776.

[22] *Ibid.*, at 777.

[23] See also Crompton J's judgment at 291, which seems to employ the two defences almost interchangeably and also—to complicate matters further—suggests that a fair comment could not be libellous in the first place, i.e. that there would be no cause of action rather than a defence to the action.

allegations of widespread fraud on the part of a prominent religious activist whose behaviour in seeking to raise huge sums of money from the public to finance his religious activities necessarily meant that he was no longer an entirely 'private' figure. Such information was—it might be suggested—of legitimate, if not essential, interest to the public at large. The reciprocal duty to disseminate/consume between publisher and audience was thus less intense than that existing in previously recognised cases of qualified privilege. This in turn implied that the efficacy of the defence which the publisher might invoke should also be reduced. A shift in the content of the defence from honest belief alone to honest belief *plus reasonable care* would clearly satisfy this reasoning. A careful reading of the various judgments offered in *Campbell* thus suggests that Cockburn CJ was moving towards a rather more perceptive understanding of the way in which the common law should respond to changes in the political culture of mid-Victorian society. Some five years later, the Chief Justice seized the opportunity to elaborate in the most explicit of terms the rationale that seemed to inform his judgment in *Campbell*.

Wason v. *Walter*

While the 1832 electoral reform legislation broke distinctly with previous tradition, the Reform Act 1867 enfranchised many more voters. In 1867, over a million voters joined the electoral roll, doubling its size and extending voting rights to the upper strata of the (male) working class. The 1867 Act, fashioned by Disraeli, took a significant Parliamentary step towards the creation of a universal franchise.[24]

Neither Disraeli nor Gladstone—then the dominant figure in the Liberal party—were 'democrats' as we now understand the term. Neither wished to enfranchise; 'the poorest, the least instructed and the most dependent members of the community'[25]. The 1867 Act nonetheless signified that the legitimacy of both Parliament and the government rested at least in part on the consent of the emergent middle classes and the most 'respectable' members of the working class. And where Parliament led, the common law—albeit in more modest fashion as it did in *Duncombe* v. *Daniel*—was soon to follow.

The plaintiff in *Wason* v. *Walter*[26] had presented a petition to the House of Lords which alleged that a judge, Sir Fitzroy Kelly, had (as a younger man) lied to a Commons Committee during an investigation into a disputed election in 1835. The petition was debated in the House, where members doubted its accuracy and made defamatory comments about Wason's integrity. Wason could not initiate libel proceedings against participants in the debate. As noted above, it had been accepted in *Stockdale* that Article 9 of the Bill of Rights 1689

[24] See Loveland, n. 1 above, ch.7.
[25] Cowling, M. *1867: Disraeli, Gladstone and Revolution* p40 (Cambridge: CUP, 1967).
[26] (1868) LR 4 QB 73.

afforded complete protection to any libellous comments voiced on the floor of either House. Nor could Wason commence an action against Hansard, the official publishers of parliamentary debates, for repeating the libel and making it available to readers, since Parliament had granted similar statutory protection to authorised publishers of parliamentary material in the Parliamentary Papers Act 1840.

Portions of the debate—with accompanying comment—were however reproduced in *The Times*. Newspapers did not enjoy any statutory immunity from defamation actions, and presumably could no longer shelter behind the rule in *R. v. Wright*. Wason thus began an action against Walter, one of the proprietors of *The Times*. There were two counts to the action: the first concerning the verbatim quotation of parliamentary proceedings; the second a *Times* leader which made factual assertions and comments based upon the relevant debate. *The Times* invoked fair comment as the defence to the second count. In respect of the first, it contended that accurate reportage of parliamentary debates should attract privilege at common law comparable to the protection bestowed by Article 9 of the Bill of Rights and the Parliamentary Papers Act 1840.

The case was heard by four judges. The Court issued a single judgment, authored by Cockburn CJ. Cockburn began by specifying the question before the Court:

> whether a faithful report in a public newspaper of a debate in either house of parliament, containing matter disparaging to the character of an individual, as having been spoken in the course of the debate, is actionable at the suit of the party whose character has thus been called in question.[27]

Cockburn saw this as a novel and important question. He suggested that there was no clear authority on the point, and relevant dicta were 'conflicting and inconclusive': most authorities invoked had concerned Article 9 of the Bill of Rights, and were of no obvious assistance. This assertion might seem surprising in the light of the apparently clear 1799 decision in *R. v. Wright* that verbatim reports of parliamentary proceedings could not be defamatory and so not found an action. The explanation would seem to be that Cockburn had accepted the shift in judicial attitude noted in *Duncan v. Thwaites* and *Stockdale v. Hansard* to the effect that accurate reportage of parliamentary and judicial proceedings could be defamatory but could also attract qualified privilege. In casting his inquiry in terms of whether such a libel was 'actionable', Cockburn CJ seems to have been asking whether it would attract absolute rather than qualified privilege—a question to which there was indeed no obvious answer.

Early in his judgment, Cockburn CJ suggested that he could discern two quite distinct scenarios arising from newspaper publication of parliamentary proceedings. There was a clear difference between:

> the publication of a speech made in parliament for the express purpose of attacking the conduct or character of a person, and afterwards published with a like character

---

[27] *Ibid.*, at 83.

or effect, and the faithful publication of parliamentary debates in their entirety, with a view to afford information to the public, and with a total absence of hostile intention or malicious motive towards anyone.[28]

The former merited no special favours from the common law; the latter, however, deserved renewed consideration.

Cockburn began with an ostensibly legalistic analysis. Lacking direct authority, he turned to the arguably analogous area of the law surrounding the publication of judicial proceedings.[29] He used a number of obiter quotations on this point to establish the principle that accurate reportage of court proceedings was 'privileged' because it brought a matter of legitimate public concern to the attention of the public. Cockburn CJ then applied this principle to parliamentary proceedings. His argument assumed that the time had now come for the values of transparency, candour and informed consent previously applied to the courts to be extended to the activities of each House of Parliament:

> Where would our confidence be in the government of the country or in the legislature by which our laws are framed . . .—where would be our attachment to the constitution under which we live—if the proceedings of the great council of the realm were shrouded in secrecy and concealed from the knowledge of the nation.[30]

Cockburn CJ was not however simply resurrecting *R. v. Wright* in a different legal form. For he then moved beyond the simple question of *where* the information was aired to consider the *substance* of what was being communicated[31]: '[t]here is perhaps no subject matter in which the public have a deeper interest than in all that relates to the conduct of public servants of the state'.[32] The court's notion of who should be seen as the legitimate audience for such information was rather limited, but perfectly in accord with then prevailing understandings of the appropriate reach of voting rights:

> every member of the educated portion of the community from the highest to the lowest looks with eager interest to the debates of either house, and considers it a part of the duty of the public journals to furnish an account of what passes there.[33]

Having discerned a strong *constitutional* argument in favour of safeguarding *The Times'* article from legal liability, Cockburn CJ then asked whether it was legitimate for the common law to offer such protection. He was—in marked contrast to Lord Campbell's evident preference in *Davison* for a static common law and thence deferential judicial role—unperturbed by the fact that he would be promulgating a new rule:

[28] (1868) LR 4 QB 73 at 85.
[29] See the cases briefly discussed at 5–6 and 10–11 above.
[30] (1868) LR 4 QB 73 at 89.
[31] As Lord Denman CJ had urged in *Stockdale*, he was not making the mistake of confounding the nature of the publication with the occasion of publication; see 22 above.
[32] N. 30 above, at 90.
[33] *Ibid.*

Whatever disadvantages attach to a system of unwritten law, and of these we are fully sensible, it has at least this advantage, that its elasticity enables those who administer it to adapt it to the varying conditions of society . . . to avoid the inconsistencies and injustice which arise when the law is no longer in harmony with the wants and usages and interests of the generation to which it is immediately applied.[34]

The 'wants, usages and interests' of contemporary society are manifestly dynamic concepts. *Wason* was decided in 1868. There would seem little scope to doubt that Cockburn CJ's judgment was influenced by the substantial extension of the parliamentary franchise introduced by Disraeli's 1867 Reform Act. In Cockburn CJ's view, the common law now had to recognise that shifts in the relationship between MPs and the general population demanded a restructuring of traditional tort law rules in accordance with newly emergent principles of constitutional morality:

[W]ho can doubt that the public are gainers by the change, and that, though public men may often have to smart under the keen sense of wrong inflicted by hostile opinion, the nation profits by public opinion being thus freely brought to bear on the discharge of public duties.[35]

It was not however entirely clear whether—in respect of the first count— Cockburn CJ concluded that publications of this nature attracted absolute or qualified privilege. The headnote to the case maintains that the privilege was only qualified, and he did, as previously noted, allude to the issue of malice. But there is a marked lack of consistency on this question in the text of the judgment itself. At the outset of his opinion, Lord Cockburn stated quite clearly that such a libel was simply not actionable,[36] a conclusion pointing towards absolute privilege. He also indicated that he regarded the privilege extended to accurate reports of court proceedings as absolute, not qualified.[37] This is perhaps the better view. Cockburn indicated quite clearly that the court was willing to refer to Hansard—as it was authorised to do by section 3 of the Parliamentary Papers Act 1840—to establish whether the report was accurate.[38] In the event that the report was inaccurate, presumably no privilege of any sort would arise.

Cockburn CJ's brief conclusion on the second count—concerning accurate but non-verbatim summary and accompanying comment on parliamentary debates—could be thought to be equally interesting and innovative. It shares the style of his judgment in *Campbell*, in that it rather blurs the distinction between

---

[34] *Ibid.*, at 93.
[35] *Ibid.*, at 94.
[36] *Ibid.*, at 83.
[37] '[F]or the publication of such reports the publishers are neither criminally or civilly responsible': *ibid.*, at 87.
[38] Perhaps more surprisingly, the opinion has a lengthy passage examining Hansard as a source from which to gather evidence as to the government's intention in promoting a subsequently enacted statute; *id.*, at 92–93. This was not authorised by the 1840 Act, and flies rather in the face of modern understandings to the effect that a court could not examine Hansard as an aid to interpreting statutes. On this point, and its supposed reversal in *Pepper* v. *Hart* [1993] 1 All ER 42, see Loveland (1996) *op. cit.* pp 317–320.

matters of fact and comment. However it might alternatively be seen as indicating that in addition to fair comment, a modified version of the ordinary qualified privilege defence, strongly reminiscent of the honest belief plus reasonable care formula used in *Campbell*, would attach to factual claims made in this type of information as long as the defendant had exercised 'a reasonable degree of judgment' in making his claims.[39]

Cockburn CJ's opinion exemplifies an avowedly functionalist approach to the courts' lawmaking role. Its method begins by conducting a survey of the political landscape and thereafter identifies a moral topography on which the most prominent features are not the disseminator and victim of the libel, but the massed ranks of voters to whom the information is directed. To attach an absolute privilege to verbatim reports of Commons and Lords proceedings was an appreciable innovation—which *de facto* resuscitated the *de jure* deceased rule aired in *R. v. Wright*—but one that seems readily comprehensible for a society taking its first hesitant steps towards becoming a representative democracy. Just the same point might be made in favour of his apparent advocacy of a modified qualified privilege defence for non-verbatim but accurate summaries of parliamentary proceedings.

Purcell v. Sowler

The Court of Appeal's judgment in *Purcell v. Sowler*[40] some ten years later ostensibly confined the *Wason* principle solely to reports of parliamentary proceedings. However a more careful reading of the case offers a more complicated picture. *Purcell*[41] concerned a newspaper report of a meeting of a Poor Law Board of Guardians which repeated accusations of malpractice made at the meeting against the plaintiff, a medical doctor employed by the Board. At trial, Brett J did not accept that the electorate, still less the public at large, had any legitimate interest in hearing allegations of corruption and malpractice against Poor Law officials. The only audience to which the possessor of such information could disseminate it with the benefit of qualified privilege would be other government officials whose legal responsibilities empowered them to investigate such allegations. This would seem perfectly in accord with the 1857 judgment in *Davison v. Duncan*. A superficial reading of the Court of Appeal's judgment in *Purcell* might suggest that this reasoning was approved. However, while the Court unanimously upheld the result reached by the lower court, its members did so in terms which suggested Brett J's approach to the question before him had been misconceived.

Counsel for the defendant (J. Edwards QC) argued that while there was no precise authority to support the availability of qualified privilege for accurate

---

[39] (1868) LR 4 QB 73 at 96, emphasis added.
[40] (1876) 1 CPD 781 (first instance); (1877) 2 CPD 215 (CA).
[41] (1877) LR 2 CPD 215.

reports of such proceedings—and that there were indeed authorities against that rule—the matter had to be revisited in the light of *Wason* v. *Walter*. Edwards suggested *Wason* should be seen as laying down a new principle—namely that qualified privilege should be presumed to attach to 'fair reports of all matters of general interest'.[42]

Cockburn CJ seemed to consider that this was a slightly extravagant way to read *Wason*. Edwards' contention was not limited to reports of proceedings of governmental bodies, but rather—in a vein perhaps reminiscent more of Cockburn's judgment in *Campbell* than in *Wason*—of all matters of general interest. In *Purcell*, Cockburn CJ limited his comments to reports of proceedings.[43] But having done so, he indicated that he had much sympathy with Edwards' contention. He observed that the 'general principle'[44] which should structure development of this area of the common law was that qualified privilege should extend to accurate reports of meetings of government bodies whenever 'publicity may be essential to good administration'.[45] This public interest extended far beyond merely reports of judicial and parliamentary proceedings:

> Take the meetings of the corporation of the City of London—the discussion at such meetings may involve strong observations on the conduct of particular individuals: so also as to the municipal councils of other cities or boroughs: so again as to the meetings of magistrates . . . not as courts of justice, but for transacting the business of their county. In all these cases I should be sorry to lay down as law that the proceedings of such meetings may not be fully reported, although the character of private individuals may be incidentally attacked.[46]

Cockburn's three colleagues delivered brief concurring opinions which were rather more reticent in style, but all of which made it clear that they did not reject the assertion that accurate reports of many governmental proceedings should attract qualified privilege.

The Court's reason for not allowing privilege in this particular case turned on the nature of the proceedings themselves. Cockburn CJ identified three factors which militated against extending privilege to the report. The first was that the proceedings were preliminary in nature. The second was that the plaintiff had not been present at the meeting, and had thus had no opportunity to respond to the allegations made against him. The third, related to the first two, was that a meeting of this sort should have been conducted in camera. In combination, these considerations indicated that privileged publication would not be for the common convenience and welfare of society.

---

[42] (1877) 2 CPD 215 at 216. In effect, this restated the wide (and rejected) claim made in *R.* v. *Lee* 70 years earlier; see 6 above.

[43] The contrast with the method used in *Davison* is fascinating. In both cases, the court decided the case on a point of law which the defendant did not actually raise. In *Davison*, the plea was greatly exaggerated by the court. In *Purcell*, it was significantly narrowed.

[44] (1877) 2 CPD 215 at 220.

[45] *Ibid.*, at 219.

[46] *Ibid.*

The ratio of *Purcell* could hardly be seen as protective of investigative or opportunist political journalism. But, like *Wason*, its significance might be thought to lie more in its reasoning than its result. The Britain of 1877 had still taken no more than timid steps along the path towards a system of universally representative governance. Its claim to a democratic constitutional morality was nascent rather than established. In that context, Cockburn CJ's analytical approach is very innovative. It suggests that the starting point for judicial analysis should be a presumption that the publication of matters of political interest—of which coverage of governmental activities was a core element—merited the protection of qualified privilege unless considerations of specific significance to the libel before the court pointed in the other direction.

While *Wason* could be seen as having followed the tentative democratic innovation introduced by Disraeli's Reform Act, the judgment in *Purcell* had no such legislative underpinnings. Indeed, it rather appears that on this occasion Parliament was prompted to follow the Court of Appeal's lead. Section 2 of the Newspaper Libel and Registration Act 1881 extended qualified privilege to fair and accurate newspaper reports of any public meeting. The privilege would not be available to newspapers which did not offer the plaintiff the opportunity to make a prompt rebuttal of or comment on the libellous allegation.

The courts did not however regard this legislation as an indication that they should be willing to return to the spirit of Lord Cockburn's judgments in *Campbell* and *Wason* to extend enhanced common law protection to 'public interest' or 'political' news reporting. Indeed, some of the leading political libel judgments of the next few years indicated that the citizenry's interest in having access to political information no longer exercised much influence over the development of the common law. Rather than being construed as a methodological innovation which required the common law to follow changing political understandings of the nature of democratic governance, *Wason* seemed to be viewed as mechanistic statement of a legal rule—a rule which applied only to reports of parliamentary proceedings. Many of Cockburn CJ's judicial colleagues were unwilling to follow his lead in requiring 'public men to smart under the keen sense of wrong inflicted by hostile opinion'. In their view, the nation apparently did not profit 'by public opinion being freely brought to bear on the discharge of public duties'.

Davis v. Shepstone and *Alexander v. Jenkins*

The Privy Council applied the same reasoning as had been deployed in *Purcell* at first instance in *Davis v. Shepstone* in 1886.[47] Shepstone was a senior Colonial Office official in Natal; Davis was the owner of *The Natal Witness* newspaper. *The Witness* had run several stories criticising Shepstone's performance in

---

[47]   (1886) 11 App. Cas. 187.

office, including lurid allegations that he had physically assaulted a Zulu chief. The story over which he sued was claimed by the paper to be a fair and accurate report of statements made by the emissaries of the Zulu King, Cetewayo, concerning Shepstone's official conduct. *The Witness* claimed that this matter was of sufficient public importance to the people of Natal to attract qualified privilege if published in the paper.

Lord Herschel's judgment for the court noted that fair and accurate reports of parliamentary proceedings and court hearings attracted privilege.[48] Davis was however asking the court to extend the protection much further than that. Lord Herschel felt unable to do this. Referring to *Purcell*, he noted that in that case the privilege had not been stretched '*even* to a report of a meeting of poor law guardians'.[49] The type of information in issue here was evidently even further outside the scope of the privilege than the report in *Purcell*. That conclusion accurately summarised the conclusion reached in *Purcell* at first instance, but it rather misrepresents the Court of Appeal's reasoning. As noted above, the appellate judgment in *Purcell* provides no authority for the blanket proposition that accurate reportage of meetings of Poor Law Guardians (and analogous local government bodies) could not attract qualified privilege. Rather it suggested that the special facts of the case justified an exception to the general principle that such reports of those proceedings should be so protected. *Shepstone* seemed essentially to reverse the order of these presumptions.

As with *Purcell* itself, the result of *Shepstone* is perhaps of less significance than the reasoning that led to it. Both decisions rejected the defendant's claim for privilege. But Cockburn CJ's judgment in *Purcell* devoted much attention to the public interest in receiving press coverage of governmental activities. In *Shepstone*, that concern was barely discernible. A few years later, in the Court of Appeal's judgment in *Alexander* v. *Jenkins*,[50] the electorate's interest in consuming and evaluating information about public officials had disappeared altogether from the judges' reasoning. The defendant had accused the plaintiff, a local councillor, of being an habitual drunkard unfit to hold public office. The action was for slander, rather than libel. As noted in Chapter 1, an action in slander was generally maintainable only if the plaintiff could demonstrate that the defamatory statement caused him/her pecuniary loss.

The slander would undoubtedly have jeopardised the plaintiff's prospects of re-election, and may also have compromised his effectiveness in office. However, the office of councillor was at that time unpaid. The plaintiff thus had to convince the court that the possibility of deprivation of public office should be recognised as a new exception to the general rule that slander required proof of pecuniary loss. At first instance, the trial court had accepted this reasoning. The Court of Appeal reversed this judgment. No action could lie in respect of unpaid offices.

---

[48] He did not distinguish between absolute and qualified privilege.
[49] (1886) 11 App Cas 187 at 191, emphasis added.
[50] [1892] 1 QB 797.

It might readily be thought that the judgment recognised the 'informed consent' principle. The conclusion reached would presumably stimulate oral discussion of a politician's or public servant's fitness for office. Since MPs were also unpaid at that time, they too would have been caught by the rule.[51] However the voters' interest did not figure at all in the Court's reasoning, which was premised simply on the view that the creation of new exceptions to the general rule was a matter better undertaken by Parliament rather than the courts.

Such reasoning indicated that Cockburn CJ's dynamic and avowedly political analysis of libel laws in *Wason* had rather drifted into the realms of jurisprudential obscurity in England, even as the representative basis of our governing institutions became ever more broadly based. The Court of Appeal's conclusion in *Alexander* and the Privy Council's judgment in *Davis* v. *Shepstone* can be contrasted with *Wason* and *Purcell* on two counts. The first is that the first pair of judgments denied that questions of political accountability played any legitimate role in guiding the development of common law defamation principles. The second implication was that if such innovations were appropriate for the 'wants and usages' of contemporary society, it should be Parliament rather than the courts which introduced the change.

Manchester Corporation v. *Williams*

One judgment in this era did seem to have the effect of protecting politically critical speech, but it did so on the basis of reasons far removed from the spirit expressed in *Wason*. The plaintiff in *Manchester Corporation* v. *Williams*[52] sued in libel in respect of a letter published in a newspaper which alleged that corruption was rife within the authority. The Divisional Court held that the council could not maintain the action, and did so on narrow technical grounds. Day J considered it to be established law[53] that a corporate body (whether governmental or in the private sector) could sue in libel over stories which caused it demonstrable property loss; however it could only sue in respect of stories attacking its political reputation if the allegations made against it amounted to a crime. Since a council *qua* corporate body could not, in Day J's view, be guilty of corruption, no action could lie.

The judgment made no allusion to questions of political accountability in its reasoning. It might also be thought unsatisfactory on other grounds. Day J was simply wrong in assuming a corporation could not be guilty of corruption. He— and, it seems, counsel for both parties -had not realised that the Public Bodies Corrupt Practices Act 1889 created such an offence. One might also think, if corporations could invoke speech tort actions to recover loss caused to their prop-

---

[51] Ministers, in contrast, held paid office, and so could have sued for slander.

[52] [1891] 1 QB 94.

[53] Citing *Metropolitan Saloon Omnibus Co. Ltd* v. *Hawkins* (1859) 4 H & N 87; [1843–60] All ER Rep. 430.

erty, that the correct remedy for them to use would be malicious falsehood rather than libel.

The judgment was strongly attacked in a leading contemporary textbook on defamation, but on the ground that corporations should be treated in exactly the same way as private individuals for libel law purposes, rather than because it ignored the political implications raised by the facts.[54] A superficial reading of *South Hetton Coal* v. *North Eastern News Association Ltd*, decided by the Court of Appeal in 1894,[55] might have created the impression that *Manchester* was not good law. The case arose from newspaper stories condemning the state of tied housing provided by the plaintiff. The primary issue before the court was whether the articles were fair comment, but before reaching that issue the judges considered whether a company was able to bring a libel action at all.

Lord Esher MR, who gave the leading judgment, made several ostensibly sweeping statements which might be thought to suggest that *Manchester* was wrongly decided: 'the law of libel is one and the same as to all plaintiffs. . . .The question is really the same by whomsoever the action is brought'.[56] However, he made no explicit allusion to *Manchester* itself, and a reading of his judgment in its entirety reveals that his references to 'corporations' were limited solely to the activities of commercial organisations. Concurring in the result, Lopes LJ did allude to the *Manchester* case, observing that it was rightly decided on its particular facts. The gist of his judgment appeared to be that—quoting Day J in *Manchester*—'[a] corporation may sue for a libel affecting property, not for one merely affecting personal reputation'.[57]

What was not made clear in either judge's opinion was whether an attack on the integrity or competence of a government body was a matter merely of 'personal reputation', or one which affected its 'property'. It would seem arguable that the Court of Appeal's implicit approval of *Manchester* suggested that such criticism fell into the former category, although none of the judges hearing the case made any explicit reference to the 'political' or 'non-political' nature of the criticism in issue.

The law relating to libel actions by government bodies would thus seem to have been rather ambiguous at the turn of the century, as was, in more general terms, the whole approach taken by both the common law and statute to the protection of political expression. In one area, however, both the judiciary and Parliament seemed to conclude that the content of the law was entirely certain.

---

[54] Spencer Bower G., *Law of Actionable Defamation* (London: Sweet & Maxwell, 1908) pp 278–279.

[55] [1894] 1 QB 133.

[56] *Ibid.*, at 138.

[57] *Ibid.*, at 142.

AN ABSOLUTE PROTECTION FOR LIBELLOUS STATEMENTS AND PUBLICATIONS
MADE DURING 'PROCEEDINGS IN PARLIAMENT'

The plaintiff in *Dillon* v. *Balfour*[58] was a midwife in Ireland. Balfour was then a minister with responsibility for Irish affairs. During the passage of the Criminal Procedure (Ireland) Bill in 1887, Balfour had made various allegedly defamatory remarks about Dillon which she felt undermined her professional reputation, and in respect of which she sought substantial damages. Balfour had applied to the court for the action to be struck out, on the basis that—as Denman CJ had concluded in *Stockdale*—speeches made in the House could not be the subject of a defamation suit.

Palles CB's judgment concluded that the plaintiff's action could not be sustained. Palles CB held that the court had jurisdiction in a defamation action only to ask if the words in issue were spoken/written as a 'proceeding in Parliament'. If it was satisfied that the words had this status, the statement enjoyed complete immunity from actions in defamation.

It may be thought that this level of absolute protection affords MPs an unnecessarily expansive legal immunity. There is no doubt force in the argument that MPs should be able to use the privilege to raise matters of public concern which subsequent investigation proves to be well-founded. However, it is also plausible to suggest that MPs might shelter behind privilege to raise wholly unfounded allegations. That was not however a consideration which the court found it necessary to address, any more than had Lord Denman in *Stockdale*.

CONCLUSION

Cockburn CJ's demonstrable concern with issues of public interest and political accountability in *Campbell* and *Wason* had, it seems, disappeared over the English common law's jurisprudential horizon by the turn of the century. But while the ideas offered in *Wason* seemed to have been forgotten or rejected in English law, they had been eagerly embraced and enthusiastically extended by many jurisdictions in the United States of America.

---

[58] (1888) 20 LR Ire. 600.

3

American Perspectives on Political Libels in the Early Democratic Era

Legal defence of freedom of speech in the United States is now most readily associated with the First Amendment to the Constitution. This provides, *inter alia*, that 'Congress shall make no law . . . abridging the freedom of speech, or of the press.'. However the application of the First Amendment to most free-speech issues is of comparatively recent origin. The US Supreme Court did not accept until the mid-1920s that the First Amendment applied to actions taken or laws promulgated by the organs of State government.[1] As we shall see in Chapter 5, it was not until the mid-1960s that the US Supreme Court concluded that the First Amendment controlled State libel laws. Freedom of expression and informed consent principles nonetheless exercised considerable influence over the development of American libel law in the nineteenth and early twentieth centuries. This was in part because some States explicitly protected freedom of speech in their own constitutions. However, in some jurisdictions, that protection emerged as a facet of the common law. And among the foremost influences on those developments was Cockburn CJ's reasoning in *Wason* v. *Walter*.

KANSAS—*COLEMAN V. MCCLENNAN*

The *Wason* rationale was approved and extended by the Kansan Supreme Court in the 1908 case of *Coleman* v. *McClennan*,[2] a judgment building upon an earlier decision concerning criminal libel. The defendant in *State* v. *Balch*[3] had been convicted of criminal libel for circulating a pamphlet during an election which (falsely) accused one candidate of vote-rigging at an earlier election. The trial judge had instructed the jury that if they considered the allegations defamatory and untrue, malice had to be presumed, irrespective of the defendant's motives and behaviour. The Supreme Court quashed the conviction. The Court held that instructions to the jury should have recognised a 'good faith' defence in respect of false and defamatory information:

---

[1] The principle was embraced by the US Supreme Court in *Gitlow* v. *New York* (1925) 268 US 652.
[2] (1908) 98 Pac 281.
[3] (1884) 31 Kan 465; 2 Pac 609.

If the supposed article was circulated only among the voters of Chase County, and only for the purpose of giving what the defendant believed to be truthful information, and only for the purpose of enabling such voters to cast their ballots more intelligently . . . the article was privileged and the defendants should have been acquitted.[4]

The 'good faith' test was cast very generously in the defendant's favour. An honest belief, even if negligently or recklessly held, would suffice.

Valentine J's opinion was based solely on Kansan common law, as was the 1908 decision in *Coleman*.[5] In 1904, Coleman held office as Kansas' Attorney-General. McClennan owned a Topeka newspaper, which ran a story accusing Coleman of illegal financial practices. The trial judge at the ensuing libel action had issued instructions to the jury which echoed the ratio of *Balch*: a false story about a candidate for public office would attract qualified privilege if published for the purpose of enabling voters to vote more intelligently and (and here the trial judge narrowed the *Balch* holding) the defendant had taken reasonable care to establish the truth of any factual allegations: in effect a 'good faith plus due diligence' test. Coleman's appeal, which contended that no qualified privilege arose in such circumstances, was firmly rebutted by the Kansas Supreme Court, in a unanimous opinion authored by Burch J.

Burch J began by referring to Article 11 of the Kansas constitution's Bill of Rights: '[t]he liberty of the press shall be inviolate; all persons may freely speak, write or publish their sentiments on all subjects, being responsible for the abuse of that liberty'. He considered the text of Article 11 of little assistance in answering the question before him, since it offered no definition either of 'liberty' or 'abuse'. Article 11 also had to be construed in the light of Article 18 of the Bill of Rights: '[a]ll persons for injuries suffered in person, reputation, or property, shall have remedy by due course of law, and justice administered without delay'. The meanings of all such terms, he felt, were found in 'the common law'.

But he did not regard the 'common law' as a simple source of formal rules. He appeared rather to construe it primarily as a methodological tool. In so doing, he closely followed the technique used by Cockburn CJ in *Wason*; the common law was an elastic phenomenon, which should be adapted to serve 'the wants and usages and interests of the generations to which it is immediately applied'.

The question facing Burch J in *Coleman* was rather different from the one before Cockburn CJ in *Wason*. The 'occasion' in issue was not verbatim recitation of legislative proceedings—nor even a summary thereof—but *all* political information affecting the voters' capacity to make informed electoral choices. In that respect, he was being invited to go much further than *Wason*. On the other hand, he was being asked to extend only qualified and not absolute privilege to the information concerned.

Had Burch J favoured a rigid, substantive conception of *stare decisis*, *Wason* would have been of little assistance in legitimising a decision in MacClennan's

---

[4] (1884) 31 Kan 465; 2 Pac 609 at 614 (Pac).
[5] (1908) 98 Pac 281.

favour. However his judgment suggested that *Wason*'s key feature was not its narrow substantive holding, but rather its political underpinning and its methodology. Burch J considered that *Wason* offered a political principle of general application. After reviewing the decision at length, he observed:

> Paraphrasing this language, it is of the utmost consequence that the people should discuss the character and qualifications of candidates for their suffrages. The importance to the state and to society of such discussions is so vast and the advantage derived are so great that they more than counterbalance the inconvenience of private persons whose conduct may be involved, and occasional injury to the reputation of individuals must yield to the public welfare.[6]

The methodological authority which Burch J extracted from *Wason* was that this principle should be applied through the common law in a form which best served 'the wants and usages and interests of the generations to which it is immediately applied'. The desirability of linking legal principle and policy in this way led Burch J to suggest that the Privy Council decision in *Davis* v. *Shepstone*[7] represented poor law, since it did not offer any substantive reason to support the conclusion it had reached. Burch J's own reasoning on this issue was *not* informed by distinctively American principles. His heavy reliance on *Wason* is obvious evidence of this. More broadly, the reasoning appeared to rest on foundations which would seem of equal applicability to any representative democracy. The first lay in the changing nature and role of the mass media in (then) contemporary society; the second in the empirical basis of the public policy considerations generally invoked to refute the argument that political information should attract qualified privilege.

On the first point, Burch J indicated that advances in communicative technology now presented the Court with the opportunity to develop the notion of the 'liberty of the press' in a manner which gave meaningful effect to the principle that government officials be accountable to their electorate:

> The press as we know it today is almost as modern as the telephone and the phonograph. The functions which it performs at the present stage of our social development, if not substantially different in kind from what they have been, are magnified many fold, and the opportunities for its influence are multiplied many times. Judicial interpretation must take cognisance of these facts.[8]

The Kansan Supreme Court then observed that a private citizen forfeited part of her constitutional entitlement to the protection of her reputation when she asked the electorate to entrust her with temporary control of even a small part of its political authority; 'by becoming a candidate . . . a man tenders as an issue to be tried out publicly before the people or the appointing power his honesty, integrity and fitness for the office to be fulfilled'.[9]

---

[6] (1908) Pac 281 at 286.
[7] See 32–3 above.
[8] (1908) 98 Pac 281 at 283–4.
[9] *Ibid.*, at 285.

Burch J then took a further analytical step. He suggested that it was a facile oversimplification to view the question as simply one of balancing the electorate's public interest in the dissemination of political information against an individual politician's private interest in having the law deter unwarranted attacks on her reputation. By seeking to become *qua* politician a *public* persona, an individual lost that element of his entitlement to the protection of reputation which was rooted in the notion of reputation as *private* property. Such protection as the common law afforded politicians against political libels therefore had to be rooted in a purely public interest, which had to stand in the balance with the public interest in maximal dissemination of political information.

In reviewing the decisions of State and Federal courts which had rejected the qualified privilege defence for political libels,[10] Burch J suggested that the 'public interest' leading them to this conclusion had been assumed rather than argued. The assumption was that diluting the purely private identity of politicians for libel law purposes would offer the press legal *carte blanche* to run the most scurrilous and unsubstantiated stories: this would in turn lead many highly qualified citizens to choose not to run for public office; and consequently voters would have a less able field from which to choose their governors. This dilemma was phrased in essentially the same terms as Cockburn CJ had used in *Campbell*[11]. But unlike Cockburn CJ, Burch J went on to say that he thought these criticisms poorly founded:

> Without speaking for other states in which the liberal rule applied in Balch's Case prevails, it may be said that here at least men of unimpeachable character from all political parties continually present themselves as candidates in sufficient numbers to fill the public offices and manage the public institutions.[12]

The Court appeared to be arguing that theoretical issues of political principle—namely to maximise politicians' accountability to their electorates—pointed firmly in favour of expansive defences to political libel suits. Such theoretical presumptions could be rebutted only by compelling empirical evidence of the pernicious effects of such a legal doctrine. Absent such evidence, the Court's responsibility was to enhance rather than restrict the likelihood that electoral decisions were made on the basis of fully informed consent.

Having concluded that qualified privilege must attach to political information, the court then offered expansive definitions both of 'political' and of 'malice'. On the first point, the court held that the privilege would apply not just to stories about occupants of and candidates for elected public office, but also to:

> all officers and agents of government, municipal, state and national; to the management of all public institutions, educational, charitable and penal; to the conduct of all

---

[10] Especially *Post Publishing Co v. Hallam* (1893) 59 Fed. 530: *King v. Root* (1829) 4 Wend. (NY) 114.

[11] See 24–5 above.

[12] (1908) 98 Pac 281 at 289.

public enterprises affected with a public interest, transportation, banking, insurance; and to innumerable other subjects involving the public welfare.[13]

The Court displayed a similar preference for protecting speech over reputation in concluding that malice demanded the plaintiff prove 'actual evil-mindedness' (i.e. knowing falsity) on the defendant's part. This test left no scope for attaching liability to even grossly negligent failures to recognise falsity.

Burch J dismissed suggestions that this conclusion left 'politicians' at the mercy of a dishonest, vindictive press. The court's holding:

> offers no protection to the unscrupulous defamer and traducer of private character. The fulminations in many of the decisions about a Telemonian shield of privilege from beneath which scurrilous newspapers may hurl the javelins of false and malicious slander against private character with impunity are beside the point. Good faith and bad faith are as easily proved in a libel case as in other branches of the law.[14]

An alternative way of expressing this is that permitting the dissemination of known political lies does not increase the amount of information available to the electorate. Rather such dissemination places necessarily places *dis*information in the political domain: it has no other purpose than to muddle, complicate and corrupt the exercise of informed electoral consent. It therefore merits no special legal protection.

The various elements of the Court's conclusion were arrived at as a matter not of Kansan *constitutional law*, but of Kansan *common law*. The state's Constitution did not require so extensive a protection of press freedom on political issues. Thus, if the Kansas legislature found the rule unacceptable, it was legally competent to alter it. Burch J thought this was unlikely to happen, given that he was applying to the civil law the rule that the court had applied to the criminal law twenty years earlier in *Balch*—a decision which the legislature had not thought it appropriate to amend or overrule.

ILLINOIS

Illinois' defamation law also drew a clear distinction between actions initiated by politicians and those begun by private citizens. The Illinois Court of Appeals' 1905 judgment in *Ambrosious* v. *O'Farrell*[15] held that the publication of political information about candidates for elected public office attracted the protection of qualified privilege at common law. *Ambrosious* was initiated by a municipal judge in Colinsville. A group of citizens presented to the city council a petition which accused O'Farrell of being in the pocket of organised crime; he 'has been guilty of the most brazen malfeasance, allowing thugs criminals and desperadoes of all character to escape without punishment'. At trial, the judge

---

[13] *Ibid.*
[14] *Ibid.*, at 292.
[15] (1905) 199 Ill. App. 265.

instructed the jury that malice was to be implied from the mere publication of libellous material (which the petition undoubtedly was); i.e. the ordinary (English) common law rules applied.

The Court of Appeals overturned this instruction. It concluded as a matter of Illinois *common law* that citizens who publicised libellous political material:

> may not be held to liability in damages even though the charge is that of a crime and may not be proved . . . if they act in good faith without malice or ill-will toward the person of the official complained of.[16]

The Court of Appeals derived this rule from what it regarded as the long-established principle of American constitutional morality that citizens should be able to petition their rulers for a redress of grievances. That base might suggest that the rule would have a limited scope—reaching only to communications to other government bodies (and ancillary publication, such as in city council minutes or reports of proceedings where the matter was discussed). However, the Court then offered a 'reason' for the rule rooted in contemporary political realities:

> Often it is a matter of common knowledge that there is failure to execute the laws and enforce the ordinances, especially those relating to the sale of intoxicating liquor, gambling and prostitution, and yet without the aid of the very officials whose conduct is questioned, the truth of the charge of maladministration could not be proved.[17]

This 'reason' would suggest the rule must have a wide scope, embracing publication in or by the press whenever the allegations maintained that large swathes of the government machinery were incompetent or corrupt.

The expansive interpretation of the *Ambrosious* principle was affirmed twenty years later in *Ogren* v. *Rockford Star*.[18] Ogren was a socialist candidate for mayor in Rockford. His suit was prompted by advertisements placed in the *Star* by one of his opponents, which suggested he was an anarchist and a terrorist. The Court of Appeals concluded that the advertisements could be construed as expressions of opinion rather than claims of fact. However, even if they were facts, their publication attracted qualified privilege. If libellous, they triggered liability only if the plaintiff demonstrated they were both false and published with malice.

The court reasoned that a candidate for public office 'put his character at issue, so far as it may respect his fitness and qualification for office'.[19] He was no longer a purely 'private' person, and so forfeited some protection bestowed on private citizens by ordinary libel law. His private interest was surrendered to the public's interest in being able to make informed choices about their governors—and the press was an entirely proper vehicle for facilitating that choice:

> It was certainly the legal right and duty of any newspaper to make such publication. It is through the medium of the public press that the people . . . become informed of

---

[16] (1905) 199 Ill. App. 265 at 269.
[17] *Ibid.*, at 270.
[18] (1925) 237 Ill. App. 349.
[19] *Ibid.*, at 357.

the record of candidates for office, and of the principles for which they stand. . . . If this right is abridged then those candidates will be deprived of a means to become fully informed of the candidates and what they represent.[20]

Victims of maliciously[21] motivated untruths could still recover damages, but the victims of honest or even careless error could not.

PENNSYLVANIA

The leading authority on this issue in Pennsylvania was the 1886 State Supreme Court judgment in *Briggs* v. *Garrett*.[22] The plaintiff was a minor political figure—a state judge seeking re-election. Garrett was the President of a Philadelphia pressure group which existed to foster discussion of the merits of candidates for public office. Garret had publicised a letter to the group which accused Briggs of corruption. The accusation was readily discovered to be false—Briggs had not sat in the case to which the letter referred. The Pennsylvania Supreme Court faced two questions. First, did the dissemination of such information in this fashion create an occasion of qualified privilege? And secondly, if qualified privilege did apply, was the defendant's failure to take the simple step needed to establish falsity tantamount to malice?

Paxson J gave the majority opinion. The Pennsylvania Constitution offered little clear guidance on these questions. As in Illinois, the state Constitution provided that '[t]he free communication of thoughts and opinions is one of the invaluable rights of man, and every citizen may freely speak, write and print on any subject, being responsible for the abuse of that liberty'.[23] Paxson J began by returning to the English common law's concept of 'qualified privilege'. He took *Toogood* as his starting point and found it led him down a path which English courts had generally been reluctant to tread. The 'common convenience and welfare' of late nineteenth-century Pennsylvania demanded that candidates for elected office necessarily cast aside substantial portions of their 'private' identity:

> When Judge Briggs accepted the nomination as a candidate . . . he threw out a challenge to the entire body of voters of the county of Philadelphia to canvass his qualifications and fitness for that position. That involved . . . not only his official conduct . . . but, generally, his fitness for the position of judge.[24]

Exposure to criticism on such matters was an unseverable concomitant of seeking important public office. Electors were both entitled and obliged to disseminate and consume information pertaining to a candidate's fitness to serve:

[20] *Ibid.*, at 358.
[21] The court did not define malice—the tone of its judgment suggests it was thinking of this test in terms of knowing falsehood.
[22] (1886) 11 PA 406; 2 ATL 513.
[23] Art 1. s.7.
[24] (1886) 2 ATL 513 at 518–19.

merely to be a citizen and a voter was sufficient to embroil an individual in a net-work of reciprocal rights and duties to circulate political knowledge and opin-ions with all her/his fellow voters. In Paxson J's opinion, it was specious to argue that citizens enjoyed effective freedom of speech on political matters if their comments were subject to the ordinary libel laws; '[i]f the voters may not speak, write or print anything but such facts as they can establish with judicial certainty, the right does not exist, unless in such form as a prudent man would hesitate to exercise it'.[25]

This presumption led Paxson J both to hold that political libels attracted qualified privilege *and* to offer a narrow definition of the 'malice' needed to defeat the defence. He suggested that malice could be established only if the plaintiff demonstrated that the defendant *knew* that the information was false: simply making a mistake did not make the defendant malicious.

Nor was Paxson J swayed by the argument that affording qualified privilege to such communications would expose political figures to constant and unfounded criticism:

> It is mistakes not lies that are protected under the doctrine of privilege . . . A man may not charge a public officer with being a thief, knowing it to be false. . . . Public officials are not outlaws, to be hounded and maligned at the will of every person who may have incurred their enmity. . . . There is no room for the application of the doctrine of priv-ilege to such instances.[26]

Chief Justice Mercer, joined by two other Justices, issued dissenting judg-ments. However, their dissent did not challenge the propriety of according qual-ified privilege to libellous political information. Their disagreement centred rather on whether Garret displayed malice in publicising the defamatory letter. In Mercer CJ's view, this test owed more to the concept of negligence than of intent. Purveyors of political libels were fixed with constructive notice of read-ily discoverable falsehoods. Since the falsity of this charge could easily have been established, Garret's failure to investigate it was tantamount to malice.

The unanimity which eluded the court in *Briggs* emerged two years later in *Press Co. Ltd* v. *Stewart*.[27] The judgment afford an extraordinarily wide lati-tude to the concept of 'political' information. Stewart owned a journalism school in Philadelphia. A Press Co. newspaper ran a story casting doubt on Stewart's competence and *bona fides*. The court concluded that such a story attracted qualified privilege:

> If we are asked why this article is so privileged, I answer because it was proper for pub-lic information. The plaintiff was holding himself out to the world as a teacher and guide of youth. He was seeking to attract them to his place by signs, placards and advertisements. . . . This gave him a *quasi* public character. Whether he was a proper person to instruct the young, and whether his school was a proper place for them to

[25] *Ibid.*, at 523.
[26] *Ibid.*, at 521 and 523.
[27] (1888) 119 Pa 584; 14 ATL 51.

receive instruction, were matters of importance to the public, and the Press was in the strict line of its duty when it sought such information, and gave it to the public.[28]

Thus by 1900 the Pennsylvania Supreme Court had pushed the boundaries of qualified privilege not simply into the sphere of *electoral* politics, but also into the much more expansive and amorphous area of the *'public interest'* generally.[29] In the mid-West, Iowa's Supreme Court had proceeded more cautiously.

IOWA

The Iowa courts had reached the conclusion arrived at in *Briggs* v. *Garrett* some years earlier. The plaintiff in the 1882 case *Bays* v. *Hunt*[30] was a candidate for public office accused by the plaintiff of religious and financial dishonesty. At trial, the plaintiff had accepted that his public status removed him from the ordinary libel laws, and exempted the defendant from liability as long as the defendant could show 'probable cause' for believing the false statements to be true; i.e. a negligence test. However the trial court instructed the jury that malice in respect of information disseminated for the sole purpose of assisting electors in evaluating the qualifications and character of candidates for public office demanded that the plaintiff show the defendant lacked an honest belief in its truth: i.e. a knowing falsity test. The Iowa Supreme Court unanimously approved this instruction, seemingly believing the point was so clear that it did not need to be justified by argument from first principles.

The court's 1899 decision in *State* v. *Hoskins*[31] reiterated this conclusion, but confined the reach of the defence to a limited geographical area. Publication of false political information about a candidate for a judgeship was privileged only if circulation was limited to the relevant electorate. State-wide publication in relation to candidates for municipal office would not attract qualified privilege.

The Iowa court also took a narrower view than its Pennsylvania counterpart of what amounted to 'public' office. In *Klos* v. *Zahorik*,[32] it accepted that a clergyman was a public officer for these purposes. However in *Morse* v. *Times-Republican Printing Co.* in 1904[33] it rejected the Pennsylvania notion that certain commercial enterprises had a 'public character'. The plaintiff in *Morse* was a life insurance salesman, accused by the defendant of unethical practices.

---

[28] At 53; original emphasis. Given the breadth of this definition of 'political knowledge', the court's decision in *Jackson* v. *Pittsburgh Times* (1893) 152 PA 406: 25 ATL 613 to grant qualified privilege status to stories concerning occupants of *unelected* public office is not surprising. The plaintiff was an officer in the State militia, accused of being drunk on duty. The Court allowed a claim of qualified privilege here, even though it was satisfied that the *Times* had run an exaggerated and sensationalistic story.

[29] i.e. it had accepted the unsuccessful argument offered in England in 1804 by the defendant in *R.* v. *Lee*; see 6 above.

[30] (1882) 60 Iowa 251, 14 NW 785.

[31] (1899) 109 Iowa 656; 80 NW 1063.

[32] (1900) 84 NW 1046.

[33] (1904) 124 Iowa 707; 100 NW 867.

Such a person, the court concluded, 'is not a public officer, nor is his character a matter of general public interest'.[34]

In *Salinger* v. *Cowles*,[35] decided in 1922, Iowa's Supreme Court confirmed the relevance of the doctrine to public officers—here one of its own members. Salinger had been falsely accused of using his judicial office to 'persuade' a railway company to employ a friend's child. The rationale behind the conclusion was but briefly argued. Candidates for public office relinquish that part of their private identity protected by ordinary libel laws; the 'public trust' which they seek necessarily exposes their behaviour and character to rigorous and potentially inaccurate criticism.

AN ABSOLUTE AND CONSTITUTIONAL PROTECTION FOR LIBELS OF GOVERNMENT BODIES

The press stories which provoked the litigation in the 1923 case *City of Chicago* v. *Tribune Co.*[36] had accused the Mayor and the city council of being so corrupt and incompetent that the city itself was bankrupt. Such stories could obviously undermine the city's reputation, both as an institution of government and as a commercial actor. Yet the Illinois Supreme Court, its unanimous opinion delivered by Thompson CJ, held that the city could do nothing at all to suppress the dissemination of such stories.

Thompson CJ made no reference at all to the First Amendment. At that time, the First was not assumed to apply to the states. However, as will become clear in Chapter 5, the Illinois jurisprudence of the early twentieth century accurately foreshadowed protections for political speech later to be recognised by the US Supreme Court. The judgment was formally rooted in Article 2 section 4 of the Illinois Constitution: '[e]very person may freely speak, write and publish on all subjects, being responsible for the abuse of that liberty'—although the court clearly drew on existing common law understandings of the limits to be placed on libel actions brought by elected politicians when reaching its decision. Thompson CJ observed that state and federal government in the USA were 'founded upon the fundamental principle that the citizen is the fountain of all authority'.[37] Such powers as government bodies possessed were granted on trust by the relevant electorate. Informed electoral choices demanded that citizens be afforded *absolute* protection against prosecution for criticising government

---

[34] *Ibid.*, at 873.

[35] (1922) 191 NW 167.

[36] (1923) 139 NE 87. For contemporary comment see Note, 'Torts—Power of a Municipal Corporation to Sue for Libel'(1923) 21 *Michigan LR* 915; Note, 'Libel and Slander—Suit by Municipal Corporation' (1923) 23 *Columbia LR* 685: Note, 'Libel and Slander—Municipal Corporations' (1929) 28 *Michigan LR* 460. For a detailed discussion and analysis of the case see Loveland I. (1998) '*City of Chicago v Tribune Co*—in Contexts', in Loveland I. (ed.), *Importing the First Amendment* (Oxford, Hart Publishing, 1998).

[37] (1923) 139 NE 87 at 90.

bodies, except in the narrow instance of criticism likely to promote violent disorder.[38] The roots of this presumption lay in the controversy engendered by the Sedition Act of 1798, enacted by the Federalist-dominated Congress to stifle criticism of its foreign policies.[39] The Act was never condemned by the Supreme Court, but had been initially enacted for a three-year period, which was not renewed by the subsequent, Jeffersonian leaning, Congress. Jefferson, when President, pardoned all those convicted under its provisions. Thompson CJ concluded that Jefferson's own view that the Act was quite beyond Congress' power should be an authoritative guide to interpreting the state constitution.

Having thus limited the legitimate scope of criminal libel, Thompson CJ saw no difficulty in drawing an analogy between criminal and civil actions. Indeed, civil actions could be substantially more effective prohibitors of speech than criminal prosecutions. Among the considerations that led Thompson CJ to this conclusion were the facts that civil libel actions, unlike criminal prosecutions, did not require a grand jury investigation; that they did not grant the defendant the presumption of innocence; that they imposed a lesser standard of proof on the plaintiff; that there was no ceiling to the damages that might be awarded; and that there was no double jeopardy rule.

Thompson CJ stressed that the protection against civil liability for criticising a government body was *absolute*; no action of any sort would be permissible. The prohibition extended as fully to the torts of slander and malicious falsehood as it did to libel, and as fully to stories which occasioned economic loss to the body as to those which attacked only its 'political' reputation. There was no question of the court trying to strike a 'balance' between freedom of political speech and the government's reputation; the government body had no corporate or public interest in its reputation to weigh in the scales. The judgment thus went much further in protecting criticism of government bodies, and did so for very different reasons, than the English High Court's earlier decision in *Manchester Corporation*.

Thompson CJ accepted that the rule the court had propounded would sometimes lead to unfounded and malevolent criticism being aired. This however was a price worth paying:

> [I]t is better that an occasional individual or newspaper that is so perverted in its judgment and so misguided in his or its civic duty should go free than that all of the citizens should be put in jeopardy of imprisonment or economic subjugation if they venture to criticise an inefficient or corrupt government.[40]

---

[38] The test thus seems broadly comparable to the 'clear and present danger' concept used by the US Supreme Court after World War I in the 1920s; see *Schenk* v. *United States* (1919) 249 US 47 and *Abrams* v. *United States* (1919) 250 US 616.

[39] The Act made it a crime (punishable with up to 5 years' imprisonment) 'by writing, speaking or printing' to threaten any federal official 'with damage to his character, person or estate'. In contrast to the English common law of sedition, the Act permitted truth as a defence. See Levy L., *Emergence of a Free Press* (Cambridge, Mass.: Harvard UP 1985), ch. IX; Lewis, ch. 7.

[40] At 91. The passage echoes Madison's celebrated observation, which Thompson CJ had earlier quoted (at 89), that: 'some degree of abuse is inseparable from the proper use of everything, and in

Thompson CJ's reasoning on this point is open to obvious criticism. Its absolutist nature can readily be seen as far too blunt a tool with which to regulate the
flow of political (dis)information, since it allowed individuals, political parties
or newspapers to disseminate what they *knew* to be lies. As such, it might corrupt rather than enhance the capacity of voters to make informed decisions
about political issues. It is difficult to see any legitimate scope for affording
protection to the 'perverted' *and* 'misguided' political commentators that
Thompson CJ was prepared to tolerate. It might sensibly be suggested that the
effect of the defence against actions brought by government bodies should be
more onerous than that applied by Illinois common law to actions brought by
elected politicians. Corporate bodies cannot, after all, suffer the emotional dis-
tress that may afflict an individual who is falsely defamed or lied about.
Moreover, they are in a position to use public funds to finance a defamation or
malicious falsehood action. The public interest in the maximal dissemination of
true political information is however unchanged, irrespective of whether the
plaintiff is a politician or a government body. A legal rule which protects publishers of deliberate deceit does not further that interest. Thompson CJ may thus
have better served Illinois' electors by modifying the *Ambrosious* principle. This
could have been achieved by permitting recovery only if the plaintiff demonstrated that the defendant knew the stories were false, or by retaining a knowing or reckless falsity test and requiring the plaintiff to prove it to a more
exacting standard than the usual balance of probabilities.

CONCLUSION

The application of qualified privilege to political libels about government officials seemed to be embraced almost without need for argument by the Iowa
court in *Salinger*. The doctrine had also been accepted as unproblematic in
Minnesota,[41] South Dakota,[42] Maine,[43] New Hampshire,[44] Vermont[45] and
Texas[46]. The American courts developed a rather more elegant variant of the
defence than the traditional English version. They reduced it to *two elements*.
The first might be labelled a matter of *'reach'*—namely *what type of information* was protected? This aspect of the orthodox defence was also streamlined by
the courts' implicit assumption that 'overbroad publication' should no longer be
seen as a facet of 'malice' to be addressed as the final part of the defence, but

no instance is this more true than in that of the press. It has accordingly been decided by the practice of the states that it is better to leave a few of the noxious branches to their luxuriant growth than
by pruning them away to injure the vigour of those yielding the proper fruits.'

[41] *Marks* v. *Baker* (1881) 9 NW 678; *Friedell* v. *Blakely Printing Co.* (1925) 203 NW 974.
[42] *Myers* v. *Longstaff* (1900) 84 NW 233.
[43] *O'Rourke* v. *Publishing Co.*, (1896) 36 Atl. 398.
[44] *State* v. *Burnham*, (1842) 9 NH 34: *Palmer* v. *Concord*, (1881) 48 NH 211.
[45] *Shurtleff* v. *Stevens*, (1888) 31 Am. Rep. 698: *Posnett* v. *Marble*, (1890) 20 Atl. 813.
[46] *Express Printing Co.* v. *Copeland*, (1895) 64 Tex. 354.

should be absorbed into the preliminary question of 'reach'. The second element could be described as one of *'effect'*—namely *how much protection* should the information attract ? Once again, the American courts streamlined the English defence, by dispensing with any examination of the publisher's motives, and focusing instead on the question of his/her culpability in publishing an untruth.

It is also clear that the American courts had adopted a flexible jurisprudential approach to all elements of the defence. As suggested in Chapter 1, the orthodox English defence had been applied to a variety of 'occasions' (i.e. its 'reach' could be adjusted) but it would always[47] have the same 'effect'. In the American jurisdictions, both 'reach' and 'effect' were modified. In some states, one can discern almost a see-saw relationship between the two elements: as the 'reach' of the defence was expanded, so its 'effect' was diluted, in a process which gave increased—albeit sometimes only modestly increased—legal protection to publishers of inaccurate political stories. The end result—as one might anticipate in a federal constitutional structure—was that the state legal systems which had rejected the English model offered varying degrees of legal protection to varying types of 'political' and 'public interest' information. In effect, these jurisdictions regarded the qualified privilege defence as an umbrella label, which simply betokened the fact that their courts had recognised that they should adopt an analytical standpoint in developing their common law which gave primacy to the constitutional rather than tort law dimension of a political libel or malicious falsehood.

This presumption led in turn to the conclusion that the dominant interest to be served in any 'balancing exercise' that courts undertook to define the conditions of liability for political libels was that of the electorate or citizenry in exercising informed consent to their system of governance and the individuals who staffed it. The reciprocal right/duty which the defence required to exist between the disseminator and recipient of the information was thus regarded as an implicit feature of citizenship when 'political information' was in issue. The individual politician's right to redress in the event that her reputation was falsely traduced and the disseminator's entitlement to publish were distinctly secondary considerations within these newly constitutionalised equations. This newly dominant audience interest in informed consent seemed in itself to require the courts to balance two countervailing concerns: how tolerant should the law be of politicians' possible inclination to try to suppress true information bearing on their fitness for office; and how indulgent should the law be of a politician's critics' possible inclination to publish deceitful information bearing on his/her fitness for office?

None of the American jurisdictions granted absolute protection to the publication of political untruths about individual politicians. None afforded citizens or the press an unfettered licence to lie to the electorate about political issues. The absolutist rule adopted in *Chicago* applied only to government bodies, not

[47] With the possible exception of Cockburn CJ's hint of a negligence-based test in *Campbell*; see 24–6 above.

to the people who staffed them. It is nevertheless obvious that the courts in these states accepted that—in varying degrees—adopting a qualified privilege defence for political libels would increase the amount of false political information in public circulation. And the broader the reach of the defence and the more substantial its effect, the higher the risk that this unwelcome consequence would ensue. But while unwelcome, this consequence was manifestly regarded as a lesser constitutional evil than the consequence of retaining the English position. If the only defence available to the publisher of defamatory political facts was truth, some citizens or press organisations would be deterred from publishing potentially true criticism for fear that they would not be able to prove its truth in court if sued by the politician concerned.

This constitutional logic was not universally accepted within the USA. Prior to World War II, many states retained a distinctively English approach to the question—a public/private libel law divide simply did not exist in much of the USA. As we shall see in Chapter 5, that situation did not last much longer. Yet before the shift to a national application of *Coleman* occurred in the USA, it appeared to have been embraced—first tentatively and then in an extremely expansive form indeed—by the English common law.

4

The English Common Law in the Early Years of the Modern Democratic Era

The Court of Appeal's 1941 judgment in *De Buse* v. *McCarthy*[1] would suggest that the *Wason* rationale had been embraced and developed only in American and not in English common law. The defendant was the Town Clerk of Stepney Council, who had placed a council committee report containing allegations of theft against the plaintiff (a council employee) in the borough's libraries, where it was available for public inspection. At first instance, Wrottesly J had instructed the jury that the publication attracted qualified privilege on the basis that the council had a duty to communicate its initial findings on such a matter to ratepayers, who had a reciprocal interest in receiving them. This instruction was overturned by the Court of Appeal,[2] which saw no basis for assuming that ratepayers and their council had any reciprocal interest or duty in communicating such information.

The court was prepared to accept that such an interest might arise in respect of such a report once the council had decided whether to act upon it. But, as Lord Greene MR put it:

> I cannot see that it can possibly be said that the council was under any duty to make that communication to the ratepayers. . . . [W]hat I may call the internal workings of the administrative machine and all the details of its domestic deliberations . . . are things which I should have thought ratepayers are not in general interested in.[3]

Goddard and Du Parq LJJ agreed with this reasoning. The conclusion might seem curious. The document in question was, after all, a committee report, not simply an unsolicited and uninvestigated accusation from an outside source. The information that such a report would contain concerning the 'internal workings of the administrative machine' would presumably be of great assistance to voters in gauging the adequacy of a council's performance, both in general and in particular in respect of investigations of fraud and dishonesty within the council itself.

---

[1] [1942] 1 KB 156. By 1941, the Commons was elected on the basis of a virtually universal franchise, the House of Lords *qua* legislative chamber had been reduced by the Parliament Act 1911 to the inferior rather than the equal of the Commons, and it was widely regarded as wholly inappropriate for the Monarch to express or act upon his own political views.

[2] Lord Greene MR, Goddard and Du Parq LJJ.

[3] [1942] 1 KB 156 at 166.

The conclusion is difficult to square with Cockburn CJ's suggestion in *Wason* that '[t]here is perhaps no subject matter in which the public have a deeper interest than in all that relates to the conduct of public servants of the state'.[4] For the Court of Appeal in *DeBuse* however, that notion was apparently a quite inappropriate concept with which to shape the contours of the common law.

In broader political terms, however, Cockburn CJ's thesis appeared evermore pertinent. By 1948, the United Kingdom had finally reached the point where almost every adult was entitled to one—and only one—vote in elections to the Commons. Whatever flaws the country's version of democracy might retain, disenfranchisement on the grounds of poverty, gender, race or religious belief was no longer among them. And just as the common law had reacted in *Wason* to the new political reality engineered by the Reform Act 1867, so it also seemed to respond (albeit tentatively) in *Braddock* v. *Bevins* to the creation of a fully representative democracy in the aftermath of World War II.

BRADDOCK V. BEVINS

The defendant in *Braddock* v. *Bevins*[5] was a Conservative candidate in a local election. He had distributed to local electors a pamphlet which accused his Labour opponent of being a communist. The defendant accepted the accusation was defamatory. However he maintained as one of his defences at trial that the pamphlet attracted qualified privilege: if the allegations were now accepted to be false he had not believed them to be so when they were made, and he had not published them to damage the plaintiff but rather to inform electors of what he honestly believed to be an important consideration of which they should be aware before casting their votes. This defence was accepted at first instance by Stable J.

On appeal, Lord Greene MR, for a unanimous court, appeared amazed that anyone could question that an occasion of qualified privilege had arisen:

> In principle, and quite apart from such assistance as can be derived from authority, we should have thought it scarcely open to doubt that statements contained in the election address of one candidate concerning the opposing candidate, provided they are relevant to the matters which the electors will have to consider in deciding which ways to cast their votes, are entitled to the protection of qualified privilege.[6]

The court considered it beyond dispute that electors had an interest in receiving such information; 'indeed the task of electors under democratic institutions could not be satisfactorily performed if such a source of relevant information bona fide given were to be cut off by the fear of an action for libel'.[7] And, relat-

---

[4] See 28 above.
[5] [1948] 1 All ER 450.
[6] *Ibid.*, at 453.
[7] *Ibid.*

edly, the publisher had a duty to disseminate it; 'we make bold to assert that [a candidate] has a duty towards the electors to inform them honestly and without malice of any matters which may properly affect their choice in using their suffrages'.[8]

The court's conclusion seemed to do no more than accept the obiter indication given by Lord Denman CJ and Coleridge J over 100 years earlier in *Duncombe* that privilege would attach to a geographically limited publication of political criticism. That Lord Greene MR thought the court was 'making bold' in reaching this decision is a strong indication that the nascent informed consent principle evident in the *Duncombe* and *Wason* judgments enjoyed little currency within the then contemporary common law, and that the court felt—with, as we shall see below, good reason—that its own understanding of the principle was not widely shared.

In that limited sense, the judgment was indeed 'bold'. But seen in the light of already long-established American principle, it was really a rather timid innovation. Lord Greene MR stressed that the judgment had a very limited 'reach': it extended only to hand-delivered election addresses pushed through the letter boxes of local voters. Had the same information been published as an article in a local or national newspaper, it appears that an occasion of privilege would not have arisen.[9]

This may suggest that the court took a curiously limited and highly localised perception of democracy in a country which possessed a unitary constitutional structure and a national newspaper industry. Alternatively, the court may simply have been adopting a conservative jurisprudential stance, in the expectation that the new principle might be given a broader reach on a case-by-case basis in ensuing years.

The former explanation is perhaps the more convincing. In terms of its political function, *Braddock* is manifestly a difficult decision to reconcile with *DeBuse*, in which Lord Greene MR had authored the leading judgment just seven years earlier. The two cases rested on formally distinct facts; *Braddock* concerning an alleged libel of a candidate for office in a rival's election propaganda, *DeBuse* a formal report produced by the occupants of a similar office. If one were to choose which of those factual situations raised the more important political issue, *DeBuse* seems the more likely contender, as it concerned the exercise of existing political power rather than the future possibility of such power being won. Yet in the Court of Appeal's scheme of things, it was the other information which merited greater protection.

---

[8] *Ibid.*

[9] As in *Duncombe*, the judges were not entirely clear in resolving whether overbroad publication went to the question whether an occasion of privilege arose or to the issue of malice. Neither was the Court of Appeal prepared to jettison questions about the defendant's motive when considering whether the qualified privilege defence should be applied. Even if the defendant did know the story was false, and was neither reckless nor negligent in failing to discover this, liability would still arise if the plaintiff proved the defendant was actuated by a hostility to him which existed independently of a desire to aid voters to make an informed electoral choice.

The outcomes of the two cases nicely illustrate the extent to which substantive political issues in political libel cases could be obscured by the complexities of the legal form in which all defamation cases were argued. But they also raise the implication that (some) judges were groping for a more coherent understanding of the way in which the common law should rebalance the conflict between freedom of political expression and the protection of individual reputation. *Braddock* did no more than breathe a little renewed life into the long moribund but far more sophisticated approach to this question taken eighty years earlier in *Wason*. This re-awakening might prove to have longer term significance, but it did not seem to have any immediate impact on the substance of the common law.

TRADES UNIONS AS NON-POLITICAL ACTORS

The sensitivity to political issues shown by the Court of Appeal in *Braddock* had been noticeably absent three years earlier in its judgment in *National Union of General and Municipal Workers* v. *Gillian*.[10] The libel concerned a squabble between two trades unions, each competing for workers in the chemical industry, in which the NUGNW had been accused of betraying the political and economic interests of the working class. The court briefly and unanimously upheld the union's right to sue in libel for any attack on its reputation. In terms somewhat reminiscent of Lord Esher MR's judgment in *South Hetton Coal*, the court held that a union possessed a legal personality just like any other corporation or individual, and could sue accordingly. As Uthwatt J put it:

> It is well-established that in certain cases a trading corporation may bring suit in respect of an imputation on its trading reputation and I see no reason why a non-trading corporation should not have the same rights as respects imputations on the conduct by it of its activities.[11]

That a trades union might be a political actor—and obviously was such during the unusual political circumstances of World War II—did not enter the Court of Appeal's reasoning at all. Nor did the members of the court discern any inconsistency between that statement and the decision in *Manchester Corporation* v. *Williams*. *Williams* was not explicitly referred to in the judgments. The court did however approve the reasoning used in *Gillian* at first instance by Birkett J, who had concluded that *Manchester* had been implicitly overruled by *South Hetton Coal*.[12] This would seem a weakly founded proposition. As noted in Chapter 2, Lord Esher MR's occasionally sweeping statements to that effect in *South Hetton Coal* are not an accurate reflection of the details of his judgment,

---

[10] [1945] 2 All ER 593.
[11] *Ibid.*, at 605.
[12] The first instance judgment is also reported at [1945] 2 All ER 593.

which was clearly concerned with the legal capacity of commercial rather than governmental corporations.[13]

Shortly afterwards, in *Willis* v. *Brooks*,[14] the High Court addressed the question whether a trades union official could sue in libel in respect of attacks on his union identifying him as involved in vote-rigging. Perhaps ironically—given that the allegedly libellous story had been concerned with the lack of democratic accountability in the management of the union's affairs—Oliver J saw no political dimension to the case. The question it posed was rather answered by existing precedent:

> It appears to me that the Court of Appeal have decided in *Gillian's* case that there is no difference in this matter between a trade union and a limited company, and that the entity of a trade union cannot be divided into different parts consisting of various of its members so as to deprive it of its right to sue if it is libelled.[15]

A COMMONWEALTH INNOVATION?

The plaintiff in *Perera* v *Peiris*[16]—who was not a politician—had been accused of bribing senior members of the Ceylonese government. The charge was made in a report by the Bribery Commission, a government body established under statutory powers. The defendant was the owner of the *Ceylon Daily News*, which had published lengthy verbatim extracts of the report. In the Ceylonese courts, the case had been argued largely on the basis of fair comment. On further appeal to the Privy Council, the issue had shifted to one of whether the publication should attract qualified privilege.

The Privy Council's task was somewhat complicated by Ceylon's traditional use of Roman Dutch rather than common law. The court (whose sole judgment was authored by Lord Uthwatt) considered that the Roman Dutch and common law rules on this point were sufficiently similar to be used almost interchangeably. Its judgment was consequently built wholly on common law authority. Lord Uthwatt referred to *R.* v. *Wright*, *Davison* v. *Duncan* and *Wason* v. *Walter* to support the proposition that it was for the common convenience and welfare of society that judicial and parliamentary proceedings be reported verbatim or fairly and accurately in the press with the protection of privilege, be it absolute or qualified. Whether press coverage of other reports should enjoy the same protection was a matter to be decided on an *ad hoc* basis; '[i]f it appears to that it is to the public interest that the particular report should be published, privilege will attach'.[17]

---

[13] See 35 above.
[14] [1947] 1 All ER 191.
[15] *Ibid.*, at 192.
[16] [1949] AC 1.
[17] *Ibid.*, at 21.

The Privy Council considered that the substance of this report was of the utmost public interest; it 'dealt with a grave matter affecting the public at large, namely the integrity of members of the Executive Council of Ceylon',[18] and should therefore receive the widest publicity. The Court also appeared to attach significance to the status of the report itself, noting that it 'contained the reasoned conclusions of a commissioner who . . . had held an inquiry and based his conclusions on evidence which he had searched for and sifted'.[19] Echoing Lord Cockburn's analysis in *Wason*, Lord Uthwatt observed that the press was under a duty to disseminate such information, and citizens had a legitimate interest in receiving it. The court stressed that it was the substance of the report rather than the status of the plaintiff that was the crucial issue here. The plaintiff, while nominally a private person, gained a 'political' identity because of his involvement in a controversy of such acute political significance.

The judgment represented a modest extension of the reach of the *Wason* principle. Seen in conjunction with *Braddock*, *Perera* could be read as indicating that English courts were beginning to embrace a more expansive understanding of the common law's legitimate constitutional role in protecting freedom of political expression than had hitherto been the case. Parliament appeared however to see a clear distinction between the two cases. Legislators were evidently not quite as receptive to this changing perception as the courts.

THE DEFAMATION ACT 1952

Despite its narrow effect, *Braddock* was not well regarded by politicians themselves, for whom considerations of preserving their reputations (or deterring criticism of their political beliefs and behaviour) evidently outweighed the interest of their respective voters, let alone of the public at large, in making informed electoral choices. The Defamation Act 1952 section 10 reversed the Court of Appeal's judgment:

> A defamatory statement published by or on behalf of a candidate in any election to a local government authority or to Parliament shall not be deemed to be published on a privileged occasion on the ground that it is material to a question in issue in the election.

The Act's terms were based largely on the report of a governmental committee (the Porter Committee) established in 1938, whose activities had been interrupted by World War II. The legislation had surfaced as a private member's bill, promoted by Harold Lever, a Labour MP. Section 10 had not originally been part of the bill, but appeared as an amendment at Committee stage, moved by Sidney Silverman, a Labour MP. Its purpose was to reverse *Braddock* and to 'encourage' candidates and their close supporters to exercise considerable care

[18] [1949] AC 1.
[19] *Ibid.*

in crafting their election literature.[20] Section 10 did not obviously reach to non-partisan press coverage of candidates for elections, nor statements made by (non-candidate) electors to each other. The availability or otherwise of the qualified privilege defence on such 'occasions' remained a matter of common law for the courts to decide.

In other respects, however, the 1952 Act extended protection for libellous 'political' speech. Perhaps most significantly, it gave an extended statutory basis to the common law privilege identified in *Perera*. Section 7 and Schedule 1 to the Act extended qualified privilege to fair and accurate reports of the public proceedings or written decisions of a wide range of national and international governmental bodies. A diluted version of the defence was extended to fair and accurate reports of the findings or decisions of various trade associations and sporting organisations, and of the proceedings of, *inter alia*, public meetings, meetings of local authorities and sittings of magistrates courts. The defence would not be available to newspapers which refused a request from the plaintiff to publish a contemporaneous explanation or rebuttal of the alleged libel.

The rest of the Act applied to all defamation actions, and offered a mix of measures which both enhanced and restricted a plaintiff's prospects of winning an action. Sections 2–3 relaxed the common law definition of 'special damage' in slander and malicious falsehood cases; plaintiffs whose professional or trade interests were disparaged would be presumed to have suffered an economic loss rather than being required to prove it. In contrast, persons who had 'innocently' published defamatory material (i.e. without knowing that the words used could relate to the person defamed) might escape liability by making a prompt 'offer of amends' to the individual defamed.[21]

Sections 5–6 also had potentially significant implications, in that they changed the legal definition of 'truth' for the purposes of both the justification and fair comment defences. Section 5 provided that a justification defence in an action concerning several libellous allegations would not fail if the defendant could not prove the truth of all his claims, so long as those which remained unproven did not materially exacerbate the harm caused to the plaintiff's reputation by those claims that had been proven true. Section 6 permitted fair comment to be invoked even if some of the facts on which the comment was based could not be justified, as long as the comment was fair in the light of such

---

[20] The original form of the amendment did not achieve that purpose. The final text of s.10 was the work of the Attorney-General; see Hansard (HC), 27 June 1952, cc. 2731–4.

[21] The amendment dealt with the problem posed by *Hulton* v. *Jones* [1910] AC 20 and *Newstead* v. *London Express Newspapers* [1940] 1 KB 377. *Hulton* had concerned a fictional character named Artemus Jones, who evidently bore sufficient similarity to a real Artemus Jones for the House of Lords to uphold a jury conclusion that the real man's reputation was injured by the account of his fictional namesake's activities. The plaintiff in *Newstead* sued in respect of a story recording that his namesake, who lived in the same town and was of similar age, had been convicted of bigamy. The jury accepted the plaintiff had been libelled, albeit unintentionally. Its view of the merits of his claim is perhaps best conveyed by the damages awarded—one farthing. See Lloyd D., 'Reform of the Law of Libel' [1952] *Current Legal Problems* 168 at 181–2. This type of 'innocent' defamation is unlikely to have any relevance to political libel cases.

assertions as were proven accurate. Both changes represented a modest advance—for defendants—from the previous common law position.

Contemporaneous analyses of the Act suggested it had provided markedly increased protection to press coverage of public-interest issues.[22] That seems something of an exaggeration. The Act did lessen the likelihood that some plaintiffs would be able to win a defamation action, but, seen in its entirety, the legislation sent confused signals about the view Parliament had adopted in respect of the relationship between defamation law and freedom of expression. In his introductory speech at second reading, Lever had expressed a wish to relax constraints on press coverage of public-interest issues, suggesting that the courts' failure to extend qualified privilege to a wider range of reports of 'official' matters had the effect of 'freezing . . . our law in Victorian times'.[23] Such sentiments seem difficult to reconcile with section 10. That specific dissonance may have been, of course, an accurate reflection of legislators' confused opinions on the likely impact of the Act more generally. In the course of the next few years, the courts indicated that the position taken by the common law was rather more clearly defined. Somewhat peculiarly, however, it seemed to be defined in very different ways.

AGAINST INFORMED CONSENT?

The plaintiff in *Silkin* v. *Beaverbrook Newspapers*[24] was a Labour peer who alleged he had been accused of hypocrisy by an article in the *Sunday Express*. The case itself revolved primarily around the issue of fair comment, in respect of which Diplock J's instructions to the jury were unremarkable. However, Diplock J had begun his summing up with what he presented as a 'common sense' explanation of the way in which libel laws treated the question of untrue allegations of fact:

> Let us look a little more closely at the way in which the law balances the rights of the public man, on the one hand, and the rights of the public on the other, in matters of freedom of speech. In the first place, every man, whether he is in public life or not, is entitled not to have lies told about him.[25]

This comment seems to make little sense as a statement of constitutional theory, and also raises obvious problems from the perspective of public policy in a supposedly 'mature' democracy.

On the public policy point, Diplock offers the politician's interest in being spared untrue attacks on her/his reputation as the starting point for analysis, a position quite different from the one adopted by the Court of Appeal in *Braddock* and by Cockburn CJ in *Wason*. By beginning one's analysis at this

---

[22] Todd E. (1953) 'The Defamation Act 1952' 16 *Modern Law Review* 198: Lloyd, n. 21 above.
[23] Hansard (HC) 1 February 1952, c.507.
[24] [1958] 1 WLR 743.
[25] *Ibid.*, at 746.

'first place', one is likely to attach paramount significance to the politician's interest in the suppression of untrue information. Any exceptions to the 'first place'—none of which Diplock J bothered to mention—then become seen very much as secondary considerations, as would the interest they are designed to protect—namely facilitating discussion of public affairs—which may in some circumstances require the politician to endure untruths (or at least make it difficult to win a defamation action in respect of such untruths). Within this analytical paradigm, suppression of political information becomes the norm, while its dissemination is portrayed as an anomalous exception. The approach is wholly irreconcilable with the premise that underpinned Cockburn CJ's judgments in *Wason* and *Purcell*.

It might also be thought that Diplock J's 'first place' analysis was misconceived as a statement of British constitutional theory. In effect, Diplock J's analytical premise elevates the common law over statute. Long before Diplock J gave judgment in *Silkin*, Parliament had unambiguously established that there were many instances in which 'every man' had to endure the most egregious of lies being told about him without having any possibility whatsoever of legal redress even if the disseminator knew the information circulated was untrue. Article 9 of the Bill of Rights is the first illustration of this principle; the Parliamentary Papers Act 1840 is another. Moreover, by extending the reach of qualified privilege in the Defamation Act 1952 to accurate reportage of various governmental sources of information, Parliament had removed that 'entitlement' not to be lied about unless the lie was disseminated with malice. The proper 'first place' for the courts' analysis of political libel law to start, therefore, might readily be thought to be that Parliament has accorded varying degrees of protection over and above those available at common law to many sorts of defamatory lies and has left it to the courts to decide whether or not other instances may arise when the public interest requires that the common law strike a new balance in respect of the suppression or dissemination of potentially true information. This is not of course a novel proposition in English law. Rather it accurately describes the approach adopted over 130 years ago by Cockburn CJ in *Wason* v. *Walter*. For Diplock J, both the spirit and letter of *Wason* seemed to have been wholly forgotten. Shortly afterwards however, they were once again afforded a prominent common law role.

A RADICAL REFORM TO THE COMMON LAW? *WEBB* V. *TIMES PUBLISHING*

The defamatory story before the High Court in *Webb* v. *Times Publishing*[26] was a *Times* report of criminal proceedings in Switzerland. In an evidently accurate report of the trial, *The Times* had repeated allegations that a British citizen previously cleared of murder in an English court had in fact been guilty. In the

[26] [1960] 2 QB 535.

ensuing libel action, *The Times* argued, *inter alia*, that qualified privilege should apply to fair and accurate reportage of the proceedings of foreign courts. As noted above, that principle long been accepted in respect of proceedings in English courts. But, as Pearson J observed in *Webb*, there was no clear authority on the question whether the defence extended to foreign courts.

There are obvious similarities between Pearson J's judgment in *Webb* and Cockburn CJ's opinion in *Wason;* not least because Pearson J relied extensively on the former decision, in terms both of its jurisprudential methodology and its understanding of the requirements of public policy. Absent clear authority, Pearson J began his judgment—as had Cockburn in *Wason*—by attempting to extract the public policy reasons which underlay the previously mentioned decisions concerning English court proceedings. He then reached the same conclusion as Cockburn—namely that the reason for the rule was to facilitate informed consent by the citizenry to their institutions of government and the laws which those institutions produced. Pearson J then expressly alluded to Cockburn's assertion that the common law was sufficiently elastic to serve the 'wants and usages' of modern society. In Pearson J's view, the 'wants and usages and interests' of 1960s Britain demanded that citizens had access to far more information than had been thought appropriate 100 years earlier.

The narrow ratio of the case confirmed that the reach of qualified privilege should encompass contemporaneous reports of foreign court proceedings which contained information of legitimate public interest to a British readership. Proceedings raising important questions of law, or concerning major political or commercial events, would fall within this category, while matters of a purely personal, trivial nature (such as divorce) would not. On the facts of the story at issue in *Webb*, which was concerned with the adequacy of the administration of justice in England, the test was clearly met.

More significantly, Pearson J indicated obiter that he believed the qualified privilege defence now reached much further than simply reports of foreign court proceedings. Adopting new terminology—which strongly echoed the way in which Cockburn CJ had blurred the edges between the fair comment and qualified privilege defences in *Campbell*—he suggested that English libel law now contained a defence of 'fair information on a matter of public interest'. The defence would embrace any information which 'a reasonable man . . . wishing to be well informed, will be glad to read. . .and would think he ought to read . . . if he has the time available'.[27]

Pearson J seemed to suggest that in a modern democracy the citizen had a moral duty as well as interest in being informed about public issues. That duty and interest obviously could not be meaningfully discharged unless one recognised the press had a reciprocal duty and interest to disseminate such information. In consequence, publication of such material was invariably an occasion on which qualified privilege arose.

[27] [1960] 2 QB 535 at 569.

Pearson J's principle would arguably stretch as far as the *Coleman* test adopted fifty years earlier in Kansas. But even if restrictively construed, it would surely reach as far as stories addressing an MP's fitness for office. In rejecting the very narrow 'reach' accorded to the political libel defence in *Braddock*, Pearson J recognised that he was dealing here with a 'national issue'. In so doing, he followed the American lead in relocating the 'overbroad publication' element of the defence from its traditional English location as the final element of the malice issue to the preliminary question of the 'occasion' of publication. This type of material could legitimately be disseminated to the public at large; overbroad publication was an impossibility.

The grant of so expansive a *reach* to the defence is perhaps the more surprising since—in accordance with the dominant English tradition—Pearson J did not narrow its *effect*. Malice would be satisfied only if the plaintiff proved that the defendant had not published in good faith, i.e. that she had knowingly disseminated false information. It might therefore readily be thought that the proposed defence was unduly indulgent of deceit, and insufficiently tolerant of suppression. A negligence-based test, drawing on the formula used by Cockburn CJ in *Campbell* v. *Spottiswoode*,[28] would perhaps have afforded a more appropriate (i.e. lower) level of protection to information which might not have had any discernible 'political' dimension.

TRUTH (NZ) LTD V. HOLLOWAY

That Pearson J had evidently taken a radical step in *Webb* is forcefully illustrated if one compares his judgment with a contemporaneous decision of the New Zealand Court of Appeal in *Truth (NZ) Ltd* v. *Holloway*.[29] Holloway was Minister of Industry and Commerce, and had been accused by *Truth*—a political magazine—of unethical dealings in the award of import licences for goods from China. *Truth*'s counsel claimed qualified privilege for the story, asserting that a 'public interest' existed in such matters as the granting of import licences and the role played by ministers and MPs therein.

The claim was perhaps too broadly based, in that it sought to encompass the potentially wide notion of 'public interest' rather than a much narrower, *Colemanesque*, 'political' interest.[30] The claim was certainly too wide for the Court of Appeal: '[t]he argument lacks nothing in boldness and originality, but, with all respect to learned counsel, in our opinion, is unsound'.[31] The court rejected *Perera* as an authority for this proposition, holding that the case did no more than extend the reach of qualified privilege to fair and accurate reports of

---

[28] See 24–6 above.

[29] [1960] NZLR 69. The judgment in *Webb* was handed down on 2 June. *Truth* was decided on 16 Nov.

[30] No reference was made to any American authorities in the judgment.

[31] N. 29 above, at 80. Its 'originality' would obviously have been difficult for American observers to discern.

official governmental proceedings. While the court accepted that a reciprocal right/duty of dissemination existed between a newspaper and its readers in respect of information of that sort, it discerned no such duty in respect of:

> news, and even, gossip, concerning current events and people. . . . [There is no principle of law, and certainly no case that we know of, which may be invoked in support of the contention that a newspaper can claim privilege if it publishes a defamatory statement of fact about an individual merely because the general topic developed in the article is a matter of public interest.[32]

Webb was not cited in the judgment, despite having been decided five months earlier. That seems a curious omission, since *Webb* obviously provided plausible support for *Truth*'s claim. The court invoked instead more aged 'English' authority, notably *Davis* v. *Shepstone*, to support the proposition that the 'common convenience and welfare of society' would not be well served by extending the defence to information of this sort. *Davis* was regarded as 'a clear and binding authority against the submission made by Mr Cooke' (*Truth*'s counsel).[33] The notion that the electorate might have a substantial interest in learning of alleged corruption and financial sharp practice by a minister and MP seemed not to enter into the court's thinking at all. Nor did it appear to entertain the possibility that, while *Davis* may have offered an acceptable common law rule for colonial Natal in 1886, it was less obviously an appropriate authority for modern New Zealand society in which the legitimacy of the governmental system could be assumed to derive from the informed consent of the New Zealand people.[34]

The court also relied on a 1908 Privy Council decision, *MacIntosh* v. *Dunn*.[35] It drew in particular on a quotation from Lord McNaghten's sole judgment in that case as authority for the proposition that no public benefit could accrue from accepting *Truth*'s argument:

> is it in the interest of the community, is it for the welfare of society, that the protection which the law throws around communications made in legitimate self-defence, or from a bona fide sense of duty, should be extended to communications made from motives of self-interest by persons who trade for profit in the reputations of other people.[36]

The obvious inference was that the Privy Council had held that a newspaper or political magazine was necessarily a self-interested traducer of reputation motivated solely by the pursuit of profit. This was an extraordinary use of 'precedent', one which creates the impression that the members of the New Zealand court had not read the case, but merely adopted an ostensibly apposite sound-bite offered up to them by the plaintiff's counsel. *MacIntosh* did not

---

[32] N. 29 above, at 83.
[33] *Ibid*, at 84.
[34] It might be recalled that the Kansan Supreme Court in *Coleman* 50 years earlier had indicated that *Shepstone* had little to commend it in a society which regarded itself as a representative democracy; see 39 above.
[35] [1908] AC 390.
[36] *Ibid*., at 400.

involve a newspaper, nor a matter of political or even public interest. It concerned information published by a credit reference agency, information which falsely imputed insolvency to the plaintiff. Lord McNaghten's next words, following on from the quotation above, make it abundantly clear that he was not enunciating a general principle: '[t]he trade [i.e. credit referencing] is a peculiar one'.[37] There is no plausible basis for extracting from his judgment authority for the proposition that he considered media investigation of political issues to be 'trading for profit in the reputations of others'. The court also overlooked, and was evidently not prompted by defendant's counsel to recall, that Cockburn CJ in *Wason* had stated quite clearly that the common law accepted that newspapers owed a public duty to voters to report information bearing on the integrity of holders of government office. That they might seek to make a profit by so doing was neither here nor there.

CONCLUSION

Webb—and the ideas it contained—did not seem to make much of an impact on other judges' understanding of the relationship between libel laws and freedom of expression on political or public-interest issues. This is nicely illustrated by the Court of Appeal's 1962 judgment in *Plummer* v. *Charman*.[38] Sir Henry Plummer was the Labour MP for Deptford. Charman was a member of the British National Party, standing for election to the London County Council in a Deptford Ward. Charman had distributed a racist pamphlet which accused Plummer of being anti-white and of supporting the establishment of 'vice dens' run by recent non-white immigrants. The pamphlet seemed to fall squarely within section 10 of the Defamation Act 1952, and the Court of Appeal rejected the defendant's ingenious attempt to circumvent this statutory restriction. The Court of Appeal's reasoning on this point is unremarkable. The judgment is however notable for a curious statement in the opinion of Diplock LJ, which was strongly redolent of the 'first place' comments he had offered in *Silkin*:

> I need hardly say that there is no privilege known to the law which entitles persons engaged in politics to misstate facts about their opponents provided that they say it honestly even though untruthfully.[39]

This is at best a very lax use of language, and at worst a flagrant misrepresentation of the then current state of English law. It is indisputable that Pearson J's 'fair information on a matter of public interest' formula in *Webb* would provide a common law rule embracing the scenario to which Diplock LJ referred. It is also clear that *Wason* would provide another common law qualified privilege defence for such stories as long as the facts concerned were part of an accurate

[37] *Ibid.*
[38] [1962] 3 All ER 823.
[39] *Ibid.*, at 827.

summary of Parliamentary proceedings, while *Perera* arguably[40] pulled accurate reportage of other governmental reports under the same common law umbrella. Moreover, statutory qualified privilege under the Defamation Act 1952 itself had been granted to any factual misstatement that formed part of a fair and accurate report of the findings or decisions of a wide range of governmental bodies. In addition, Article 9 of the Bill of Rights and the Parliamentary Papers Act 1840 went much further in defence of falsely stated facts about a person's political opponents, by providing absolute privilege against libel proceedings even to individuals who knew the statements they were making were false.

Pearson J's judgment in *Webb* did not invoke American case law. Yet, like the Kansan Supreme Court's judgment in *Coleman*, he reached his conclusion largely on the basis of long-established English common law principles; principles which seemed rather to have been forgotten by English courts in the previous eighty years. This might suggest that there is more common ground than one might suppose between English and American approaches to this particular legal problem. *Webb's* subsequent use in English law is a subject to which we return in Chapter 6. Chapter 5 turns again to the United States, and to the US Supreme Court's seminal 1964 judgment in *Sullivan* v. *The New York Times*.

---

[40] Privy Council decisions not being in the strict sense part of English law.

5

Sullivan *v.* The New York Times

The litigation in *Sullivan* v. *The New York Times*[1] was yet another stage in the continuing struggle between civil rights activists and racist white politicians in the southern USA over desegregation of public services. Sullivan was a city Commissioner (an elected office) in Montgomery, Alabama, who had specific responsibility for the management of the city's police force. Sullivan and other senior figures in the state government[2] had systematically sought to frustrate the efforts of black citizens to enforce their civil rights. In addition to such overt tactics as the beating, arrest and intimidation of civil rights activists, state officials in Alabama had used state libel laws to discourage criticism of their behaviour within Alabama and to prevent dissemination of such information in the national media.[3] Much of the civil rights campaigning centred upon segregation in state schools and universities. Almost ten years had passed since the US Supreme Court had handed down its landmark ruling in *Brown* v. *Board of Education*,[4] which held that racial segregation in state schools was an unconstitutional infringement of the equal protection clause of the Fourteenth Amendment. Like many of its southern neighbours, Alabama had taken few steps to implement that judgment.

Alabama's libel laws were particularly well-suited to the harassment of its government's political opponents. The law afforded a complete defence to defamation actions only if the disseminator proved truth in *all* particulars; even trivial inaccuracy made the defence inapplicable.[5] The fair comment defence was available only if the defendant demonstrated the absolute truth of facts to which such comment was directed. Defendants might avoid liability for punitive (but not general) damages by publicly retracting the alleged libel at the plaintiff's request. Relatedly, punitive damages were recoverable only if the plaintiff proved 'actual malice' on the defendant's part. This test was met by showing the defendant was negligent in failing to ascertain the truth of factual allegations. One might further add, of course, that neither the Alabama judiciary nor

---

[1] (1964) 376 US 254.

[2] The term 'government' is used in the broad sense, to encompass members of the Alabama legislature and judiciary as well as its executive.

[3] See Lewis A. *Make No law* (New York: Vintage Books 1991) ch. 5; Bass J. *Taming the Storm* (New York: Auchen, 1993) at 158–62: Black J in *New York Times* v. *Sullivan* (1964) 376 US 254 at 294.

[4] (1954) 347 US 483.

[5] This was a more severe rule than the one traditionally imposed by English common law, and markedly more severe than the statutory formula introduced in England and Wales by the Defamation Act 1952.

Alabama juries were likely to discharge their legal functions in a spirit of non-partisan objectivity towards critics of their state's racist political culture.

The subject of the suit in *Sullivan* v. *The New York Times* was an advertisement placed in *The Times* by a civil rights pressure group, which accused the Montgomery authorities[6] of persistent harassment of Martin Luther King and violent intimidation of black student activists. The advertisement contained several minor factual errors, which the trial court concluded *The Times* had negligently failed to spot. *The Times* thus had no defence under Alabama law in respect of either general or punitive damages.[7] *The New York Times* had been joined as a defendant in the suit by several black Alabama residents whose names (unbeknown to them) had been attached to the advertisement in *The Times*. All of these individuals had been active for the past ten years in Alabama's school desegregation movement: all perceived Sullivan's actions as a state-sponsored effort to punish them for having sought to have *Brown* enforced and to deter others from continuing such action in future.[8] The trial jury awarded Sullivan the phenomenal sum of $500,000 damages, without specifying which proportion of it was general and/or punitive. That conclusion was upheld by the Alabama Supreme Court.[9]

THE APPEAL TO THE US SUPREME COURT

For *The Times'* co-defendants, the judgment meant personal bankruptcy and the indignity of having their belongings seized by state officials and sold to satisfy their judgment debts. Even for a major business enterprise such as *The Times*, a judgment of half a million dollars was not to be taken lightly. *The Times* engaged Herbert Wechsler, a professor at Columbia University Law School, to produce a written brief for the US Supreme Court and to represent the newspaper at the subsequent oral hearing.[10] Wechsler's brief for *The Times* rested primarily on the assumption (which had been made explicit by *Balch* and *Coleman* and then again by *Chicago*) that criminal sedition and civil libel laws could be used with equal felicity by government officials to suppress criticisms of their policies and official behaviour; an enormous damages award in a civil suit could be just as effective a way to punish critics and deter others from voic-

---

[6] Sullivan was not named in the advertisement. The evidently uncertain question in Alabama law of whether he personally was defamed by the advertisement was (unsurprisingly) resolved in his favour by the Alabama courts.

[7] Some dispute arose over whether Sullivan had demanded a public retraction. The Alabama courts settled this ambiguity in Sullivan's favour.

[8] See especially Tushnett M. *Making Civil Rights Law* (Oxford: Clarendon Press, 1995) ch. 11.

[9] 273 Ala. 656; 144 So. 2d 25.

[10] See Lewis, n. 3 above, chs. 11–13. Perhaps ironically, Wechsler had recently argued in a highly controversial law review article that *Brown* itself did not withstand close jurisprudential scrutiny, and was more properly seen as a usurpation of political power by the Court rather than a 'legal' decision in the orthodox sense: 'Towards Neutral Principles of Constitutional Law' (1959) 73 *Harvard LR* 1.

ing similar views as a gaol sentence or fine imposed after criminal proceedings. The Supreme Court had by this juncture clearly accepted that criminal libel laws were incompatible with the free speech and free press clauses of the First Amendment except in very limited circumstances involving the incitement of imminent violence and public disorder. To allow state governments to use their respective civil justice systems to achieve ends denied to them under the criminal law effectively undermined those First Amendment prohibitions. Wechsler nonetheless reasoned that the Supreme Court would be unwilling to accept a complete bar on civil defamation actions as had been offered in *Chicago*, and suggested instead that the Court might use the First Amendment to lend a constitutional status to the innovative qualified privilege defence that many states had by then adopted in respect of political libels. He placed particular reliance on *Coleman*, which he presented (notwithstanding its strong links to *Wason* v. *Walter*) as an example par excellence of the American political tradition. Wechsler saw no need to travel abroad in support of his argument. The recent English High Court decision in *Webb* v. *Times Publishing*, which essentially restated *Coleman* as a principle of English common law, did not feature in his brief.

THE JUDGMENT

Wechsler's arguments evidently found a receptive audience on the Supreme Court bench. All nine Justices concluded that the Alabama laws violated the First Amendment, and held that the judgment of the Alabama Supreme Court should be reversed.

The core of William Brennan's majority opinion lay in its acceptance of Wechsler's analogy between civil litigation in libel and criminal prosecutions for sedition. The majority considered it a well established principle of First Amendment jurisprudence that neither Congress nor the states could enact criminal laws punishing the expression of political speech except in the most limited of circumstances.[11] Like Thompson CJ in *Chicago*, Brennan alluded to the controversy over the 1798 Sedition Act to support this conclusion. Similarly, Brennan noted that it had been generally accepted following the *Chicago* judgment that no elected government body could maintain a civil action in libel, slander or malicious falsehood to defend its reputation against criticism, whether in the form of fact or opinion, from citizens.

William Brennan suggested that the rationale underpinning such principles was self-evident. Legislatures derived their constitutional authority from the

---

[11] Political speech which incited imminent violence and breach of the peace, or which directly jeopardised national security in time of war, could legitimately be proscribed. Much of the controversy within the Court has been generated by the application of this principle to given facts, rather than by the principle itself: see, for example, *Schenk* v. *US* (1919) 249 US 47; *Abrams* v. *US* (1919) 250 US 616; *Gitlow* v. *New York* (1925) 268 US 652; and latterly *Brandenburg* v. *Ohio* (1969) 395 US 444.

consent of 'the people', and within the constraints of that authority derived legitimacy for their preferred policies from the consent of their respective electorates. Such consent had to be 'informed', a state evidently best achieved by affording individual citizens (*qua* members of the populace and its various sub-electorates) the opportunity to disseminate and receive as much information as possible about political matters. Information which criticised government policies and officials was particularly valuable in this respect, since it alerted citizens both to the potential failings of those they had chosen to govern them and to the existence of alternative ideas and officials in whom their trust might be vested. Legislatures which enacted laws to punish expression of such material undermined governments' accountability to the citizenry and thereby corrupted the principle of informed consent on which America's revolutionary settlement was presumed to have been built.

Brennan's opinion invoked numerous supportive quotations from previous Supreme Court decisions on other free expression issues to support his conclusion. Many were lifted directly from Herbert Wechsler's brief for *The Times*.[12] The Court had previously suggested, for example, that the First Amendment recognised that it 'is a prized American privilege to speak one's mind, although not always with perfect good taste, on all public institutions'; its purpose was to ensure 'the widest possible dissemination of information from diverse and antagonistic sources'; or to 'assure unfettered interchange of ideas for the bringing about of political and social changes desired by the people'.[13] All such statements could be readily accommodated, as Wechsler's brief had inferred, in the common law principles that many states had by now developed when regulating political libel actions.

The majority on the Court regarded the informed consent principle as entirely functional in nature. It purpose was to remove *unwarranted* restraints on the dissemination and circulation of political speech, irrespective of the legal form such rules took. It was thus as readily applicable to rules of state common law as to legislative enactments. State libel laws did not enjoy any 'talismanic immunity'[14] from First Amendment regulation simply because they had a common law basis. Similarly, the plaintiff's identity was not determinative of the legal regime to be applied in libel actions. A government body could not entirely be separated from the individuals who staffed it; '[t]here is no legal alchemy by which a State may thus create the cause of action which would otherwise be denied'.[15] That a state itself could not prosecute its critics for libel was a factor that weighed heavily in the scales when the Court had to decide whether a state official should be permitted to pursue the same objectives indirectly by attacking those critics through a civil suit.

[12] Lewis, n. 3 above, chs. 12–13.
[13] Respectively (1964) 11 L Ed. 2d 686 at 700, quoting *Bridges* v. *California*, 314 US 252 at 270; at 698, quoting *Associated Press* v. *US*, 326 US 1 at 20: and at 698 quoting *Roth* v. *US*, 354 US 476 at 484.
[14] (1964) 376 US 254 at 269.
[15] *Ibid.*, at 271.

The judgment considered that Alabama's defamation law was an effective tool for politicians and government officials to 'chill' (deter) political speech. That Alabama law allowed truth in *every* particular as a defence to defamation actions was an inadequate guarantee of an acceptable flow of political information within and beyond the state:

> It is often difficult to prove the truth of the alleged libel in all particulars. And the necessity of proving truth as a defence may well deter a critic from voicing criticism, even if it be true, because of doubt whether it can be proved or fear of the expense of having to do so.[16]

Brennan did not tinker with such tests as 'degrees of truth' in determining whether civil or criminal sanctions could be attached to political speech. Rather he accepted that false speech was an inevitable ingredient of vigorous political discourse. But to permit the dissemination of 'false' speech by making it difficult for plaintiffs to recover was a lesser constitutional evil than to risk the suppression of 'true' speech by making it easy for plaintiffs to succeed.

Elected politicians would therefore in future have to prove 'actual malice' on the disseminator's part to recover libel damages in respect of speech concerning their political activities and/or suitability for office. William Brennan's understanding of 'actual malice' was quite distinct from the meaning attached to the term in English or Alabaman common law. It bore, however, a marked similarity to the common law principles that had been developed some sixty to seventy years earlier in Kansas, Iowa, Illinois and Pennsylvania. Brennan quoted extensively from *Coleman* both in justifying the political rationale underlying his 'actual malice' principle and in identifying the reach and effect of the principle itself.

As in *Coleman*, the rationale underlying *Sullivan* was to reduce the possibility that voters were deprived of potentially valuable political information by the deterrent (or, as Brennan termed it, 'chilling') effect that ordinary libel laws might exert on the dissemination of political information. However, the 'reach' of the *Sullivan* test was markedly less expansive than the version of qualified privilege applied in *Coleman*.[17] As noted in Chapter 2, the Kansan Supreme Court defined 'political information' very broadly.[18] *Sullivan*'s reach was much more modest. It extended only to 'actions brought by public officials against critics of their public conduct'.[19] The 'effect' of the *Sullivan* test was also, in one important respect, less indulgent of false speech than the *Coleman* formula. While *Coleman* had demanded that the plaintiff proved 'actual evil-mindedness'

[16] *Ibid.*, at 279.
[17] Or indeed Pearson J's 'fair information on a matter of public interest' variant of the qualified privilege defence in *Webb*.
[18] The concept was to embrace stories relating to the public activities of 'all officers and agents of government, municipal, state and national; to the management of all public institutions, educational, charitable and penal; to the conduct of all public enterprises affected with a public interest, transportation, banking, insurance; and to innumerable other subjects involving the public welfare': (1908) 98 PAC 281 at 289.
[19] (1964) 376 US 254 at 283. Brennan appeared to limit the rule to *elected* politicians.

in the defendant's publication of lies (i.e. intentional deceit), *Sullivan* would per-mit the plaintiff to recover if she could prove either intentional deceit or reck-lessness as to truth on the defendant's part; i.e. either that the defendant knew the story was untrue or, having grounds to doubt its accuracy, took no steps to verify it. But having offered this less exacting 'knowing or reckless falsity' test, Brennan then added a further reinforcement to his constitutional variation of the *Coleman* defence. The various state court judgments discussed in Chapter 2 all appeared to accept that the problem posed to free political speech by libel laws derived from the legal rules *per se*, and not from any dishonest manipula-tion of their contents by judges and juries. The plaintiff's burden was thus to prove 'actual evil-mindedness' on the usual civil standard of the balance of probabilities. Brennan was clearly unwilling to rely on the good faith and integrity of the Alabama legal system. The *Sullivan* test would require that knowing or reckless falsity be proven not simply on the balance of probabilities, but on the more exacting standard of 'convincing clarity'. This enhanced bur-den of proof would make it far easier for federal courts to overturn state court decisions and substitute their own judgments—as indeed the US Supreme Court did in *Sullivan* itself[20]—rather than return the case for a new trial to the state concerned.

A Balancing Test, Not an Absolutist Principle

Brennan's presumption seems to have been that his 'actual malice' test, being difficult for any plaintiff to surmount, would preclude governmental use of libel laws as a tool for concealing its activities from wide-ranging public scrutiny. But the majority opinion did not provide *carte blanche* for the criticism of politi-cians, whether by their peers, their citizens or the press. It offered no protection to deliberate lies or to falsehoods promulgated through reckless carelessness. Brennan did not explain this point fully in *Sullivan*. However his reasoning was revealed in a judgment he delivered the following year, in *Garrison* v. *Louisiana*, a criminal libel case; 'the use of a known lie as a tool [for political ends] is at once at odds with the premises of democratic government and with the orderly manner in which economic, social or political change is to be effected'.[21] Brennan's reasoning on this point in *Sullivan* seemed to owe little to a desire to protect an individual's reputation; his concern centred rather on protecting a societal interest in maintaining the integrity of political discourse.

Three Justices in *Sullivan*—Black, Douglas and Goldberg JJ—rejected any need for balance and were prepared to interpret the First Amendment in a way which, extending the reach of *Chicago* from government bodies to elected

---

[20] Brennan considered that his 'convincing clarity' test demanded that he review the trial evidence in the interests of 'effective judicial administration'. On doing so, he held that the record offered no support for a finding in Sullivan's favour.
[21] (1965) 379 US 64 at 75.

officials, offered *absolute* protection even to disseminators of deliberate lies. Black J suggested that a test which afforded juries in southern states any scope at all to impose libel liability on political speech would be unconscionably manipulated whenever the speech related to racial equality issues. He assumed that the 'actual malice' test would prove to be no more than a 'stop-gap', which the majority would amend as soon as they realised how open it was to abuse. His conclusion was typically trenchant: '[a]n unconditional right to say what one pleases is . . . the minimum guarantee of the First Amendment'.[22] Goldberg was equally forthright, asserting that the First Amendment granted citizens and the press 'an absolute, unconditional privilege to criticize official conduct despite the harm which may flow from excesses and abuses'.[23]

There is little obvious merit in this extremist or absolutist position. The imposition of a complete bar on any form of civil or criminal defamation action in respect of political speech encourages individuals and organisations prepared to disseminate deliberate lies, or to display the most reckless disregard for the truth of their claims, in order to discredit their political opponents. These consequences would be doubly objectionable. They would presumably result in unwarranted damage being done to individual politicians. But they also have a wider and more seriously detrimental effect, in so far as they may lead citizens to make choices about political matters which are based on quite erroneous understandings of the facts.

In contrast to the Black/Douglas/Goldberg position, Brennan's *Sullivan* test acknowledges that the problem of false political speech does not present a simple choice between good and evil. Nor can the equation be reduced to a straightforward clash between the political figure's 'individual interest' in not being 'lied' about, and the 'public interest' in having access to 'true' political information. The electorate has an interest in not being lied to. Similarly, individual politicians have an interest in true information about other politicians entering the public arena. Whatever solution is adopted in these circumstances will cause undesirable consequences. But the Goldberg/Douglas/Black solution to the problem affords too much opportunity for deliberate deceit to infect political discourse. That result would do little to foster the process of enhancing the citizenry's informed consent to the government process.

Conclusion

The methodology informing much of the majority's reasoning in *Sullivan* was a process of argument by extrapolation from First Amendment case law concerning other aspects of freedom of expression, notably on sedition, criminal libel, obscenity and religious autonomy. Yet Brennan's substantial reliance on *Coleman* indicates that *Sullivan's* knowing/reckless falsity test was not so much

---

[22] (1964) 376 US 254 at 297.
[23] *Ibid.*, at 298.

a principle inherent in the First Amendment itself, but rather a common law principle in respect of which the First Amendment served merely as a vehicle to give it supra-legislative and nationwide effect. Brennan's use of *Coleman* did not acknowledge that judgment's English roots in *Wason* v. *Walter*, and indeed rather created the erroneous impression that a principle so protective of political speech was wholly incompatible with English constitutional traditions. The significance of this point to the subsequent development of libel law in Britain will be returned to in later chapters. In the second section of this chapter, attention is focused instead on the way in which the Supreme Court substantially extended the reach of *Sullivan* while simultaneously also seeming to accept the need to modify its effect.

EXTENDING THE DOCTRINE

William Brennan was later to suggest that his reasoning in *Sullivan* was shaped in part by a thesis advanced some years earlier by an eminent political philosopher, Alexander Meiklejohn.[24] Meiklejohn had argued that the constitutional function of the First Amendment was to provide a tool to safeguard the process of what he termed 'self-government' among the American people and its many electorates.[25] Meiklejohn's thesis seemed to be itself an elaboration of the principles drawn upon by Cockburn CJ in *Wason* v. *Walter*, which, as noted in Chapter 2, were themselves further developed by various state Supreme Courts in the late nineteenth and early twentieth centuries. But for politicians and the press in the USA, *Sullivan* would prove to be of interest not so much for where it came from, as for where in future years it might go.

Remedial Considerations

A close reading of the text of *Sullivan* itself raised two ambiguities which were settled shortly afterwards in *Garrison* v. *Louisiana*.[26] The first uncertainty arose over whether the *Sullivan* rule extended only to the award of *damages*, and left other remedial devices, such as a declaration or injunction, available if the plaintiff could surmount the relevant state law hurdles. The second concerned whether the 'actual malice' requirement was limited only to *libel*, or also embraced the nominally separate causes of action in slander and malicious falsehood. Brennan's frequent references to 'damages' and 'libel' in his text suggested that the other remedies and causes of action were available. Those

[24] Brennan W., 'The Supreme Court and the Meiklejohn Interpretation of the First Amendment' (1965) 79 *Harvard LR* 1. See especially Meiklejohn A., 'The First Amendment Is An Absolute' [1961] *Supreme Court Review* 245.

[25] For an English view see Sir John Laws, 'Meiklejohn, the First Amendment and Free Speech in English Law', in Loveland I. (ed.) *Importing the First Amendment* (Oxford, Hart Publishing, 1998).

[26] (1964) 379 US 64.

conclusions would however obviously run counter to the political underpin-nings of the judgment, and particularly to his early conclusion that the Supreme Court should not permit the labels attached by a state to a particular legal prin-ciple to divert its attention from the effect that the law in question would have.[27]

Garrison appeared to settle both questions in a single passage which indicated that political plaintiffs would have to overcome the actual malice standard before receiving any remedy at all for the publication of false facts, irrespective of whether or not they were defamatory:

> [O]nly those statements made with the high degree of awareness of their probable falsity demanded by *New York Times may be the subject* of either civil or criminal sanctions.[28]

These were not trivial issues. Permitting a political plaintiff to seek a declara-tion in libel would have lessened the anti-chilling effect of the *Sullivan* rule, as some critics may have been deterred from publishing by the fear of having to bear their own costs in a libel action.[29] Similarly, the orthodox malicious false-hood action was more chilling than the *Sullivan* rule, since the plaintiff's burden as to falsity and malice had to be proven only on the balance of probabilities, and not to the standard of convincing clarity. *Garrison* indicated that the Court would not allow technical quibbles to dilute *Sullivan's* practical impact. And the Court did not take long to confirm that it was also willing to extend that impact beyond its original boundaries.

From Elected to Appointed Officials . . .

The plaintiff in *Rosenblatt* v. *Baer*[30] had been the manager of a municipal ski resort in New Hampshire. His libel action was brought in response to an article in a local newspaper which he claimed accused him of embezzling public funds during the course of his employment. He had won his action at trial under New Hampshire law, which permitted a plaintiff to recover damages for negligently published falsehoods. On appeal, the New Hampshire Supreme Court had con-cluded that the *Sullivan* test applied only to senior, elected public officials, a cat-egory into which Rosenblatt obviously did not fall.

In the US Supreme Court, Brennan J delivered the majority opinion. Brennan held that 'the rationale that had driven the Court's reasoning in *Sullivan*—'that debate on public issues should be uninhibited, robust and wide open'—demanded that the concept of 'public official' be broadly defined:

---

[27] (1964) 376 US 254 at 269.

[28] (1964) 379 US 64 at 74, emphasis added.

[29] Most state jurisdictions did not follow the English rule that the loser should pay the victor's cost as well as her own.

[30] (1966) 383 US 75.

The 'public official' designation applies at the very least to those among the hierarchy of government employees who have, or appear to the public to have, substantial responsibility for or control over the conduct of governmental affairs.[31]

Brennan J again stressed that this conclusion did not ignore the public interest in safeguarding an individual's reputation from unwarranted criticism. Rather it recognised that the public interest in that value was outweighed by its interest in maximising discussion of political issues.

The Court unanimously agreed that Rosenblatt was a public official for *Sullivan* purposes. It thereby extended the reach of the knowing/reckless falsity defence quite substantially. Douglas J, however, evidently still attracted to his absolutist view of First Amendment freedoms, suggested somewhat implausibly in a concurring opinion that the majority's holding broadened the reach of the defence beyond any identifiable limits; 'if free discussion of public issues is the guide, I see no way to draw lines that exclude the nightwatchman, the file clerk, the typist, or, for that matter, anyone on the public payroll'.[32] Moreover, Douglas J felt the Court's concern with an individual's function rather than her status should lead it to extend the *New York Times* test into the nominally private sector, to include 'the industrialists who raise the price of a basic commodity? Are not steel and aluminium in the public domain? And the labour leader who combines trade unionism with bribery and racketeering?'.[33]

Douglas' concurrence was rather disingenuous. It was, for example, hard to imagine that a 'nightwatchman' would in the ordinary course of events exercise any 'substantial responsibility' over the conduct of public affairs. Brennan's insistence that the *Sullivan* test applied only to plaintiffs exercising 'substantial governmental power' suggested that the majority was yet to be persuaded by Douglas' reasoning. Yet Douglas' observation that nominally private figures might exercise great influence over political issues raised a point of considerable significance. And in the following year, the Court produced a judgment that appeared to grant the *Sullivan* test a reach which did not just accept Douglas' position in *Rosenblatt* but went far beyond it.

. . . to Matters of Interest to the Public . . .

The cause of action in *Time Inc* v. *Hill*[34] was not libel, but an action for breach of privacy under a New York statute. The statute created a right of action in tort, which enabled individuals to recover damages for unauthorised publication of details about their lives. Publishers had a defence if the individuals concerned were 'newsworthy' as long as the information published was substantially true.

---

[31] (1966) 383 US 75 at 86.
[32] *Ibid.*, at 89.
[33] *Ibid.*, at 89.
[34] (1967) 385 US 374.

Hill had some years previously been the victim of a violent crime, in which he and his family had been held hostage by an armed gang. The family were eventually released unharmed, and made every effort to escape the glare of press publicity that immediately shone down upon them. Some years later, a play loosely based on their experience (and written without their approval) opened on Broadway. *Time* magazine ran a feature on the play, in which it substantially misrepresented the ordeal which the family had suffered. As a result of the feature, the family once again became subject to intense media interest. At trial in New York, Hill recovered $50,000 general damages and $25,000 punitive damages for breach of privacy. The award was based on the court's finding that, while Hill was a 'newsworthy' person as the result of having been held hostage, the story published about him was substantially untrue. The jury had been instructed that it could award general damages for false stories even if the publisher honestly and reasonably believed the stories to be true. Punitive damages required the plaintiff to prove that the lies were published because the publisher either knew them to be untrue, or recklessly or negligently failed to establish their accuracy.

The Supreme Court reversed the judgment. Brennan's majority opinion concluded that the *Sullivan* knowing reckless/falsity test should be applied to this situation. Brennan's judgment wholly abandoned the 'informed consent to government' rationale that had apparently underlain his opinion in *Sullivan*. In a passage which seemed to ignore the common law roots of the *Sullivan* principle in favour of a substantive test extracted from the First Amendment itself, Brennan observed that '[t]he guarantees for speech and press are not the preserve of political expression or comment on public affairs, essential as these are to healthy government'.[35]

The 'guarantees'—of which the *Sullivan* test formed a part—extended to all newsworthy events and necessarily to the people involved in them. Brennan refused to be drawn into trying to distinguish between information which was valuable for informed consent purposes, and that which was simply entertaining to the public at large. All such information merited rigorous First Amendment protection. Only lies published as the result of deliberate deceit or reckless indifference to the truth could found liability in tort.

The majority's position in *Hill* has little to commend it. It appeared to have departed radically from the common law rationale which underlay the Court's judgment in *Sullivan*—namely that an individual's presumptive entitlement not to have her reputation besmirched by untruths was waived by her voluntary involvement with 'political matters'. It seems unlikely that even *Coleman*'s broad definition of 'political' would have encompassed a play of this sort, and still less unlikely that Burch J would have accepted that the 'wants and usages' of modern American society necessarily made victims of crime into political figures. Both Coleman and Sullivan had *willingly* given up their respective private

[35] *Ibid.*, at 388.

identities by seeking to occupy elected political office. Moreover participants in all the other forms of activity included in *Coleman's* very wide definition of 'political' would have made positive choices to participate in the relevant process. The plaintiffs in *Hill* had done no such thing. Rather they had had their private identity forcibly removed from them, and had subsequently given every indication in their conduct that they wished to have it restored.

The fragility of Brennan's reasoning was evident to four of his colleagues, all of whom dissented. Harlan J would have accepted a negligence test for plaintiffs in Hill's position. The other three Justices, Warren CJ and Fortas and Clark JJ, adopted a more starkly differentiated position which seemed perfectly consistent with Brennan's judgment in *Sullivan*—namely that the crucial issue was whether the story in issue was of a type which would enable voters to make informed choices about the people they elected to govern them. While accepting that privacy rights should be subjected to a *Sullivan* defence 'where political personalities or issues are involved', the dissenting judges saw no reason to extend that protection to a false story which 'irresponsibly and injuriously invades the privacy of a quiet family for no purpose except dramatic interest and commercial appeal'.[36]

... to Political and Public Figures ...

Hill was much criticised in the academic press.[37] An indication that some members of the *Hill* majority entertained immediate doubts about the judgment was offered shortly afterwards in the joined cases of *Curtis* v. *Butts* and *Associated Press* v. *Walker*.[38] Both cases clearly raised issues of 'public interest' within *Hill*. However rather than relying expressly on that test, the Supreme Court applied the *Sullivan* principle to the cases before it on the basis that both plaintiffs could properly be classified as 'public figures'. Butts was Athletic Director of Georgia University, a state institution. He had been accused in a newspaper article of giving away the football team's game plans to a rival coach in order to effect a betting swindle. Although Harlan J for the majority did not characterise college football as a governmental function, he observed that the framers of the First Amendment took a broad view of the type of speech worthy of protection, which encompassed 'truth, science, morality and the arts in general'.[39] Given the great importance which the contemporary American public attached to college football, Harlan J saw no difficulty in concluding that the game's administrators became 'public figures' when charged with dishonesty or corruption. These individuals too would therefore have to surmount the reckless/knowing

---

[36] (1967) 385 US 374 at 415–16.

[37] See especially Nimmer, M., 'The Right to Speak from *Times* to *Time*' (1968) *California LR* 935: Kalven, H., 'The Reasonable Man and the First Amendment' [1967] *Supreme Court Review* 267.

[38] (1967) 388 US 130.

[39] *Ibid*., at 147.

falsity test if they were to succeed in a libel action concerning criticism of their public functions.[40] All nine judges approved this conclusion.

The judgment in *Butts* suggested that the reach of the *Sullivan* defence still extended beyond 'political information' in a narrow sense, as Douglas had advocated in *Rosenblatt*. The conclusion which the Court reached in *Walker* seemed to rest on rather more narrowly defined political and jurisprudential grounds. Walker had commanded the federal troops sent by Eisenhower to desegregate schools in Little Rock, Arkansas, in 1957 following that state's refusal to comply with *Brown* v. *Board of Education*. Walker was evidently much moved by this experience, for, following his retirement from the Army, he became a prominent supporter of Southern resistance to *Brown*. The alleged libel at issue in *Walker* v. *Associated Press* arose over his involvement in racially motivated civil disorder at the University of Mississippi in 1962.

Walker clearly did not hold either elected or appointed government office. Nor was there even any obvious indication that he intended to use his activities in Mississippi as part of a campaign to seek such a position. The Court nonetheless unanimously held that press coverage of Walker's involvement in these events attracted *Sullivan* protection. By involving himself so intimately and visibly in a subject of such acute political sensitivity, Walker had 'thrust himself into the vortex of public controversy'.[41] He was—at least in respect of this issue—a political figure.

That the Court placed such emphasis on Walker's voluntary involvement with political issues—and that it chose to describe this involvement with so forceful a word as 'thrust'—seems difficult to reconcile with the test it applied in *Hill*. On the facts of *Hill*, it was doubtful that the plaintiff was involved in an issue of 'public controversy'. And even if he was, he was more appropriately described as having been sucked unwillingly into the relevant vortex. It is difficult to avoid the conclusion that some members of the *Hill* majority were seeking to distance themselves from their decision in the former case without having to suffer the embarrassment of immediately overturning the judgment.[42]

... to Candidates for Office

The Supreme Court had little difficulty in accepting that individuals who sought elected political office presented a strong case for being subjected to the *Sullivan*

---

[40] Butts was successful on the facts. The newspaper had taken its story from a source with no track record of accurate reporting, who had criminal convictions for fraud, and who claimed to have uncovered the story when he fortuitously overheard a conversation between Butts and the rival coach on a crossed telephone line. The Court had little difficulty in holding that publication of such a story amounted to a 'reckless disregard' for the truth.

[41] (1967) 388 US 130 at 146, *per* Harlan J.

[42] In strictly legalistic terms, *Hill* would not have to have been overruled, as it was not a libel case, but one involving privacy. In substantive terms, however, it was clearly an extension of *Sullivan*, and so might defensibly be thought to apply to all future libel actions.

principle. In *Monitor Patriot* v. *Roy*,[43] a local New Hampshire paper had described a US Senate Democrat primary candidate as a 'former small time bootlegger'. As in *Curtis* and *Walker*, the Court did not rely on the *Hill* test. Rather it returned to the core 'political' rationale invoked in *Sullivan*. Stewart J's majority opinion held that it was:

> abundantly clear that . . . publications concerning candidates must be accorded at least as much protection under the First and Fourteenth Amendments as those concerning occupants of public office.[44]

Indeed, he continued: 'the constitutional guarantee has its fullest and most urgent application precisely to the conduct of campaigns for public office'.[45]

The Court considered that publicising a candidate's criminal conduct—'no matter how remote in time or place'[46]—would always attract *Sullivan* protection for the publisher. Its judgment nevertheless stressed that entry into the political arena did not deprive a candidate or office holder of every aspect of her private identity for defamation law purposes. There could still be some aspects of her private life to which the actual malice test would not apply. The extent of this private realm was in part a consequence of the style of a candidate's campaign. Thus, a politician who featured her spouse and children in the campaign could not argue that her immediate family circumstances remained a private concern. Similarly, a candidate who stressed her honesty and integrity would have to surmount the actual malice test if those qualities were questioned.

Recklessness—a Subjective or Objective Test?

Harlan J's opinion in *Curtis/Walker* hinted that the recklessness limb of *Sullivan*'s actual malice formula was more appropriately seen as a test of gross negligence; i.e. that it could be satisfied if the plaintiff proved that the publisher had engaged in 'highly unreasonable conduct constituting an extreme departure from the standards of investigation and reporting ordinarily adhered to by responsible publishers'.[47] This formula is difficult to reconcile with the majority view in *Rosenblatt*, where the Court appeared to adopt a 'recklessness' test that focused solely on the mind of the disseminator, not on the reasonableness of her beliefs.[48]

The difference between an objective and subjective recklessness test is not merely semantic, even if it betokens a distinction trial juries may find elusive.

---

[43] (1971) 401 US 265.
[44] *Ibid.*, at 271.
[45] *Ibid.*, at 272.
[46] *Ibid.*, at 277.
[47] (1967) 388 US 130 at 155.
[48] 'The test we laid down in [*Sullivan*] is not keyed to ordinary care; defeasance of the privilege is conditioned, not on mere negligence, but on reckless disregard for the truth': (1966) 383 US 75 at 84.

The latter formula offers disseminators an incentive to be incompetent and ignorant; it serves as an inducement to irresponsibility. First Amendment jurisprudence has frequently used the metaphor of 'breathing space' to explain the protection afforded to various forms of political speech. The analogy has adverse as well as positive implications. While we might readily agree that suffocating potentially true political speech is undesirable, we might also wish to prevent the halitosis of deceit being blown too vigorously into the political atmosphere.

A test which leaves the plaintiff uncompensated and (more importantly) leaves the disseminator unpunished, even if the plaintiff can prove that the defendant acted in complete disregard of even rudimentary standards of journalistic integrity, pollutes rather than purifies political discourse. This might suggest that negligence as to truth offers a more satisfactory criterion for liability than knowing/reckless falsity. The test would not be a difficult one for any reputable news organisation or moderately prudent politician to surmount, but it would be likely to chill the activities those media organisations for which truth is an unwelcome encumbrance rather than an ideal.

The Court has however been equivocal on this issue. Its 1968 judgment in St Amant v. Thompson[49] is widely regarded as having confirmed a subjective test. Yet the majority judgment in St Amant (joined by six members of the Court) was internally incoherent on this issue. One can identify several formulae which point forcefully towards a purely subjective notion of recklessness, dwelling solely on the publisher's beliefs. Thus the publisher must be; 'aware of the likelihood that he was circulating false information'; he/she must have had a 'high degree of awareness of probable falsity' or 'entertained serious doubts as to the truth of his publication'.[50] The most oft-quoted line of the judgment appears quite unambiguous: '[f]ailure to investigate [the reliability of] the source does not in itself establish bad faith'.[51] Yet other parts of the judgment equate recklessness with a standard that looks much more like gross negligence. So, recklessness could be satisfied if the publisher relied solely on 'an unverified anonymous telephone call' as her source; or, more broadly, 'where there are obvious reasons to doubt the veracity of the informant or the accuracy of his reports'.[52]

There is an obvious temptation to conclude that the majority on the Court was being deliberately opaque on this point. The lack of clarity in its reasoning made it rather difficult for trial courts to be sure that they were giving juries constitutionally defensible instructions on the effect of the Sullivan defence. This difficulty was compounded by the very rapid way in which the reach of the defence was being altered—from politician, to government official, to public figure, to matters of public interest all within the space of six years. In the context

---

[49] (1968) 390 US 727; 88 S Ct. 1323.
[50] Ibid. at 731 (S).
[51] Ibid., at 733 (US).
[52] Ibid. at 732 (US). Note that the formula is not 'obvious reasons for the publisher to doubt . . .'.

of such doctrinal uncertainty, the Supreme Court could be sure that it would be presented with innumerable instances of 'unconstitutional' state libel laws which it could use further to refine its *Sullivan* holding.

Narrowing the Reach and Effect of the *Sullivan* Defence

That *Hill* was an unwarranted extension of the *Sullivan* principle was further implied by the Court's 1974 and 1975 decisions in *Gertz* v. *Robert Welch Inc.*[53] and *Time Inc.* v. *Firestone*, cases which appreciably narrowed both the reach and the effect of the *Sullivan* defence. By this time, the Court contained several members appointed by President Nixon, and was clearly a more 'conservative' body than it had been some six or seven years earlier.

The suit in *Gertz* v. *Robert Welch Inc.* arose following the shooting in 1968 of a man called Nelson by a Chicago policeman. Following the policeman's conviction, the John Birch Society—a radical right-wing pressure group—published an article claiming that prosecution witnesses lied at the trial, and that the episode was part of a communist conspiracy against the police. Gertz was a lawyer who had represented Nelson's family in a related civil action, but had not been involved in the criminal trial. The article falsely claimed that Gertz had a criminal record, and identified him as the 'architect of the frame-up'.[54]

At trial in Illinois, the judge—also, it seems, ignoring *Hill*—rejected the defendant's assertion that Mr Gertz would have to surmount the *Sullivan* defence. The plaintiff was neither an elected official *per Sullivan* nor a public figure *per Butts/Walker*. Nor did the judge consider Mr Gertz to come with the scope of the rule in *Ambrosious* and *Ogren*.[55] Under the ordinary Illinois common law rule of strict liability for the publication of defamatory falsehoods, Gertz was clearly entitled to judgment in his favour. The jury awarded $50,000 compensatory damages. On appeal, the Illinois Supreme Court overturned the trial verdict, following the rationale of *Hill*. Gertz then appealed to the US Supreme Court, in effect asking it to hold that *Hill* was wrongly decided.

A majority on the Court accepted this contention. It held that the actual malice formula should be applied only in respect of 'public figures', and only then if the public figure concerned was involved in a matter of 'public controversy'. This two-pronged test moved away substantially from *Hill's* public-interest criterion. The Court stressed in particular that a private individual could not become a 'public figure' involuntarily.[56] The designation applied only to people who possessed:

---

[53] (1974) 418 US 323.

[54] On Gertz himself and his approach to the trial and subsequent Supreme Court hearings see Irons P. *The Courage of Their Convictions* ch. 14 (Los Angeles: University of California Press 1990).

[55] See 41–2 above.

[56] 'Hypothetically, it may be possible for someone to become a public figure through no purposeful action of his own, but the instances of truly involuntary public figures must be exceedingly rare': (1975) 418 US 323 at 345.

especial prominence in the affairs of society. Some occupy positions of such persuasive power and influence that they are deemed public figures for all purposes. More commonly, those classed as public figures have thrust themselves to the forefront of public controversies in order to influence the resolution of the issues involved.[57]

In respect of such plaintiffs, the *Sullivan* defence was entirely appropriate. Mr Gertz, however, did not fall into this category. The Court noted that he had been active in community matters, and published law books and articles, but he had 'no general fame or notoriety in the community. . . . [W]e would not lightly assume that a citizen's participation in community and professional affairs rendered him a public figure for all purposes'.[58] Gertz had played a minimal, non-partisan role in this controversial political episode; '[h]e plainly did not thrust himself into the vortex'.[59] *Sullivan* therefore did not apply.

The states' interest in protecting the reputation of private individuals justified a different rule. It was legitimate for states to fashion their libel laws in a way that provided effective *compensation* for reputation injuries caused by defamatory falsehoods: states should thus enjoy a 'substantial latitude' in determining the defences available in libel actions brought by such plaintiffs. But this latitude did not extend to permitting—as was the case under *Sullivan*—liability for publishing falsehoods without any proof of fault at all. The new bottom line of culpability in respect of *all* libel actions in respect of *compensatory damages* would be negligent falsity on the publisher's part, with the burden of proof (to the balance of probabilities standard) evidently lying on the plaintiff. States could if they wished impose a higher level of fault, but not a lower level. In essence, a new defence with a *universal reach* and a *significantly more protective effect* than English common law was being created in respect of compensatory damages.[60] However the Supreme Court's tolerance of a negligence-based standard of liability for private plaintiffs encompassed only compensatory damages. *Punitive damages* could only be awarded to private plaintiffs if plaintiffs established actual malice (to a standard of convincing clarity). In essence, a new defence with a *universal reach* and a *substantial, Sullivan effect* was now available in respect of *all* claims for punitive damages.

The majority discerned two constitutional difficulties with punitive damages in libel cases. The first lay in their nature. Punitive damages had no compensatory purpose. They were, rather, a vehicle for the punishment of unpopular views, almost, in effect, a disguised form of criminal libel. The second difficulty lay in their size:

> In most jurisdictions, jury discretion over the amounts awarded is limited only by the gentle rule that they not be excessive. Consequently, juries assess punitive damages in wholly unpredictable amounts bearing no necessary relation to the harm caused. . . .

[57] *Ibid.*

[58] *Ibid.*, at 352.

[59] *Ibid.*

[60] Gertz's case was consequently returned to Illinois to be decided anew on the basis of a negligence test. The award of damages was upheld under that new test.

[J]ury discretion to award punitive damages unnecessarily exacerbates the danger of media self-censorship.[61]

The rationale underlying this conclusion is not immediately apparent. It would seem that the majority's intention was to facilitate the vindication of an individual's reputation without at the same time imposing potentially such vast costs that newspapers would self-censor 'newsworthy' stories of political interest. The judgment made no difference at all to the treatment of political libels involving false statements of fact.[62] In essence what the case did was to make it easier than under *Hill* for private individuals to receive at least some damages for defamatory falsehoods contained in press coverage of their involuntary involvement in issues of public interest. And by so doing, of course, the case made identification of the dividing line between 'political' and 'public interest' issues of considerable importance.

The Court did however resolve a lingering uncertainty within defamation law that *Sullivan* had not addressed. *Sullivan* itself was concerned with assertions of fact, not opinion or comment, and it was not clear how the judgment had affected—if at all—the fair comment defence. The *Gertz* majority offered a simple answer to this question. That a defamatory statement was comment— whether fair or no—was a complete defence to any speech tort action or criminal prosecution:

> Under the First Amendment there is no such thing as a false idea. However pernicious an opinion may seem, we depend for its correction not on judges and juries but on the competition of other ideas.[63]

That a majority on the Court in *Gertz* felt that *Sullivan* had been pushed too far from its political roots in respect of matters of fact was suggested shortly after *Gertz* by the judgment in *Time Inc. v. Firestone*.[64] *Time*, perhaps buoyed by the substantial protection afforded to its mendacious reportage of private individuals' lives in *Hill*, was appealing against a $100,000 (compensatory damages) libel judgment against it by a Florida court, affirmed on appeal by the Florida Supreme Court. The plaintiff was a wealthy socialite. The subject-matter of the allegedly libellous *Time* story was her divorce, which in a farrago

---

[61] (1974) 418 US 323 at 350.

[62] Brennan, dissenting, accepted that Mr Gertz was not a public figure. He held that this was not a pertinent conclusion, since Gertz was intimately caught up in a matter of great public interest. He therefore fell within *Hill*. Douglas also dissented, maintaining his usual position that no libel actions were permissible concerning stories on issues of public interest. White J and Burger CJ dissented from a different perspective. Both deplored the extension of *Sullivan* to civil libel suits other than those analogous to criminal libel prosecutions. In their view, Mr Gertz was a private citizen. He had not, like General Walker, thrust himself qua political activist into a public controversy, but had become involved in his private capacity as an attorney. For such citizens, the law regulating libel actions was to be determined by their respective states. And if a state wished to have a rule of no-fault liability in such cases, it could do so.

[63] *Ibid.*, at 339–40. Subject one assumes to the 'clear and present danger' caveat. See pp 46–7 above.

[64] (1976) 424 US 448.

of press publicity about the respective spouses' sexual inclinations, had been granted on the basis of an irretrievable breakdown of the marriage. A subsequent *Time* article quite falsely alleged that the divorce had been granted on the grounds of the plaintiff's adultery and 'extreme cruelty' to her then husband. Florida's ordinary common law of libel, fashioned on the English model, allowed only truth as a defence in such circumstances. The Florida courts had assumed that the *Sullivan* rule did not apply against this type of private figure suing in respect of a non-political story.

The Supreme Court upheld the Florida courts on that question. Building on *Gertz*, the majority reiterated that the actual malice test reached only to public figures involved in matters of 'public controversy'. To be a socialite did not *per se* turn one into a 'public figure'. Neither was a divorce, no matter how salacious or fascinating, necessarily a matter of public controversy. To so define it would be to confuse—as did *Hill*—'public controversies' with 'controversies of interest to the public'.[65] Nor would the majority accept that seeking a divorce was a 'voluntary' action in the *Gertz* sense. Resort to court proceedings could hardly be so described if it was the only means of ending an unsatisfactory marriage. The majority nonetheless overturned the Florida judgment, on the ground—as laid out in *Gertz*—that Florida law did not require that the plaintiff prove at least negligence as to publishing falsehoods on the defendant's part.[66] Significantly, however, the majority implied that it would not subject a state court's findings on the negligence issue to particularly rigorous scrutiny.

CONCLUSION

From an English perspective, *Sullivan* and the litigation which followed it offer several important issues to consider when evaluating the adequacy of our domestic libel laws. The first two relate to issues of policy: the others to matters of law and legal methodology.

The first policy issue is that the *Sullivan* defence did not grant the press or individuals an absolute freedom to defame or lie about elected politicians. That extreme position, favoured by three Justices in *Sullivan* itself, has never commanded majority support on the Court. In terms of its effect, the *Sullivan* defence placed substantial rather than insuperable obstacles in the plaintiff's path. At no time has a majority of the Supreme Court approved the absolutist position.

The second policy point, on which the Court's post-*Sullivan* manoeuvrings were, at least initially, far less satisfactory, concerned the reach of the defence.

---

[65] This is of course also the distinction that had been made at common law in England some ten years earlier by Pearson J in *Webb*.

[66] Brennan, joined by Marshall J, again dissented, arguing in effect that *Hill* was correctly decided. White once more dissented from the other direction, arguing that no-fault liability was acceptable in non-political cases.

Hill was clearly an aberrant and abhorrent decision. By stretching the reach of the actual malice principle so far, the *Hill* majority severely undermined the legitimacy of the principle's effect. *Sullivan* was a readily defensible judgment in a liberal democratic polity; it both involved an elected politician as plaintiff and arose from that politician's attempts, along with his political allies, to continue to act in consistent defiance of the law on the fundamental issue of racial equality and to conceal that defiance from observers beyond Alabama's borders. In such circumstances, the notion of informed consent or Meiklejohn's theory of self-government has obvious relevance to the development of legal principle. But in a legal system in which the protection of an individual's reputation against mendacious criticism is in itself a valued political principle, any legal rules which outweigh that protection must be grounded in compelling policy arguments. *Hill* had no such basis. This might suggest that invoking the notion of 'public interest' as a moral justification for deviating from the original common law norm is a dangerous course for a court to adopt, as it may tend to obscure the intensely and intimately political nature of the controversies in issue in the litigation where the 'political libel' defences first appeared. Retaining the label of 'political interest' may be a more sensible strategy for a court to follow.

The first legal issue which British observers might consider is the source of the knowing/reckless falsity principle itself. It would be quite incorrect to present the *Sullivan* defence as rooted substantively in the First Amendment. Brennan's reliance on *Coleman* indicates that the substance of the defence derived from the common law. The role played by the First Amendment in the judgment was as a transmission device through which the substance of that long-established Kansan[67] common law could be imposed on all elected politicians occupying either state or federal office. Moreover, the substantial reliance placed in *Coleman* on *Wason* v. *Walter* indicates that those common law principles had a transatlantic rather than indigenously American root. While the English origins of the *Sullivan* defence may not be explicitly alluded to in the judgment itself, they are very easy to trace. For English courts to adopt the defence as a principle of common law would not require them to embrace a concept whose substantive content was 'foreign' to the English constitutional tradition.

Were they to do so however, the second legal point of note emerging from the post-*Sullivan* case law is that they would perhaps be well advised to create and maintain a simple, easily understood test. Even *Sullivan* itself, given its lack of clarity on whether 'recklessness' bore an objective or subjective meaning, could be held wanting on that issue. The case law which followed it became increasingly byzantine in its substantive holdings, with the result that the law on this question became both very complicated and distinctly unstable. Neither quality seems particularly commendable if one's understanding of the rule of law embraces a high degree of predictability and certainty in the substance of judge-made laws.

---

[67] (And Iowan, and Pennsylvanian *et. al.* common law).

The final point to note is that the formulation of the *Sullivan* rule and the subsequent US Supreme Court development of the defence all happened in something of an empirical vacuum. *Sullivan* itself had an obvious, if crudely characterised, empirical base. Alabama's libel laws were manifestly aiding the state government to ignore much of the Supreme Court's case law on the meaning of the equal protection clause of the Fourteenth Amendment. But, in later cases, the Court's effort to evaluate the empirical significance of existing libel laws and the likely consequences of altering them was at best hypothetical and perfunctory, and quite often wholly absent. This point was forcefully made by White J in *Gertz*:

> To me, it is quite incredible to suggest that threats of libel suits from private citizens are causing the press to refrain from publishing the truth. I know of no hard facts to support that proposition, and the Court furnishes none.[68]

In much the same way as the Kansan Supreme Court had done in *Coleman*, the US Supreme Court conducted its 'actual malice' debate largely at the level of abstract theory. This may have been—as was the case in Kansas sixty years earlier—unavoidable. There was little empirical evidence for judges to draw on.[69] But in those circumstances it would seem somewhat disingenuous to try to suggest that they are responding to political fact rather than political theory.

As we shall see in subsequent chapters, the limitations of *Sullivan* and its progeny have been well understood by courts in some other countries. In Chapter 6, we consider how the ideas that underlay *Sullivan* were initially understood and received in the United Kingdom.

---

[68] (1974) 418 US 323 at 390.
[69] In the US context, see now Smolla R. *Suing the Press* (Oxford: OUP, 1986); *Jerry Falwell v. Larry Flynt* (1988).

6

The Sullivan *Principle in 'English' Law*

The prospect that *Webb* might herald a new, more protective regime for publishers of political libels was soon put to the test. Before considering that issue however, one other related development merits attention. While *Sullivan* was winding its way through the US court system, English courts were addressing an ostensibly more prosaic facet of English libel law—namely the heads and quantum of damages that a plaintiff might recover.[1]

ON DAMAGES

As noted in Chapter 1, damages were recoverable under several heads. The total sum itself was presumed to be 'at large'—namely a matter for the jury itself to determine, subject only to very loose judicial supervision. The courts had consistently declined to interfere with awards unless they were manifestly absurd. This principle had been expressed in various formulae. In the 1879 case of *Phillips* v. *London and South Western Railway Co.*, James LJ had observed that[2]:

> Judges have no right to overrule the verdict of a jury as to the amount of damages, merely because they take a different view and think that if they had been the jury they would have given more or given less.

Similarly, ten years later in *Praed* v. *Graham*, Lord Esher had held that a court should interfere only if 'the damages are so excessive that no twelve men could reasonably have given them'.[3] Hamilton LJ had offered a more succinct formula in *Greenlands Ltd* v. *Wilmshurst and London Association for Protection of Trade*[4] in 1913, observing that an award should only be disturbed if it was 'excessive', a term intended to convey that there was no reasonable relationship

---

[1] Although, as the first instance judgment in *Sullivan* made clear, the size of a damages award played a crucial role in determining the extent to which reporting might be chilled by the prospect of losing a libel action, *Sullivan* itself was ignored in English academic circles. The decision did not attract so much as a case note in the 1964 or 1965 editions of the *Law Quarterly Review*, the *Modern Law Review*, *Public Law*, the *International and Comparative Law Quarterly* or the *Cambridge Law Journal*.

[2] (1879) 5 QBD 78 at 85–6.

[3] (1889) 24 QBD 53 at 55.

[4] [1913] 3 KB 507.

between the sum awarded and the loss to reputation that the plaintiff suffered. This principle of minimal intervention related as readily to low as to high damages; the award made in the bizarre case of *Newstead*[5] was only a farthing.

Hamilton LJ's formula is potentially misleading. The laxity of judicial supervision of quantum in libel cases was compounded by the assumption that punitive/exemplary damages were readily available. Such damages were not designed to compensate the plaintiff, but to penalise the defendant for particularly disreputable behaviour. There was not necessarily any linkage between the loss the plaintiff suffered and the moral degeneracy of the defendant's actions. A small loss, caused by the defendant's most egregiously outrageous conduct, could in principle lead quite legitimately to a enormous sum in damages. This had long been recognised as a factor which would make it still more difficult for an initial award to be overturned.[6]

Formulae offered in later judgments seemed to subsume the plaintiff's loss and the defendant's behaviour under an umbrella test concerning quantum premised on a notion of proportionality which addressed all facets of the libel. In 1959, Morris LJ suggested in *Scott* v. *Musial* that awards should be quashed if they were 'out of all proportion to the circumstances of the case'.[7] Three years later, in *Lewis* v. *Daily Telegraph Ltd*, Holroyd Pearce LJ observed that an award should stand unless 'it is out of all proportion to the facts or such that twelve reasonable men could not have made such an award'.[8] More succinctly, he suggested an award should be overturned if it was 'divorced from reality'.

Nor were juries required to apportion the total sum awarded between the different heads. There was thus no way of knowing what proportion of the award was intended to compensate the plaintiff for injury to her reputation (i.e. general, special and aggravated damages) and what was intended to punish the defendant for her unlawful behaviour. This imprecision became potentially problematic in 1964, when the House of Lords held in *Rookes* v. *Barnard*[9] that exemplary/punitive damages in all tort actions should be awarded only in a limited range of circumstances. The core of the judgment lay in a presumption that punitive damages were more akin to a criminal than civil penalty. In civil cases, they should thus be available only where specifically authorised by statute, where the tort concerned involved oppressive conduct by a government official, or—the category most relevant to defamation actions—where the defendant knew that his proposed actions were unlawful but decided to proceed anyway

---

[5] See 57 above.

[6] Cf. Cockburn CJ in *Phillips*: '[t]he fact that the jury may give exemplary damages for libel must always make it very difficult for the defendant to show that the award is out of all proportion': (1879) 4 QBD 406 at 409.

[7] [1959] 3 All ER 429 at 437.

[8] [1962] 3 All ER 698 at 716–17.

[9] [1964] 1 All ER 367.

on the assumption that the profits generated by the tortious action would outweigh any compensatory damages that a court might award.[10]

In principle, *Rookes* v. *Barnard* might have been thought to reduce the chilling effect of libel actions in respect of all kinds of information. That a defendant
in a libel action was careless or reckless as to truth, or even knew the information concerned to be false, would not in itself be sufficient to justify an award of
punitive damages. There would have to be in addition to this a deliberate calculation as to profitability. This would presumably have not been provable in
respect of most of the political libel cases discussed thus far, in which pecuniary
profit would not seem to have featured in the various defendants' reasons for
disseminating libellous material.

In practice, the consequences of *Rookes* would be much more opaque. This
was primarily because the courts did not recognise any clear dividing line
between many of those aspects of the defendant's behaviour which went to
punitive damages, and those which went to aggravated damages, a sub-division
of compensatory damages. Lord Devlin's judgment in *Rookes* made it quite
clear that such matters as the motive and conduct of the defendant could legitimately be taken into account in assessing aggravated damages.[11] Malevolence
or spite on the defendant's part was a legitimate ground on which to increase
aggravated damages, as would be a failure to apologise for or retract an unjus-
tified libel.

The Court of Appeal was presented with the opportunity to try to disentan-
gle the potential complication that *Rookes* raised for libel damages in *McCarey*
v. *Associated Newspapers Ltd*.[12] The plaintiff was a surgeon whose negligence
had caused the death of an elderly patient. The action concerned clear misre-
porting by several newspapers of events at the subsequent coroner's inquiry
which implied quite falsely that the surgeon was trying to evade taking responsibility for the error which led to the death. The jury had awarded him some
£9,000 damages.

Pearson LJ delivered the leading judgment. His opinion indicated that it
would now be less difficult for the higher courts to overturn libel awards than
had hitherto been the case. He suggested that there were now likely to be few
cases—and this was certainly not one of them—where the *Rookes* test would be
met. This meant that the damages awarded had to be purely compensatory in
nature. An award of £9,000 on these facts, which did not contain any aggravat-
ing behaviour by the defendant, was 'much, much too large . . . [I]t is an excessive and extravagant and exorbitant sum'.[13] Diplock and Wilmer LJJ concurred
in this result. Diplock LJ also suggested that the quantum of awards in libel
cases could be kept to more sensible levels if juries were instructed to have

[10] See Dias, R. and Markesinis, B., *Tort Law* (Oxford: Clarendon Press, 1984) pp 389–392:
Rogers W. *Winfield and Jolowicz on Tort* (London: Sweet and Maxwell, 1994 12th ed) pp 617–620.
[11] [1964] 1 All ER 367 at 407.
[12] [1964] 3 All ER 147.
[13] *Ibid.*, at 958.

regard to awards made in personal injuries cases. He draw a disparaging comparison between the £9,000 awarded to McCarey and a sum of £2,000 recently awarded to a young woman who had suffered the amputation of a leg. If those awards represented a correct statement of the law; 'so much the worse for the law'.[14] *Rookes* and *McCarey* had not made entirely clear whether the fact that newspapers generally existed to make a profit necessarily meant that every libel they published fell within the *Rookes* test. The Court of Appeal promptly resolved this uncertainty in *Broadway Approvals* v. *Odhams Press*.[15] As Sellers LJ put it:

> If Lord Devlin had intended newspapers in publishing items of news as here to fall within a punitive penalty and not merely a compensating liability, I would have expected it to be expressly so stated. Newspapers would never be immune from the risk of penalty if that is the right interpretation. They, in the ordinary sense of their business, publish news for profit. It would seem that a more direct pecuniary benefit would have to be shown to make a newspaper or any other defendant liable for punitive damages.[16]

This position thus seemed to be clearly stated, and while it was of no especial significance to political libels, the newly restrictive rules on punitive damages would arguably have reduced the chilling effect of libel laws in respect of all types of press reportage. All was however thrown into confusion shortly afterwards by the Court of Appeal's judgment in *Broome* v. *Cassels & Co.*[17] The libellous allegations at issue in *Broome* would undoubtedly have been regarded as intensely 'political' in the United States, and seemed also to fall squarely within the Pearson J's concept in *Webb* of information of legitimate interest to the public. The suit concerned a book, *Convoy PQ17*, written by the right-wing historian David Irving and published by Cassells, which purported to describe the circumstances which led to the destruction of a convoy of merchant ships by German ships during World War II. Broome was a senior naval officer, who was accused quite falsely in the book of cowardice and dereliction of duty which had contributed to the convoy's destruction.

At trial, the jury found in Broome's favour, and awarded him £15,000 compensatory damages and £25,000 punitive damages. The trial judge had appeared to take account of *Rookes* v. *Barnard* in his summing up, although he was not as explicit in his instructions as Lord Devlin had been in *Rookes* itself. On the facts of the case, there seemed sufficient evidence for the jury to have concluded

---

[14] *Ibid.*, at 960. The apparently clear guidance offered in *Rookes* and then *McCarey* apparently escaped the attention of some judges. At trial in *Broadway Approvals* v. *Odhams Press* ([1965] 2 All ER 523) Lawton J had told the members of the jury that they could award punitive damages if the defendant had behaved 'outrageously'. This direction was disapproved by the Court of Appeal.

[15] [1965] 2 All ER 523 at 537.

[16] *Ibid.*, at 537. See also Widgery J's judgment in *Manson* v. *Associated Newspapers*: 'If a newspaper, in the ordinary way of business, publishes news in regard to a particular item, and happens to make a mistake, the mere fact that it is publishing for profit does not open the door to an award of exemplary or punitive damages' ([1965] 2 All ER 954 at 958–9).

[17] [1971] 2 All ER 187.

that Cassells had realised that the allegations against Broome were untrue, but decided to publish anyway, assuming either that he would not sue or—if he did—that profits from the book would outweigh any damages award. The case seemed clearly to fall within the *Rookes* parameters.

On appeal, it became evident that the case had raised a 'constitutional' issue, but not one that had anything to do with political libels. The members of the Court of Appeal[18] formed the view that *Rookes* v. *Barnard* had been wrongly decided, and that they need not therefore regard it as a binding precedent on the issue of punitive damages. There was some constitutional basis to this argument, which proceeded on the various grounds that Lord Devlin had overlooked previous House of Lords authorities, that the point had not been fully argued by counsel, that the judgment had subsequently been subject to savage criticism in other common law jurisdictions and that the conclusion defied common sense and logic. The Court noted almost as an aside that, if *Rookes* were correct, it had been properly applied by the trial judge and the quantum of damages awarded was by no means excessive. The judgment was nonetheless an extraordinary enterprise for the Court of Appeal to undertake. Its (to put it kindly) unorthodox view of the hierarchical relationship between the Court of Appeal and House of Lords was forcefully dismissed by the Law Lords themselves, who took the matter so seriously that a panel of seven, rather than the usual five, judges sat to hear the case.[19]

The House of Lords also firmly restated the view that *Rookes* v. *Barnard* was correctly decided, and the majority accepted that the trial judge's instruction to the jury in the initial hearing adequately described the law. This was a case in which punitive damages could appropriately be awarded. As Lord Hailsham put it, 'the jury were clearly entitled to infer that [the publishers] went ahead with the most cold-blooded and clear sighted appreciation of what they were doing'.[20] Nor did the Court accept that the award was excessive.

On the issue of punitive damages, therefore, the House of Lords' judgment in *Cassell* suggested that fewer such awards could now be made. The anti-chilling effect of this conclusion was however tempered by the Court's clear recognition that a defendant's outrageous behaviour could found an award for aggravated damages, and by the fact that the majority also rejected Diplock LJ's suggestion in *McCarey* that personal injuries awards be invoked as a comparator in libel actions. For the purveyor of political libels therefore, the brief flurry of litigation on the head and quantum of damages in tort actions made it no less likely that he/she would lose his/her case, but offered the possibility

---

[18] Lord Denning MR and Salmon and Phillimore LJJ.

[19] Lord Hailsham's views typified the sentiments expressed by his colleagues: 'it is not open to the Court of Appeal to give gratuitous advice to judges of first instance to ignore decisions of the House of Lords in this way, and if it were open to the Court of Appeal to do so, it would be highly undesirable. . . . The fact is, and I hope it will never be necessary to say so again, that in the hierarchical system of courts which exists in this country, it is necessary for each lower tier, including the Court of Appeal, to accept loyally the decisions of the higher tiers': [1972] 1 All ER 801 at 809.

[20] *Ibid.*, at 812.

that defeat would be rather less expensive in the future than it had been in the past.

The courts' responses to the more narrowly tailored question of the reach of the qualified privilege defence in political libel cases were markedly inconsistent in the period from 1970 to the mid-1980s. The Court of Appeal's judgment in *Cook v. Alexander*[21] concerned a controversy arising over the closure of an approved school following allegations of staff brutality made by Cook, a former teacher at the school. Cook's action was against the parliamentary sketch writer of *The Daily Telegraph*, who he alleged had authored an unfairly selective account of a House of Lords debate on the matter, an account which would leave readers with the impression that Cook was himself both a child abuser and a liar.

The Court of Appeal unanimously concluded that such publications attracted qualified privilege as long as they offered a fair impression of the relevant proceedings. The opinions of two of the three judges were mildly reminiscent of the 1891 judgment in *Manchester Corporation*, in which the court had arrived at a conclusion which was protective of political speech without in explicit terms giving any substantial consideration to the contemporary political significance of so doing. That assumption may perhaps have been implicit. Lord Denning MR's leading judgment took *Wason* as its starting point. He accepted that a parliamentary sketch was 'different' from a verbatim report or a précis of parliamentary proceedings[22]: it was inevitably selective and impressionistic in the information it conveyed. However the public interest in its publication was similar enough to the public interest in verbatim or précis reporting to demand that the common law grant its publishers qualified privilege as long as the sketch was 'fair'.[23] This test afforded the writer appreciable leeway. As Buckley LJ put it, a sketch would only be unfair if it was 'so tendentious or otherwise so slanted as to make it a distorted report of that part of the proceedings to which it relates'.[24]

Lawton LJ showed a rather clearer understanding of the value of explicitly grounding his conclusion in the changing nature of the relationship between the press, the public and the Houses of Parliament. His reasoning echoed the analytical perspective adopted by Cockburn CJ in *Wason* and *Purcell*; namely that the common law should develop in ways which reinforced emergent societal understandings of the type of political information which citizens had a legiti-

---

[21] [1973] 3 All ER 1037.

[22] Denning seemed to view the verbatim report and the precis as identical creatures for the purposes of privilege, a conflation which certainly has no basis in *Wason* itself.

[23] The decision was certainly not reached as a result of construing the report as a matter which fell clearly within the 'fair information' principle used by Pearson J in *Webb*. *Webb* was cited in argument by defence counsel, but not referred to in any of the judgments.

[24] [1973] 3 All ER 1037 at 1043.

mate interest in receiving. He observed that since 1939, few newspapers carried substantial verbatim reports of parliamentary proceedings; journalistic 'fashions' had changed, perhaps because 'the newspapers have found that the public are not interested in that kind of [verbatim] report'.[25] Although he did not use the formula explicitly, the implicit point of his argument was that the 'common convenience and welfare' of modern society required that selective and perhaps sensationalistic reporting of parliamentary proceedings now merited substantial protection against defamation actions.

In absolute substantive terms, the reach of the *Cook* rule is obviously much wider than that of the rules promulgated in *Wason* and *Purcell* almost 100 years earlier. In methodological terms, however, the three cases are virtually identical.[26] And this might lead to the observation that, if the substance of the respective judgments is measured in relative terms—with the varying levels of democratic maturity of British society in 1868–77 and 1973 providing the yardsticks—there is little to choose between them. On the ostensibly related question of a local authority's capacity to sue in libel however, the common law of the 1970s and the 1890s seemed to share little common ground.

Bognor Regis UDC v. Campion

The defendant in *Bognor Regis UDC* v. *Campion*[27] had waged a protracted and polemical campaign against what he considered to be corruption and incompetence in his local authority. The object of the suit was a pamphlet authored by Campion which he handed out at a public meeting in the local area. The pamphlet was an hysterical polemic, not couched in party political terms, which accused the ruling group on the council of ineptitude and dishonesty and—less directly—levelled the same accusations against several councillors. Rather than ignore the pamphlet, the council's ruling group resolved that the council itself should sue Mr Campion in libel for what it claimed were false and defamatory attacks on its reputation.

The issue before Browne J in the High Court was whether the authority could maintain such an action. The decision in *Manchester Corporation* seemed to hold quite clearly that a council could sue only in respect of allegations occasioning economic loss or accusing it of a crime. That judgment had not been directly overruled by the Court of Appeal or the House of Lords. Browne J refused to follow the earlier judgment however. Rather, he held that:

> Just as a trading company has a trading reputation which it is entitled to protect by bringing an action for defamation, so in my view the plaintiffs as a local government

---

[25] *Ibid.*

[26] Even to the extent that only one of the judges in each case alluded explicitly and at any length to the public's legitimate interest in consuming political information.

[27] [1972] 2 QB 169.

corporation have a 'governing reputation' which they are equally entitled to protect in the same way.[28]

Browne was led to this conclusion by the Court of Appeal's judgment in *Gillian*. His rationale was in effect that *all* corporations, be they limited companies, trades unions or local authorities, enjoyed the same legal capacity for libel law purposes. *Gillian* had in turn been strongly influenced by Lord Esher's statement in *South Hetton Coal* in 1894 that all plaintiffs were alike for libel law purposes. As suggested in Chapter 4, a careful reading of Lord Esher's judgment in *South Hetton Coal* indicates that his rather careless phraseology was not intended to include governmental bodies, but only commercial organisations. *Campion* thus rested in large part on the perpetuation of an error made twenty-five years earlier in *Gillian*.

Judgment was eventually delivered against Mr Campion. The award of damages was only £2,000, but this was accompanied by an order to pay the council's costs, which amounted to some £30,000.[29] A bill of £32,000 (at 1972 prices) might be thought to have a decidedly chilling effect on citizens or newspapers wishing to criticise a local authority's behaviour.

There is nothing in Browne J's judgment to indicate that he perceived the case to have any 'political' or constitutional dimension at all. *Webb* was not cited, nor was any reference made in the decision or in argument to *Chicago* or to *Sullivan* and its progeny. The judgment is a masterly illustration of jurisprudential insularity: insularity both in the doctrinal sense of seeing the issue as one of tort law rather than constitutional law, and in the geographical sense of its evident incomprehension that other common law jurisdictions might offer useful lessons about the role properly to be played by libel law in regulating political expression in democratic countries.[30]

As suggested in Chapter 2, it would be erroneous to regard *Manchester* as a judgment formulated in defence of a constitutional principle of safeguarding freedom of political expression. That the judgment had that outcome was a fortuitous but wholly incidental side-effect of a judicial methodology grounded in narrowly 'apolitical' legalistic principles. The High Court's failure in *Campion* to recognise this dimension of the problem before it is perhaps surprising. But Browne J was by no means the only member of the senior judiciary who saw no need to engage explicitly with the constitutional dimension of political defamation actions.

---

[28] [1972] 2 QB 169 at 175.

[29] Weir, A., 'Local Authority v Critical Ratepayer—a Suit in Defamation' [1972] *Cambridge LJ* 238.

[30] For a splendidly splenetic critique of the judgment see *ibid*. See also Gatenby, J., 'More Bother in Bognor' (1973) 36 *MLR* 307.

Horrocks v. Lowe

The House of Lords displayed a little more awareness of these political implications in *Horrocks* v. *Lowe*.[31] The plaintiff was a Conservative member of Bolton Town Council. He was verbally accused by Lowe during a council meeting of using his political position to further his business interests. In an action for slander, it was accepted by both parties that the occasion was one of qualified privilege. This appeared to be for distinctly 'political reasons'. As Lord Diplock put it in the House of Lords:

> What is said by members of a local council at meetings of the council or of any of its committees is spoken on a privileged occasion. The reason for the privilege is that those who represent local government electors should be able to speak freely and frankly, boldly and bluntly, on any matter which they believe affects the interests or welfare of the inhabitants.[32]

The *reach* of this occasion is very narrow, extending only to words spoken by councillors in council meetings, and not to the type of publication in question in *Campion*. What was in issue in *Horrocks* was the *effect* of the privilege. At first instance, the trial judge had accepted that Lowe honestly believed his accusations to be true. He nonetheless directed the jury that the defendant's speech was made with malice if it was premised on 'gross and unreasoning prejudice'—a test perhaps best described as one of gross negligence. The Court of Appeal had reversed the judgment, holding that the plaintiff had to prove that the defendant's subjective state of mind was one which regarded the information disseminated as false.

Lord Diplock delivered the leading judgment in the House of Lords. His understanding of 'honest belief' indicated that the plaintiff would have to prove either knowing or reckless falsity on the defendant's part. The latter test would be met by demonstrating that the plaintiff was 'indifferent' to whether the information was true or false. That the plaintiff was 'stupid' or 'prejudiced' in dealing with the information in issue did not in itself amount to malice. No reference was made in the judgment to Cockburn CJ's evidently long-forgotten suggestion in *Campbell* v. *Spottiswoode* that a negligence based test might be appropriate gauge of malice in some 'public interest' libels.[33]

The judgment was obviously very protective of a limited category of political speech. But Lord Diplock's analysis did not afford any special status to 'political' information. His reasoning was evidently intended to settle an apparent uncertainty as the meaning of 'malice' which was of equal applicability to all occasions when qualified privilege arose. This apparent indifference to

---

[31] [1975] AC 135.
[32] *Ibid.*, at 152. Para. 9 of the Sched. to the Defamation Act 1952 had extended qualified privilege to fair and accurate reports of council proceedings. This was presumably yet another exception to the 'first place' analysis Diplock had offered up in *Silkin*: see 58–9 above.
[33] See 24–6 above.

constitutional considerations continued to be embraced more than a decade later by the Court of Appeal in a case involving the alleged incompetence of a senior civil servant.

Blackshaw v. Lord

The litigation in *Blackshaw* v. *Lord* [34] arose from a *Daily Telegraph* story written by Lord investigating the Department of Energy. The story alleged that the Department had apparently breached Treasury guidelines and overpaid some £52 million in grants to various oil companies. Several civil servants were reprimanded following internal disciplinary proceedings. The Commons Public Accounts Committee (PAC) investigated the affair, and issued a report. The article linked the report to the resignation of a senior civil servant, Blackshaw, who held the rank of Under-Secretary. The Permanent Secretary at the Department of Energy had told the PAC that an Under-Secretary had been reprimanded. Just after Lord's story ran, the Permanent Secretary informed the PAC that this was false; no Under-Secretary had been reprimanded. Blackshaw claimed to have resigned purely for pre-existing, personal reasons. He considered the story defamatory in that it implied that his professional incompetence had cost the taxpayer £52 million.

At trial, the judge upheld Lord's claim that the story attracted qualified privileged, on the grounds that 'the defendants had a legitimate interest or duty to publish the words complained of and the readers of the *Daily Telegraph* had a corresponding or common interest therein'.[35] He suggested that an allegation of governmental maladministration involving large sums of money:

> is a matter which, I think, it is beyond argument would be for the ordinary English person who would be interested in the workings of government, a matter which is so important in my judgment, that it would be the duty of the press to bring it to the attention of the public, and any right thinking person who wanted good administration in this country, and who was interested in the running of the country, would want to know those facts:. . .and furthermore, a newspaper proprietor . . . of any proper standing . . . would have a strict duty to bring those matters to the attention of the public.[36]

Reduced to essentials, the summing up suggests that allegations that senior government officials have incompetently misused substantial sums of money are political (in the broad sense) matters which all responsible citizens would wish to know about and evaluate. As such, it falls squarely within a fairly narrow interpretation of *Webb*. Unlike Browne J in *Campion*, the first instance judge in *Blackshaw* perceived that a libel alleging incompetence within government raised an issue of constitutional law as much as of tort law.

---

[34] [1984] 1 QB 9 (CA).
[35] *Ibid.*, at 23.
[36] *Ibid.*, at 24.

In the Court of Appeal, Stephenson LJ. adopted an extremely limited view of the ratio of *Webb*. He reviewed previous authorities on qualified privilege and concluded that:

> I cannot extract from any of those authorities any relaxation of the requirements. . . . No privilege attaches yet to a statement on a matter of public interest believed by the publisher to be true in relation to a matter in which he has exercised reasonable care.[37]

This rather overlooked the statements made to precisely that effect by Cockburn CJ. in *Campbell* v. *Spottiswoode*.[38] But, as noted in the earlier discussion of *Horrocks* v. *Lowe*, that aspect of judgment appeared to have been erased from the judiciary's collective memory. Stephenson LJ then rejected the argument that *Webb* established a qualified privilege of 'fair information on a matter of public interest'. Its *ratio* reached only to the reporting of foreign judicial proceedings.

Dunn LJ concurred. His judgment was ostensibly based in large part[39] on the Court of Appeal's decision in *Purcell* v. *Sowler*,[40] but it was reasoned in a fashion that created the impression (like the New Zealand court's use of *MacIntosh* v. *Dunn* in *Truth*) that he probably had not read, and certainly had not understood, the full judgments in *Purcell*. In Dunn LJ's view, '*Purcell*, which has stood for over 100 years, remains good law'.[41]

This might be thought an uncontentious claim, until one begins to consider just what Dunn LJ seemed to think 'the law' laid out in *Purcell* actually was. Dunn LJ seemed to take a very narrow view of *Purcell*, regarding it as confirming that the reach of privilege in respect of as yet unproven allegations was limited to the dissemination of information to an audience which had a legal duty to investigate the claim. In *Purcell* this legitimate audience would presumably have been Poor Law Board officials; in *Blackshaw* it would have been MPs and officials in the Department of Energy. It did not embrace the public at large. Dunn LJ concluded that, since a newspaper and its readers were under no such reciprocal obligation to disseminate and consume political stories in 1877, they could not be so in 1984. *Webb* was thus 'good law' only if narrowly interpreted to apply only to reports of foreign judicial proceedings raising matters of 'legitimate and proper public interest'.

Dunn LJ's reasoning was supported by the other two judges. The Court of Appeal concluded unanimously in *Blackshaw* that the press had no duty to publish its story to the public at large. Fox LJ doubted that the general public had any 'audience interest' in this sort of story. He concluded simply that 'an allegation of improper or negligent conduct against a public servant may be privileged if made to persons having a proper interest to receive it—such as the police

[37] *Ibid.*, at 26.
[38] See 24–6 above.
[39] Stephenson LJ alluded to *Purcell* only briefly, invoking it as an authority against the grant of privilege on the facts before the court in *Blackshaw*.
[40] (1877) LR 2 CP 215.
[41] [1984] 1 QB 9 at 35.

or senior officials'.[42] The electorate had no legitimate interest in such information. The contrast with the sentiments expressed in *Wason* is marked. Cockburn
CJ had, it may be recalled, suggested that '[t]here is perhaps no subject matter
in which the public have a deeper interest than in all that relates to the conduct
of public servants of the state'.[43]

It might however be suggested that the Court of Appeal in *Blackshaw* wholly
misunderstood and then unthinkingly misapplied 'the law' articulated by
Cockburn CJ in *Purcell*. As suggested in Chapter 2, the principle underpinning
Purcell was a presumption that privilege should apply to political information
in which the citizenry had a legitimate interest. If one construes *Purcell's* significance as 'law' primarily as a source of broad principle rather than a narrow
rule, *Blackshaw* can be seen as a poorly founded judgment. It is of course important that 'the law' in this broad sense not be read ahistorically when one applies
the principle to fashion a legal rule. It is unlikely that the type of information in
issue in *Blackshaw* would have been accorded privilege by the *Purcell* court, but
that is because the principle it espoused was located in the political context of a
very primitive form of democratic constitutionalism. In the constitutional context of a mature democracy, one would expect the principle to yield a much
more expansive rule.

The Court's methodology in *Blackshaw* is wholly formalistic, as was Browne
J's reasoning in *Campion*. It compares poorly not just with the techniques used
in *Wason* and *Purcell*, but also with Pearson J's much more purposive approach
in *Webb* and with Lord Greene MR's 'bold' analysis in *Braddock*. Pearson J's
and Lord Greene MR's methodology in those cases required them to ask themselves whether contemporary (i.e. 1960 and 1948 respectively) British political
culture now demanded a 'new' common law rule be recognised.[44] Their answer
to the question was a clear 'Yes'. In *Blackshaw*, the Court of Appeal evidently
did not accept that such a question should even be raised. Instead, it effectively
held that the relationship between elected government bodies and the electorate
had not undergone any meaningful change since 1877.

That was a most peculiar assumption to make. In 1877, Britain could not be
regarded as a representative democracy in the sense in which we now understand the term. Barely one third of adults were entitled to vote for members of
the Commons; the House of Lords enjoyed co-equal legal status in the legislative process with the lower House; and the Monarch seemed to think it quite
appropriate to interfere with most aspects of government decision-making. The
legitimacy of the governmental system did not rest on the consent of the governed in any active sense. In so far as the government was to be accountable, it
was to be accountable to the Houses of Parliament, rather than to the citizenry.

[42] *Per* Fox LJ at 41.
[43] (1868) 4 QB 73 at 89.
[44] The tone of Lord Greene MR's language suggests he was recognising a new rule, although, as
suggested above (at 52–3), his court seemed to be doing no more than applying a rule easily discernible in the 1837 case of *Duncombe* v. *Daniel* (see 20 above).

Wason and *Purcell* can thus be seen as unusually far-sighted and progressive examples of common law reasoning. Assessed against the same yardstick, *Blackshaw* stands as an illustration of extraordinarily myopic and reactionary judicial decision-making.

Templeton v. Jones

The English Court of Appeal's judgment in *Blackshaw* might usefully be analysed alongside the contemporaneous decision of its New Zealand counterpart in *Templeton v. Jones*.[45] The defendant was an MP and government minister; the plaintiff was an opposition party candidate contesting the minister's seat in the coming election. The minister had made a speech to his local constituency party in which he accused the plaintiff of anti-Semitism. He had then distributed copies of the speech to newspaper and television correspondents in the press gallery of the New Zealand legislature. His claims were thereafter extensively reported in the national press and on television.

The Court of Appeal's judgment was delivered by Cooke J—who, it might be recalled, had, at an earlier stage of his career, unsuccessfully floated a *Webb* argument before the New Zealand High Court in *Truth (NZ) Ltd v. Holloway*. Twenty-five years on, Cooke J delivered a judgment which rejected the defendant's claim that he could invoke the defence of qualified privilege. The claim was much less ambitious in its reach than Cooke's formula (as counsel) in *Truth*, asserting merely that 'the defendant had a social or moral duty to make a statement to the general public as to the conduct and fitness for office of a declared parliamentary candidate'.[46]

Cooke J's judgment was far more alert to questions concerning the electorate's interest in receiving information about governmental issues than the opinions delivered in *Blackshaw*. He quoted extensively from *Braddock v. Bevins* to support the principle that electors in a given constituency had a legitimate interest in hearing candidates' views of their opponents.[47] However he noted that Lord Greene MR had limited the reach of the *Braddock* defence to leaflets distributed in the relevant electoral district—it did not extend to dissemination to the public at large. This distinction lay at the core of his decision in *Templeton*. He was prepared to accept that qualified privilege would arise in respect of information that the Minister had targeted precisely at his own constituents, even if the information thereby became incidentally available to people who were not electors in his constituency. However, by giving copies of his speech to the national media, the Minister had in effect published to the entire country. The court could see no basis for assuming that the requisite reciprocal duty/interest to disseminate this information arose between the

---

[45] [1984] 1 NZLR 448.

[46] *Ibid.*, at 459.

[47] The *Braddock* rule had not been reversed by legislation in New Zealand as it had in England.

defendant and the people of New Zealand as a whole; '[o]ne must not lose sight of the fact that the publication sued on is only that in the television programme of 3 March 1983'.[48]

Braddock was of course decided some forty years earlier, in an era when very few electors possessed television sets. It was also concerned with a local, rather than—as in *Templeton*—national election. It might plausibly have been thought that the 'common convenience and welfare of society' would by 1984 have demanded that the reach of *Braddock* be extended. That the plaintiff sued only in respect of a television broadcast perhaps indicates that television had by then become in New Zealand the most effective way of communicating political information. Cooke J's opinion was evidently not as 'bold' as that offered by Lord Greene MR in *Braddock*, and the judgment seemingly lacked the awareness of the changing nature of the news media that the Kansan Supreme Court had displayed to a much earlier stage of technological evolution eighty years previously in *Coleman*.[49] In other respects, however, it demonstrated an appreciable degree of insight.

In marked contrast to *Blackshaw*, the judgment in *Templeton* dwelt at some length on *Sullivan* and the political purposes that a knowing/reckless falsity test might serve, and Cooke J indicated that he did not rule out the argument that *Sullivan* could be a legitimate influence on the future development of New Zealand common law. The judgment also created the impression that the court would have welcomed a reform which would permit purveyors of political information to plead a negligence-based defence. The judges felt however that this was a step more appropriately taken by Parliament than by the court, particularly as Parliament had recently enacted libel reform legislation which did not alter this facet of the common law.[50]

The Report of the Faulks Committee

That the Court of Appeal in *Blackshaw* paid no regard to *Coleman*, to *Sullivan*, or to the US Supreme Court's by then substantial body of elaborative post-*Sullivan* case law[51] is presumably explained by the same judicial insularity that drove Browne J's conclusion in *Campion*. The issue had been addressed by the Report of the (Faulks) Committee on Defamation, which was issued in 1975. The Committee's treatment of *Sullivan* was however rather unsophisticated. It began by revealing a deep misunderstanding of the substantive roots of the decision, arguing that:

---

[48] [1984] 1 NZLR 448 at 459.
[49] See 37–9 above.
[50] Like his English counterparts, Cooke J evidently did not appreciate that the roots of such a defence might be found in *Campbell* and *Wason*.
[51] The facts of *Blackshaw* were virtually on all fours with those in *Rosenblatt*; see 73–4 above.

the foundation of the Supreme Court's decision was the provisions of the 1st and Fourteenth Amendments of the United States Constitution. . . . Here we have no written constitution to interpret; we apply the common law.[52]

That *Sullivan* was itself an application of the common law (and of common law only one step removed from an English source) had evidently passed the Committee by. Its members, apparently motivated primarily by the supposed 'foreignness' of the *Sullivan* defence, stated that '[w]e oppose it most strongly because we believe that here it would in many cases deny a just remedy to defamed persons'.[53] This was a peculiar argument to make. The US Supreme Court had appreciated that *Sullivan* would have just that same effect in the USA. The point that Brennan had grasped in *Sullivan* was that the denial of a 'just remedy' to the victims of defamation was the price to be paid for enhancing the flow of political information to the public.[54]

Conclusion

The suggestion in the Faulks Report that English law should regard *Sullivan* as both irrelevant and undesirable indicated that the case's invisibility at the English libel bar was unlikely to be remedied in the near future. What is perhaps less easy to explain is why the judges hearing *Campion, Horrocks* and *Blackshaw*, along with the members, judges or otherwise, of the Faulks Committee, paid no attention to a 'constitutional' principle defending freedom of expression whose legal roots ostensibly lay rather closer to home.

THE REQUIREMENTS OF THE EUROPEAN CONVENTION ON HUMAN RIGHTS

Prior to the passage of the Human Rights Act 1998, the provisions of the European Convention on Human Rights (ECHR) were not directly enforceable in the United Kingdom courts. The UK had however been one of the initial signatories to the Convention, and British politicians and lawyers had played a major part in determining its contents.[55] In the early 1960s UK citizens were granted the right directly to petition the European Commission on Human Rights if they considered a government body had infringed one of their Convention rights.

---

[52] Paras. 6.10 and 6.17.

[53] Para. 6.17.

[54] Nor had the Court forgotten that point. While the Faulks Committee was concluding its deliberation, the Supreme Court was deciding *Gertz*, in which the majority judgment noted that: 'plainly, many deserving plaintiffs, some intentionally subjected to injury, will be unable to surmount the barrier of the New York Times test': (1974) 418 US 323.

[55] See Marston, G., 'The United Kingdom's Part in the Preparation of the European Convention on Human Rights' (1993) 42 *ICLQ* 796: Hunt, M., *Using Human Rights Law in English Courts* (Oxford: Hart Publishing, 1997) pp 31–3.

Stricto sensu, the Convention's status in UK law was that of an international treaty. In the event that a provision of UK law was found by the European Court on Human Rights (ECtHR) to breach the Convention, the government would accept its treaty obligation to modify the law concerned, a step which would generally require it to promote a bill which, when enacted, would alter domestic law accordingly. Constitutional lawyers had long accepted that domestic courts could not invoke international law rules to invalidate government action that was clearly authorised by statute.[56] But if a statutory provision could bear several meanings, only one of which corresponded with the Treaty's requirements, a court could legitimately afford the provision that meaning. It also seemed, although the point was not entirely without ambiguity, that the courts would be willing to modify common law rules to ensure that they complied with the UK's international law obligations. In the context of the Convention, this might be done reactively, in response to a judgment issued by the ECtHR. It could however be done pro-actively, in anticipation of what the ECtHR might conclude if a common law rule that appeared to breach the Convention were to come before it. More speculatively, it might be suggested that the courts would be willing to modify clear common law rules if they reached the conclusion that the rules concerned did not comply with the Convention.[57] From either the reactive or prospective viewpoint, the UK's accession to the Convention could readily be seen (to borrow from *Wason*) as an indication that the 'wants and usages and interests' of modern Britain were now better served by the moral values articulated in the Convention's various Articles than by longstanding principles of common law. Accession could legitimately be seen as an invitation to the domestic courts to lend a renewed vigour to the adaptability of the common law. The invitation was evidently one of which domestic courts were unaware. The Convention was referred to by English courts on only one occasion in the 1960s, and that in a case involving the status of the European Commission on Human Rights.[58] It did not begin to feature in English case law with any regularity until the mid-1970s.[59]

Political Libels and Article 10 ECHR

The provision of the Convention of most relevance to libel laws is Article 10, which—like the First Amendment to the US Constitution—deals in general terms with freedom of expression;

---

[56] *Mortenson v. Peters* (1906) 14 SLT 227; *Cheney v. Conn* [1968] 1 WLR 242; discussed in Loveland, *Constitutional Law* (London: Butterworths, 1996) 44–7.

[57] The complexities of the courts' views on these questions are best conveyed in Hunt, n. 55 above, ch.1.

[58] *Zoernsch v. Waldock* [1964] 1 WLR 675 (CA).

[59] See generally Hunt, M., *Using Human Rights Law in English Courts* (Oxford: Hart Publishing, 1997), especially 131–9, 326–7.

1. Everyone has the right to freedom of expression. This right shall include freedom to hold opinions and to receive and impart information and ideas without interference by public authority and regardless of frontiers. This Article shall not prevent States from requiring the licensing of broadcasting, television or cinema enterprises.

Unlike the US Constitution, however, Article 10 ECHR contains a clause which explicitly limits the scope of the freedoms it protects:

2. The exercise of these freedoms, since it carries with it duties and responsibilities, may be subject to such formalities, conditions, restrictions or penalties as are prescribed by law and are necessary in a democratic society, in the interests of national security, territorial integrity or public safety, for the prevention of disorder or crime, for the protection of health or morals, for the protection of the reputation of others, for preventing the disclosure of information received in confidence, or for maintaining the authority and impartiality of the judiciary.[60]

This constitutional methodology pervades the Convention. In the main, the Convention's Articles identify and afford protection to a broadly defined civil right; the text then permits signatory states to intrude into the nominally protected sphere in defence of certain specified objectives; but it then in turn requires that intrusion to comply with certain safeguards. The ECHR's decision-making in Article 10 cases can thus be broken down into four stages:

(a) Has a governmental body in some way interfered with the applicant's right of free expression?

(b) If so, has it done so to satisfy a legitimate objective arising from one or more of the factors identified in Article 10(2), i.e. national security, territorial integrity etc.?

(c) If so, is the basis for that interference 'prescribed by law'; i.e. precisely identified in the domestic legal system?[61]

(d) If so, is the measure taken 'necessary in a democratic society'; i.e. is the substance of the interference a 'proportionate' means to achieve the legitimate objective in the sense that it curtails the protected right to as limited an extent as possible?[62]

---

[60] The substantive distinction between Art. 10 and the First Amendment on this point is much narrower than their respective texts would suggest. Although the First Amendment is cast in absolute terms, the Supreme Court has consistently held that its guarantees are impliedly subject to considerations similar to those articulated in Art. 10(2). See e.g. *Schenk* v. *United States* (1919) 249 US 47 (sedition); *Gitlow* v. *New York* (1925) 268 US 652 (criminal syndicalism); *Beauharnais* v. *Illinois* (1952) 343 US 250 (racist abuse); *Brandenburg* v. *Ohio* (1969) 395 US 444 (public order); *Palko* v. *Connecticut* (1908) 302 US 319 (authority of the judiciary). *Sullivan*, of course, diluted the absolutism of the text in deference to Alabama's legitimate interest in providing (some) protection for the reputations of public officials.

[61] The concept had been explained in the following terms by the ECHR in *Sunday Times* v. *United Kingdom*: 'a norm cannot be regarded as a "law" unless it is formulated with sufficient precision to enable the citizen to regulate his conduct; he must be able—if need be with appropriate advice—to foresee to a degree that is reasonable in all the circumstances, the consequences which a given action may entail': 2 EHRR 245 (1979) at para. 49.

[62] For a general introduction to the area see Harris, D., O'Boyle, M. and Warbrick, C., *Law of the European Convention on Human Rights*, ch.11 (London: Butterworths, 1995): Janis, M., Kay and Bradley, A., *European Human Rights Law* ch. 6 (Oxford: Clarendon Press, 1995).

That Pearson J had made no reference in *Webb* to Article 10 is hardly surprising. In general terms, UK courts in that era seemed not to realise (or perhaps to accept) that the Convention might be a relevant factor to consider in a wide range of areas of domestic law. More specifically, there was at that point no obvious indication[63] that Article 10 had any bearing on civil libel laws. Nor until the US Supreme Court decision in *Sullivan* four years later was there any clear authority to support the proposition that broad 'constitutional' provisions protecting free expression in western democracies might have significant implications for common law rules of defamation. The *Sullivan* lesson as to the potential relevance of Article 10 to libel laws seemed however to go largely unnoticed in Europe and particularly in the United Kingdom. *Campion* and *Horrocks* were decided in the mid-1970s. Neither judgment, nor it seemed the arguments raised in both cases,[64] made any reference at all to the Convention. The same point can be made of two contemporary academic critiques of *Campion*. While both alluded to the 'constitutional' dimensions of the case, neither perceived that the ECHR was a germane consideration for the court to have taken into account.[65] Of the seven judges who authored opinions in *Broome* v. *Cassell & Co. Ltd*, only Lord Kilbrandon made any mention of the Convention, and even his reference was no more than a casual aside.[66] Nor was any allusion whatsoever made to the Convention in the Faulks Report.

The First Wave of Convention Case Law

In the same era, the European Commission and Court of Human Rights had seemed similarly unreceptive to the argument that Article 10 might exert a *Sullivanesque* influence on domestic libel laws. The *Engel* judgment in 1974 was concerned primarily with the Article 6 right to a fair trial: the defendants had been convicted of criminal libel in France for making defamatory criticisms of government officials.[67] However, in the course of its decision, the Court observed—apparently without recognising the need for argument on the point—that defamation laws were an appropriate means for a state 'to protect the reputations of others'; their interference with freedom of expression was thus justified under Article 10(2). The following year, in *X* v. *Germany*,[68] the Commission followed this reasoning when declaring manifestly ill-founded an

[63] Although the reference in Art. 10(2) to the protection of reputation certainly implied it might reach to that issue.

[64] The defendant had represented himself in the litigation.

[65] Weir, n. 29 above; Gatenby, n. 30 above.

[66] He commented that allowing a defendant's profit motive to be sufficient justification for the award of punitive damages 'would be seriously to hamper what must be regarded, at least since the European Convention was ratified, as a constitutional right to free speech': [1972] 1 All ER 801 at 876.

[67] (1974) Pub. Ct. B, Vol 20, 82.

[68] App. No. 6988/75, 3 D & R 159.

application which claimed that Germany's defamation laws interfered unacceptably with freedom of expression.

The Commission seemed to be maintaining this position in the early 1980s. The applicant in *Lingens* v. *Austria*[69] was the editor of a political magazine. Lingens ran a story accusing a prominent politician of lying to the electorate. He was subsequently convicted of criminal libel following a private prosecution initiated by the politician under Article 111 of the Austrian Criminal Code. Article 111 imposed a sentence of a fine or up to twelve months' imprisonment on the publisher of material which accuses any person of 'possessing a contemptible character or attitude or of behaviour contrary to honour or morality and of such a nature . . . to lower him in public esteem'. The publisher had a defence if he could prove his story was true. Lingens was convicted by the Austrian courts.

In his application to the Commission, Lingens argued that the requirement that defendants have to prove the truth of their factual claims in political stories was an unnecessarily draconian interference with freedom of expression, and as such not justified under Article 10(2). The Commission accepted that Article 10 was of 'fundamental importance' in the field of political discussion. It also noted that defamation laws:

> should not be used to curb legitimate criticism in the press of the behaviour and statements of a politician since it is the very function of the press in a democratic society to participate in the political process by checking on the development of the debate of public issues carried on by political officeholders.[70]

As a result, politicians had to be prepared to accept 'harsh criticism'.[71]

Such rhetoric is strongly reminiscent of Brennan's reasoning in *Sullivan*. But unlike the US Supreme Court, the Commission did not go on to assess the chilling effect that Article 111 might have on political discussion in Austria. Rather it stated simply that politicians could not be expected to accept untrue allegations about their integrity. Article 111 thus fell within the range of legitimate state interference with free expression recognised in Article 10(2) of the Convention. The Commission did not even address the argument that this objective might be achieved through less restrictive means.

Blackshaw v. *Lord*, a Court of Appeal judgment issued in 1984, followed the Faulks Report in not making any reference at all to Article 10. This is perhaps unsurprising, given the Commission's early understanding of the Convention's (non-)impact on libel laws. But by 1984 it could no longer be presumed that English courts did not realise that Article 10 was of potentially broad significance in evaluating the adequacy of domestic laws regulating freedom of expression. By the mid-1980s, the compatibility of several provisions of UK law with Article 10 had been raised before the European Commission on Human Rights

---

[69] App. No. 8303/79, 26 D & R 171.
[70] *Ibid.*, at 181.
[71] *Ibid.*

or before the ECtHR itself.[72] Litigation had been initiated and concluded in respect of obscenity laws,[73] of the use of contempt of court proceedings to restrain publication of newspaper stories,[74] of prosecutions under the law of blasphemy,[75] and of the prosecution of CND (Campaign for Nuclear Disarmament) campaigners for distributing pro-nuclear disarmament literature to members of the armed forces.[76] It was not difficult to extract from these cases the lesson that the function of Article 10 was to provide a legal device which courts might invoke to safeguard the democratic basis of western societies. As such, it articulated a principle of sweeping application. The point is best conveyed by a passage from the ECtHR's 1976 judgment in *Handyside* v. *UK*:

> Freedom of expression constitutes one of the essential foundations of [democratic] society, one of the basic conditions for its progress and for the development of every man. Subject to paragraph 2 of Article 10, it is applicable not only to 'information' or 'ideas' that are favourably received or regarded as inoffensive, but also to those that offend, shock or disturb the state or any sector of the population. Such are the demands of that pluralism, tolerance and broadmindedness without which there is no 'democratic society'.[77]

Article 10 arguments had by then also been raised in English courts on a variety of free-expression issues concerning contempt of court,[78] commercial confidentiality[79] and industrial relations.[80] That the defendant's counsel in *Blackshaw* failed to appreciate the potential significance of Article 10 to their client's defence is perhaps indicative of a lack of jurisprudential imagination, but may be excusable in the light of the Commission's conclusions in *X* v. *Germany* and *Lingens*. It is perhaps less excusable if one notes that Lord Diplock had produced a judgment as long ago as 1979, in a case called *Gleaves* v. *Deakin*,[81] which suggested that England's law of criminal libel breached Article 10. Lord Diplock—pre-empting the Commission's contrary indication in *Lingens*—observed that the English law's requirement that the defendant prove truth as a defence rather than that the prosecution prove falsity was unacceptable.[82]

There could be no doubt that the United Kingdom's civil defamation laws pursued a legitimate governmental objective within Article 10(2). It was similarly clear that those libel laws satisfied the Article 10 requirement that such

[72] Prior to 1999, the Commission acted as a filter mechanism for the Court. A case could not come before the Court unless the Commission had evaluated its merits and declared it to be admissible.

[73] *Handyside* v. *United Kingdom*, 1 EHRR 737.

[74] *Sunday Times* v. *United Kingdom*, 2 EHRR 245.

[75] *Gay News* v. *United Kingdom* (1982) 4 EHRR 123.

[76] *Arrowsmith* v. *UK* (1981) 3 EHRR 218.

[77] 1 EHRR 737 at para. 49.

[78] *Attorney-General* v. *BBC* [1981] AC 303 and *Harman* v. *Secretary of State for the Home Department* [1983] 1 AC 280.

[79] *Schering Chemicals Ltd* v. *Falkman Ltd* [1982] QB 1.

[80] *Associated Newspapers Group Ltd* v. *Wade* [1979] 1 WLR 697.

[81] [1979] 2 All ER 497.

[82] See also *Desmond* v. *Thorne* [1983] 1 WLR 163.

restrictions be 'prescribed by law'. A defendant in a political libel action might well suggest that English law placed her/him at a considerable disadvantage when compared to the legal regime in the USA, but that disadvantage was undoubtedly clearly defined.

What was not clear, however, was whether a disadvantage of that degree was 'necessary in a democratic society'. It would require but little reflection to conclude that there was an uncomfortable mismatch between the Court's grand rhetoric as to the significance of freedom of political discussion in democratic society and its own and the Commission's evidently unthinking assumptions in *Engel* and *Lingens* and the Court's conclusion in *X* v. *Germany* that state libel laws which curbed such expression need not be subjected to exacting judicial scrutiny. The jurisprudential relationship between Article 10 and libel laws position seemed remarkably similar to that between the First Amendment and state libel laws in the USA in the early 1960s.

This opacity was in part a result of the imprecision of the ECtHR's jurisdiction, which could plausibly be characterised as having a supervisory rather than appellate character. The ECtHR had rapidly developed a doctrine known as 'the margin of appreciation' when evaluating the 'necessity' of state interference with Convention rights. This doctrine, like the 'prescribed by law' principle, had also been elaborated in litigation involving English law. In *Handyside*, the ECtHR had emphasised that it did not see its role as articulating a common legal rule that would apply uniformly in all signatory states:

> By reason of their direct and continuous contact with the vital forces of their countries, state authorities are in principle in a better position than the international judge to give an opinion . . . on the necessity of a 'restriction' or 'penalty'.
>
> Nevertheless, Article 10(2) does not give the contracting states an unlimited power of appreciation. The Court . . . is empowered to give the final ruling on whether a 'restriction' or 'penalty' is reconcilable with freedom of expression as protected by Article 10.[83]

The ECtHR had confirmed by the late 1970s that the boundaries of the 'margin of appreciation' would vary in Article 10 cases according to which of the many factors in Article 10(2) the state was invoking to justify its interference with freedom of expression. The Court's initial political libel jurisprudence had indicated that the margins on this issue would be extraordinarily wide. But in the mid-1980s, that jurisprudence began rapidly to change.

'Political' Defamation and Article 10 ECHR—the Second Wave of Cases

The evident failure of the UK's legal profession and media organisations to appreciate the pertinence of Article 10 to determining the content of libel laws seemed to be shared in other European jurisdictions. Prior to 1990, the ECtHR

---

[83] 1 EHRR 737 at para. 48.

had not heard any cases dealing with 'political' libels in civil law. Nor, until the mid-1980s, did it begin regularly to decide cases involving criminal libel laws. Since that date, the Court has issued a series of decisions either upholding or quashing criminal libel convictions against journalists accused of publishing defamatory political stories.

These cases have obvious relevance to the compatibility with Article 10 of a state's civil law of defamation. Brennan's judgment in *Sullivan* had accepted that one could not neatly distinguish criminal libel laws from their civil law counterparts when political information was in issue. He suggested that the prospect of having to pay substantial civil damages could silence potential critics of a politician's behaviour just as effectively as the prospect of being gaoled or fined for breaking the criminal law. Brennan's concern was with the substantive effect that libel laws had on political discussion, not merely with the form that such law took. The ECtHR's Article 10 jurisprudence showed a similar preference for substance over form. Its free-expression decisions had by the mid-1980s addressed issues of civil as well as criminal law.[84] The ECHR's 'second phase' of criminal libel judgments is discussed below. As will readily become apparent, the principles developed in those cases fall some way short of the robust common law defence of political expression formulated by some American state courts at the turn of the century and subsequently given national constitutional status in *Sullivan*. The decisions are also in part rather opaque. An inevitable consequence of the ECtHR's adoption of the margin of appreciation doctrine is that a judgment may define a particular national law as unacceptable, but it will rarely—as did the US Supreme Court in *Sullivan*—specify with any precision just how that law should be changed. What would seem quite obvious from a reading of these cases, however, is that the English common law's refusal to draw any distinction between government bodies, elected politicians and 'private individuals' when it came to deciding what legal obstacles they had to surmount to succeed in a libel action was quite irreconcilable with the ECtHR's newly emergent understanding of Article 10. The first of these cases, *Lingens* v. *Austria*[85] was decided shortly after *Blackshaw* v. *Lord*.

Lingens *v*. Austria

Lingens had published two articles in a political magazine which suggested that Kreisky, then the Chancellor of Austria, had used his office to shield a political ally from investigations into that person's alleged role in Nazi atrocities. Kreisky issued private criminal proceedings against Lingens under Article 111 of the Austrian Criminal Code. Lingens was convicted. Undeterred by the fate of his application to the Commission a few years earlier, Lingens again argued that Article 111 amounted to an unnecessarily intrusive interference with freedom of

---

[84] See the cases cited at n. 73–76 above. More generally see Jacobs, F., and White, R., *The European Convention on Human Rights* (Oxford: Clarendon Press, 1995) ch. 12; Janis, M., Kay, R., and Bradley, A., n. 62 above; Harris, O., O'Boyle, M., and Warbrick, C., n. 62 above.

[85] (1986) 8 EHHR 407.

political expression. The Commission had evidently undergone something of a change of heart since 1982, for its members not only admitted the application but unanimously considered that Lingens' conviction breached Article 10.[86] The Commission observed that it considered its decision in the first *Lingens* application to be correct, and appeared to distinguish this case on the basis that this alleged libel concerned Kresiky's 'political' identity, whereas the previous case involved defamation of a politician's private persona. The distinction is unconvincing. The tone of the second Commission opinion is notably different from its previous decision, in that it dwells at greater length on the significance of political discussion to the maintenance of a democratic society. This rather suggests that the Commission was *de facto* reversing itself without *de jure* acknowledging it was doing so. Whatever its rationale, the Commission concluded that on these facts Article 111 of the Criminal Code was unnecessarily restrictive of freedom of political expression.

The ECtHR began its review of Lingens' conviction with a broad evaluation of the purpose Article 10 was intended to serve. Echoing its words in *Handyside*, the ECtHR reiterated that the Convention recognised freedom of speech as 'one of the essential foundations of a democratic society and one of the basic conditions for its progress and for each individual's self-fulfilment'.[87] Within this general scheme, freedom of speech on political questions had a particularly high level of protection; 'freedom of political debate is at the very core of the concept of a democratic society which prevails throughout the Convention'.[88]

Implicitly adopting Brennan's chilling rationale, the Court observed that restraints on political debate such as those imposed by Article 111 of Austria's Criminal Code could effectively deter journalists from voicing useful political information and opinions in future, thereby depriving the public of access to political discussion and undermining the press's role as a watchdog on governmental behaviour. Nor could that watchdog role be limited to the mere transmission of facts: the press also had an important constitutional role to play as a commentator on such information.

The ECtHR held that the 'core' status of political speech had significant implications for the extent to which member states could restrict its dissemination to protect the reputation of individuals, a criterion explicitly adverted to in Article 10(2). Protection was permitted only to the extent 'necessary in a democratic society'. Politicians did not forfeit all entitlement to have their reputations protected by defamation laws, nor could they expect to be treated as 'private citizens' for these purposes. In respect of attacks on a politician's political beliefs and behaviour, 'the requirements of such protection have to be weighed in relation to the interests of the open discussion of political issues'.[89] In the ECtHR's view, that weighing demanded that:

---

[86] (1985) 7 EHRR 446.
[87] (1986) 8 EHRR 407 at para. 41.
[88] *Ibid.*, at para. 42.
[89] *Ibid.*

The limits of acceptable criticism are accordingly wider as regards a politician as such than as regards a private individual. Unlike the latter, the former inevitably and knowingly lays himself open to close scrutiny of his every word and deed by both journalists and the public at large, and he must consequently display a greater degree of tolerance.[90]

The ECtHR's language in this passage is sufficiently expansive to suggest that the principle it was expounding was as applicable to civil as to criminal defamation laws. However, the ratio of the *Lingens* judgment was narrow. His conviction was held to be incompatible with Article 10 on two grounds. The first was that in respect of *facts*, Article 10 demanded that criminal defamation laws placed the burden of proving falsity and that the defendant had no reasonable grounds for believing the story to be true on the prosecutor,[91] rather than, as did Article 111 of Austria's Criminal Code, requiring the accused to prove truth or the reasonableness of his belief. The safeguard 'necessary' to protect a politician's reputation had to contain obstacles which a prosecutor would find difficult to surmount.

The Court also dealt with the issue of *opinion/comment* or, as the ECtHR termed them, 'value judgements'. On this point, the ECtHR reached a conclusion similar to the 'no such thing as a false idea' principle adopted by the US Supreme Court in *Gertz*. Since a value judgement could not be proven 'true' or false, its dissemination could not be punished at all.

The judgment made no reference to *Engel, X v. Germany* or Lingens' previous application to the Commission. It could not be doubted however that those cases no longer represented good law on the political libel question. And in the next few years, in rather the same way that the US Supreme Court had found itself dealing frequently with the ramifications of *Sullivan* in the late 1960s, the Court was presented with several opportunities to refine its initial restatement of Article 10's requirements.

Barfod *v*. Denmark

The ECtHR took a markedly less protective attitude towards freedom of 'political' expression in *Barfod* v. *Denmark*.[92] Barfod had been convicted of criminal libel for an article in which he accused two part-time lay judges of bias in a tax case. Since the two judges were full-time employees of a government body which was one of the parties to the proceedings in which they sat, the accusation would appear quite unremarkable. The Greenland criminal law under which he was convicted forbade 'insulting words or acts' which 'degraded the honour of another person'. The accused had a defence if he proved the truth of the accusation, unless the words were 'unduly insulting', in which case even truth was no defence.

---

[90] (1986) 8 EHRR 407.

[91] Lord Diplock's observations some seven years earlier on the incompatibility of English criminal libel law with Art. 10 was thus proven well-founded; see 106 above.

[92] (1989) 11 EHRR 493.

The Greenland law appeared to intrude even more severely on freedom of expression than the Austrian provision at issue in *Lingens*, particularly in placing the burden of proof of truth on the defendant rather than the prosecution. Barfod's conviction was nonetheless upheld. The ECtHR's judgment was brief and not clearly reasoned. Its core assumption—echoing the Commission's reasoning for distinguishing *Lingens (No.1)* from *Lingens (No.2)*—seemed however to be that Barfod's attack on the judges was not a 'political' criticism, but rather a personal matter. As such, the state could legitimately subject it to onerous restrictions in order to protect the judges' reputations.[93]

The reasoning stands in marked contrast to that adopted in Iowa a century earlier. In both *State* v. *Hoskins* and *Salinger* v. *Cowles*,[94] the Iowa Supreme Court unquestioningly accepted that judicial activities were 'political' for libel law purposes. The US Supreme Court reached the same conclusion in *Garrison* v. *Louisiana* in 1965.[95] The ECtHR appeared to be at this stage construing 'political' very narrowly when libel laws were in issue. To revisit familiar terminology—the *effect* of the '*Lingens* defence' was potentially significant, but its *reach* appeared to be quite limited. This initial impression was reinforced by the next two criminal libel cases which came before the ECtHR.

Oberschlik *v.* Austria

In 1983, Herr Grabher-Meyer, the leader of the Austrian Liberal party, proposed that family allowances to Austrian mothers be doubled, while those paid to immigrant mothers should be halved. Oberschlik tried to bring a private prosecution against Grabher-Meyer, alleging that his comments amounted to advocacy of Nazism, which is a crime under Austrian law. The prosecuting authorities declined to proceed with the case. Oberschlik then reproduced the charge he laid against Grabher-Meyer in full in a political journal called *Forum*. Grabher-Meyer subsequently brought a private prosecution against Oberschlick under the same law used in *Lingens*.[96] Oberschlick was convicted.

Argument before the ECtHR[97] again centred on whether a conviction under Article 111 of the Austrian Criminal Code was 'necessary in a democratic society'. The ECtHR's general musings on the purpose of political speech bore strong echoes of the Meiklejohn view of the First Amendment:

> freedom of expression . . . constitutes one of the essential foundations of a democratic society and one of the basic conditions for its progress and for each individual's self fulfilment.[98]

---

[93] The ECHR did not decide the case on the basis of the 'authority of the judiciary' provision in Art. 10(2).

[94] At 45–6 above.

[95] At 70 above.

[96] (1991) 19 EHRR 389.

[97] Art. 111 of the Criminal Code.

[98] (1991) 19 EHRR 389 at para. 57.

After reiterating its holding in *Lingens* that 'freedom of political debate is at the very core of the concept of a democratic society which prevails throughout the Convention',[99] the Court observed that this principle did not merely bestow rights to 'speak' on the press or individuals. It also set the press a 'task': 'to impart information and ideas on political issues and other matters of general interest', and granted individuals the right to receive as well as disseminate such information.[100]

As in *Lingens*, the Court stressed that this end could not be achieved unless member states' legal systems drew a distinction between defamation actions launched by politicians in respect of political information and those initiated by private citizens. The reasoning is very reminiscent of the common law principles underpinning *Coleman* and *Sullivan*—all citizens and the media are inextricably caught up in a reciprocal relationship of rights and duties to disseminate and consume political information. The outcome of the case also had *Sullivan-esque* echoes. The ECtHR considered that Oberschlick's accusations of Nazism were opinion or 'value judgements' rather than factual assertions. As such, they could be proven neither true nor false, and in accordance with *Lingens* could therefore not serve as the basis for a criminal prosecution.

Castells *v*. Spain

Castells, a member of the Spanish Senate, published articles in a Basque newspaper which accused 'the government' (without naming names) of complicity in murders and violence against the Basque people. He was prosecuted under Article 161 of Spain's criminal code, which permitted 'long-term prison sentences' to be imposed on those 'who seriously insult, falsely accuse or threaten the government'. Article 162 permitted lesser sentences when the insult was not 'serious'. Neither provision permitted a defence of truth. Castells was convicted under Article 162, and received a one year sentence.

The ECtHR's judgment[101] was not a model of clarity. The Court accepted that the government had brought this action not to protect any person's reputation, but to preserve public order—the Basque area was in considerable turmoil when the articles were published in 1979. The restraints 'necessary' to achieve this objective were more severe than those justified by the protection of reputation: criminal law sanctions could be imposed against untruths or accusations 'formulated in bad faith'. However, if such sanctions were to comply with Article 10, the defendant had to have the chance (which Castells had not been granted) to prove the truth of his claims and his good faith.

As in *Lingens*, the ratio of *Castells* has no direct bearing on civil defamation law. But the conceptual framework surrounding the Court's narrow holding

[99] (1991) 19 EHRR 389 at para. 58.
[100] 'This is underlined by the wording of article 10 where the public's right to receive information and ideas is expressly mentioned': *ibid*.
[101] (1992) 14 EHRR 445.

was broadly stated, and seemed to coincide in many respects with the rationale informing William Brennan's opinion in *Sullivan*. Thus the Court observed that:

> [T]he pre-eminent role of the press in a State governed by the rule of law must not be forgotten. . . . [F]reedom of the press affords the public one of the best means of discovering and forming an opinion on the ideas and attitudes of their political leaders.[102]

Building on this political presumption, the Court suggested that domestic legal systems had to recognise a tri-partite division within their defamation laws. At paragraph 46, the Court observed that 'the limits of political criticism are wider with regard to Government than in relation to a private citizen, or even a politician'. This clearly implies that the 'government' *qua* corporate body must endure more criticism than a 'politician', who in turn must endure more than a private citizen. The judgment did not make it clear whether this would require that a government body be wholly deprived of any recourse to a civil defamation suit (as, *per Chicago*, seems to be the case in the USA). Nor did it specify precisely how the three categories of plaintiff should be treated by state libel laws: what the judgment unambiguously did demand, however, was that domestic law should draw *some* meaningful distinction between them.

Thorgeirson *v.* Iceland

As suggested in Chapter 5, the substantially more expansive reach that the US Supreme Court accorded to the knowing/reckless falsity principle in cases after *Sullivan* prompted considerable controversy both within and outside the Court. That reach was extended beyond stories relating to elected politicians to embrace those about public officials, political activists and even private individuals unwillingly involved in 'newsworthy' events. The ECtHR's initial understanding of 'political' appeared to reach no further than *Sullivan* itself. But just as the US Supreme Court promptly pushed the scope of the defence beyond the limit category of elected politicians, so the ECtHR seemed quickly to do the same.

The applicant in *Thorgeirson v. Iceland*[103] had written several newspaper articles which alleged that certain unnamed members of the Rejkjavik police had repeatedly engaged in excessively brutal behaviour towards local residents. He was subsequently convicted of criminal defamation under Article 108 of the Icelandic Penal Code, a provision couched in sweeping terms:

> Whoever vituperates or otherwise insults a civil servant in words or actions or makes defamatory allegations against or about him when he is discharging his duty, or on account of the discharge of his duty, shall be fined, detained or imprisoned for up to three years. An allegation, even if proven, may warrant a fine if made in an impudent manner.

[102] *Ibid.*, at para. 43.
[103] (1992) 14 EHRR 843.

During argument before the ECtHR, the Icelandic government sensibly suggested that *Barfod* permitted states to impose quite stringent restrictions on
speech to protect reputations if the speech did not address a 'political' issue. It
then argued that the activities of the police, like those of the judiciary at issue in
Barfod, were not 'political' in the *Lingens* sense. This contention met with a
peculiar response from the Court, which denied that *Barfod* had drawn any distinction between 'political' and 'non-political' stories:

> [T]he Court observes that there is no warrant in its case law for distinguishing, in the
> manner suggested by the Government, between political discussion and discussion of
> other matters of public concern.[104]

There is little scope to doubt that *Barfod* had drawn just this distinction, and
it is not to the ECtHR's credit that it refused to acknowledge this point.
Thorgeirson nonetheless leaves the impression that the *reach* of 'public libels'
under Article 10 was now to be very broad, extending beyond *Sullivan* and
stretching perhaps as far as that identified in *Coleman* or *Webb*. What was much
less clear, however, was the *effect* that Article 10 had on the defences available
to defendants in 'public libel' actions. On this point, the 'margin of appreciation' doctrine would seem to imply that states would enjoy appreciable discretion in determining just how difficult it should be for a 'political' plaintiff to win
a libel action.

CONCLUSION

One need not credit the ECtHR's jurisprudence with a particularly elastic character to assume that *Lingens*, *Castells* and *Oberschlik* offered principles which
might be as readily applicable to civil as to criminal defamation laws. That those
cases had by the early 1990s yet to be forcefully argued in an English court on
behalf of a defendant being sued by an elected politician in respect of a 'political' libel is something of a puzzle. It thus transpired that the defendant in the
first English defamation case in which counsel and judges made extensive reference to both American and ECtHR jurisprudence was not a politician, but, as in
Manchester Corporation and *Campion*, an elected government body.

---

[104] (1992) 14 EHRR 843 at para. 64.

7

English Law—The First Phase of Reform

By 1990, some English judges had accepted Article 10 as a relevant source of law to consider when addressing free expression issues. More significantly, judges in the House of Lords had suggested during the '*Spycatcher*' saga of the mid to late 1980s that English common law was wholly compatible with Article 10's requirements. *Spycatcher* was triggered by the Thatcher government's repeated attempts to suppress publication and newspaper serialisation and reporting of a book published by a former member of MI5.[1] The episode culminated in the House of Lords refusing to grant the government an injunction to prevent publication, in a judgment which referred extensively to the European Court of Human Rights' jurisprudence. Lord Goff, having observed somewhat inanely that 'we may pride ourselves on the fact that freedom of speech has existed in this country as long as, if not longer than, anywhere else in the world', went on to suggest that English law on free speech issues was in perfect harmony with Article 10:

> It is established in the jurisprudence of the European Court of Human Rights that the word 'necessary' in this context implies the existence of a pressing social need, and that interference with freedom of expression should be no more than is proportionate to the legitimate aim pursued. I have no reason to believe that English law, as applied in the courts, leads to any different conclusion.[2]

Judicial protestations that all facets of English common law complied with the Convention could have been regarded sceptically by defamation lawyers. English judges still displayed a lack of imagination about the scope of Article 10. In *Sutcliffe* v. *Pressdram*,[3] a case decided in 1989, the Court of Appeal set aside an award of £600,000 to Sonia Sutcliffe. Sutcliffe was the wife of Peter Sutcliffe, the mass murderer known as the Yorkshire Ripper. She has sued the *Private Eye* magazine over a story which alleged she was trying to profit from her husband's activities. The court followed Pearson LJ's approach in *McCarey* to justify quashing the award, and implied that so large an award must have included a substantial element of punitive damages, which—*per Rookes* v. *Barnard*—should not have been awarded on these facts. It displayed no awareness

---

[1] The saga is summarised in Loveland (1996) *op. cit.* 578–81: Ewing, K., and Gearty, C., *Civil Liberties Under Thatcher* (Oxford: OUP, 1989) 152–69.

[2] *Attorney-General* v. *Guardian Newspapers Ltd* (No. 2) [1988] 3 All ER 545 at 660.

[3] [1990] 1 All ER 269.

whatsoever of the idea that the quantum of damages in libel actions might raise an Article 10 issue.

Moreover, *Lingens* did strongly suggest that civil as well as criminal libel laws had to recognise a distinction between political and non-political actions. There was manifestly no acceptance of that proposition in English law in 1990.

This point was reinforced by the Report of a Supreme Court Procedure Committee on Practice and Procedure in Defamation, chaired by Neill LJ, which was published in 1991. In the course of its deliberations, which were concerned primarily with matters of procedure, the Committee considered and dismissed the idea of recommending that Parliament introduce a statutory version of the *Sullivan* defence into domestic law:

> Standards of care and accuracy in the press are, in our opinion, not such as to give any confidence that the 'Sullivan' defence would be treated responsibly. It would mean, in effect, that newspapers could publish more or less what they liked, provided they were honest, if their subject happened to be within the definition of a public figure.[4]

This passage misrepresents *Sullivan* in two respects. The first is that *Sullivan* itself did not address the issue of public figures, but only of politicians. That the *Sullivan* defence may have been over-extended in subsequent Supreme Court decisions does not provide a convincing ground for rejecting the defence as it was originally applied. The second misrepresentation, which applies as readily to *Sullivan* as to subsequent cases, is the failure to acknowledge that the Supreme Court has consistently recognised that political and public figures still retain 'private' lives; libels addressed to the private facets of a political or public figure's identity will be caught by the rules in *Gertz*, not *Sullivan*.[5]

The prospects of statutory reform thus seemed remote. However, an indication that some members of the House of Lords might be persuaded to amend the common law was offered early in 1990 by the Privy Council's judgment in *Hector* v. *Attorney General of Antigua and Barbuda*.[6] Hector was a criminal libel case. The defendant had been convicted under a law which made it a crime to publish false statements 'likely to undermine public confidence in the conduct of public affairs'. The Privy Council overturned the conviction, concluding that the crime was incompatible with the free expression provisions of Antigua and Barbuda's own constitution.

The judgment was extremely brief, and made no reference to any case law from any jurisdiction on freedom of speech issues. However, in a passage with potentially broad scope, the court suggested that it was alert to the constitutional implications of restrictive libel laws:

> In a free democratic society it is almost too obvious to need stating that those who hold office in government and who are responsible for public administration must

---

[4] At 164–5.
[5] I.e. that negligent falsehood be proved in respect of compensatory damages, and knowing/reckless falsehood in respect of punitive damages: see 81–3 above.
[6] [1990] 2 All ER 103.

always be open to criticism. Any attempt to stifle or fetter such criticism amounts to political censorship of the most insidious and objectionable kind.[7]

Lord Bridge then suggested that the stifling of political speech was objectionable because it then hindered the citizenry's capacity to make informed electoral choices:

[I]t is no less obvious that the very purpose of criticism levelled at those who have the conduct of public affairs by their political opponents is to undermine public confidence in their stewardship and to persuade the electorate that the opponents would make a better job of it.[8]

Such sentiments echoed those expressed over 100 years earlier by the Kansan Supreme Court in *Coleman*, in the 1920s by the Illinois Supreme Court in *Chicago*, and more recently by William Brennan in *Sullivan*. In each of those cases, the sentiments had been coupled with a significant amendment to the relevant jurisdiction's civil libel laws. Shortly after the judgment in *Hector* was handed down, Derbyshire County Council presented the English courts with an opportunity to decide how far the Privy Council's distrust of criminal libel laws should influence the contents of the civil law of defamation.

THE IDENTITY OF THE PLAINTIFF—*DERBYSHIRE COUNTY COUNCIL V. TIMES NEWSPAPERS*

The story at issue in *Derbyshire* was a *Sunday Times* feature which accused the county council (then controlled by the Labour party), its senior Labour members and a wealthy businessman, Owen Oyston, of engaging in unethical and possibly illegal transactions involving the council's pension funds. Oyston, the council itself and David Bookbinder—the council leader—all commenced libel proceedings. Oyston's case was promptly settled for an undisclosed sum of damages. Bookbinder's action was stayed pending the High Court's answer to a preliminary question in the action launched by the council. The question was ostensibly a simple one: did the common law permit a local authority to maintain an action in libel?

The High Court

The action was heard before Morland J.[9] Anthony Lester QC, an advocate with an unrivalled reputation at the English bar for his knowledge of domestic and comparative free-expression law, acted as lead counsel for the *Sunday Times*. Lester's argument was explicitly constitutional in its terms, and—unsurprisingly,

[7] *Ibid.*, at 106.
[8] *Ibid.*
[9] [1992] 4 All ER 795.

given the paucity of constitutionally literate English case law on civil libel laws—heavily reliant on principles extracted from foreign jurisdictions. Lester placed particular emphasis on *Chicago*, *Sullivan*, *Lingens* and *Hector* as illustrations of the way in which broad principles accepting the importance of freedom of political expression might be expressed as rules of common law. Lester suggested that the two existing English authorities on the question—*Manchester* and *Campion*—were contradictory. The common law position was thus unclear, and so ripe for development in a direction that was sensitive to the requirements of a modern, democratic society. His preferred solution lay mid-way between *Chicago* and *Sullivan*: the common law should not allow a local authority to sue in libel, but should permit it instead to defend its reputation through an action in malicious falsehood.

Morland J's judgment was reminiscent in style of Browne J's opinion in *Campion*. He dismissed many of the non-English cases referred to in Lester's brief as 'of only peripheral relevance'; and, while alluding in passing to the 'utmost importance' of freedom of speech in a democratic society, suggested it was neither 'appropriate or necessary for me to comment on many of the matters raised by Mr Lester'.[10] The narrowness of Morland J's methodology was best conveyed by this response to Lester's invocation of *Sullivan* and *Chicago*: 'I must decide this case according to the English law of tort and not American constitutional law, however admirable those sentiments may be'.[11] Morland J further considered that since English law was so clear on this point, there was no need for him to pay any attention to Article 10 of the Convention and the jurisprudence of the ECtHR.

The answer to the question before the court was to be found in English case law on the capacities of corporations. Misguidedly following—as did Browne J in *Campion*—Lord Esher MR's grand rhetoric in *South Hetton Coal*, Morland J concluded that a local authority was a corporation just like any other, and so entitled to sue in libel to vindicate its reputation. *Manchester* was decided per incuriam, and *Campion* was therefore a correct statement of the law.[12]

The Court of Appeal

Both Morland J's conclusion and the reasoning he deployed to reach it were unanimously rejected in the Court of Appeal.[13] All three members of the court (Balcombe, Ralph Gibson and Butler-Sloss LJJ) proceeded on the assumption that the divergent outcomes of *Manchester* and *Campion* did indeed confirm that the common law was uncertain. In consequence, the court was bound to

[10] [1992] 4 All ER 795 at 799.

[11] *Ibid.*, at 805.

[12] Curiously, Morland J evidently attributed more than 'peripheral relevance' to foreign authorities (notably several Canadian common law cases) which supported his conclusion.

[13] [1992] 3 All ER 65.

refer to the European Convention to determine what the common law position should be.

While all three judges identified Article 10 as the legal source of their conclusion, they indicated that its political contents derived substantially from American jurisprudence. All referred approvingly to the 'chilling effect' analysis offered by Brennan in *Sullivan*, and both Ralph Gibson and Balcombe LJJ quoted extensively from *Chicago*. American constitutional principle was, it seemed, shaping their answer to the Article 10 question whether the interference with free expression that would result from allowing a council to sue in libel was 'necessary in a democratic society'. The court—the point is best expressed (although by no means fully reasoned) in the judgment of Ralph Gibson LJ[14]— concluded that libel was so easy a remedy for a plaintiff to satisfy that it presented a substantial threat to freedom of political expression. That a council might sue in the less easily established tort of malicious falsehood was a good indication that the libel remedy was not 'necessary'.

The Court of Appeal seemed to take however a very restrictive view of 'political' plaintiffs. Butler-Sloss LJ held, as did her colleagues, that one of the reasons that it was not 'necessary' for a council to be able to sue in libel was that its individual members could initiate action in a private capacity, thereby—if successful—indirectly vindicating the council's reputation *qua* political body. No member of the court gave any indication that a councillor pursuing such an action would face the kind of obstacles identified in *Coleman*, *Briggs*, *Salinger*, *Sullivan et al*. This was perhaps because they misunderstood *Sullivan*, reading the case as supporting the absolutist position favoured by Black, Douglas and Goldberg JJ rather than the more subtle balancing approach which the majority actually advanced. Butler-Sloss LJ's confusion on this point was the most evident:

> The American law of libel, including as it does no protection for the individual politician as well as political institutions goes further along the road of freedom of the press than the English law.[15]

Castells had not by then been decided by the ECtHR, so the trichotomous approach evidently required by Article 10 in respect of government bodies, elected politicians and private individuals had yet to be elaborated. However as noted in Chapter 4, *Lingens*, which was decided in 1986 and was referred to in the court's judgment, did state explicitly that:

> The limits of acceptable criticism are . . . wider as regards a politician as such than as regards a private individual. Unlike the latter, the former inevitably and knowingly lays himself open to close scrutiny of his every word and deed by both journalists and the public at large, and he must consequently display a greater degree of tolerance.[16]

[14] *Ibid.*, at 88–9.
[15] *Ibid.*, at 95, emphasis added.
[16] (1986) 8 EHRR 407 at 419.

Unless one construed *Lingens* very narrowly—as applying only to *criminal* libel laws—it is impossible to reconcile the Court of Appeal's failure to draw a distinction between political and private plaintiffs in libel cases with the requirements of Article 10. Moreover, the failure makes no sense even in terms of the court's own reasoning. At one point in her judgment, Butler-Sloss LJ appeared wholeheartedly to endorse the analytical premise on which *Coleman* and contemporaneous decisions in other American states were based, namely that, in becoming politicians, citizens voluntarily surrender part of their private identity and thence deprive themselves of any legitimate claim to be able to protect their reputations *qua* politicians through easily satisfied remedies in libel:

> Elected councillors are politicians in the public domain. They are and expect to be exposed to criticism and comment from many quarters. . . . Such comment may and no doubt does from time to time overstep boundaries acceptable to the individual or local authority so criticised.[17]

If politicians have voluntarily put themselves in the public domain, it is difficult to understand why they should still benefit from the same safeguards for defending their reputation that they enjoyed while living wholly 'private' lives. The judgment rather leaves one with the impression that the members of the Court of Appeal had not carefully thought through the implications of the judgment they were producing.

The House of Lords

On further appeal,[18] the House of Lords issued a single opinion authored by Lord Keith. The judgment approved the Court of Appeal's conclusion, but arrived at it through a different legal route. Lord Keith rejected Lord Esher MR's assertion in *South Hetton Coal* that all corporations were alike for libel law purposes. A local authority was a quite different creature from a charity, trade union or private company:

> The most important of these [distinguishing] features is that it is a government body. Further, it is a democratically elected body. . . . It is of the highest public importance that a democratically elected governmental body, or indeed any governmental body, should be open to uninhibited public criticism. The threat of a civil action for defamation must inevitably have an inhibiting effect on freedom of speech.[19]

Lord Keith's reasoning on this point was much influenced by his understanding of *Chicago* and *Sullivan*, which he described as judgments underpinned by public-interest considerations no less valid in modern Britain than in the USA.

---

[17] [1992] 3 All ER 65 at 95.

[18] [1993] 1 All ER 1011.

[19] *Ibid.*, at 1017. It seemed that Lord Keith also read Lord Esher MR's judgment in *South Hetton Coal* solely at the level of its grand rhetoric. As noted in Ch. 2, a close reading of the opinion suggests Lord Esher's thoughts were directed only towards commercial corporations.

Lord Keith also invoked the Privy Council's judgment in *Hector* as an apposite indicator of the approach that the common law should take when regulating political libels. He found further guidance in a 1948 judgment of the Appellate Division of the South African Supreme Court, *Die Spoorbond* v. *South African Railways*.[20] *Die Spoorbond* had concluded that a government department could not sue in libel as this would entail a 'serious' interference with freedom of political expression.

In combination these sources of authority ostensibly led Lord Keith to conclude that the common law did not permit a council to initiate libel proceedings. Its reputation could adequately be protected by simple rebuttal at council meetings, by an action in malicious falsehood, or indirectly through libel actions begun by individual councillors. He saw no need to invoke the European Convention to justify this finding, but reasoned rather that this was—and indeed had been for some time[21]—the position in English common law.

The Weaknesses of the Judgment

In broad terms, *Derbyshire* represented a substantial innovation in English law. Yet the precise ratio of Lord Keith's judgment is difficult to identify. The text of his opinion offers several contradictory intimations as to the specific decision he actually reached. In terms of its statement of broad legal principle, the judgment's crucial passage would seem to be this one:

> I regard it as right for this House to lay down not only is there no public interest favouring the right of organs of government, whether central or local, to sue for libel, but that it is contrary to the public interest that they should have it. It is contrary to the public interest because to admit such actions would place an undesirable fetter on freedom of speech.[22]

This statement seems perfectly clear. All facets of the libel remedy are now denied to government bodies, but those bodies may invoke other remedies in defamation (slander and malicious falsehood[23]) to protect their reputations. However, towards the end of his argument, Lord Keith observed that:

> The conclusion must be, in my opinion, that under the common law of England a local authority does not have the right to maintain an action of damages for defamation.[24]

Two significant ambiguities arise from this statement. The first is whether, when using the word 'defamation', Lord Keith meant simply libel or also included slander and malicious falsehood. In the ante-penultimate paragraph of

---

[20] [1946] AD 999. For an account of the case see Loveland, I., *By Due Process of Law* (Oxford: Hart Publishing, 1999) pp 224–225.

[21] Lord Keith held that *Campion* was wrongly decided, rather than that the case was correctly decided in the light of prevailing political understandings of the early 1970s but had now become obsolete as society had embraced a more sophisticated understanding of free expression principles.

[22] [1993] 1 All ER 1011 at 1019.

[23] Using this latter term in the loose sense.

[24] [1991] 1 All ER 1011 at 1021.

the judgment, Lord Keith spoke approvingly of the Court of Appeal's reasoning to the effect that malicious falsehood and criminal libel would be acceptable remedies for a defamed council to invoke. He thereby inferred that he agreed with this conclusion, but did not say so expressly. On the other hand, his enthusiastic approval of *Chicago*, a judgment which denied local authorities any remedy in tort—be it defamation or malicious falsehood—points us in the other direction. The second ambiguity derives from Lord Keith's reference to 'an action for damages'. That phrasing holds out the possibility that a council might initiate a libel action (or slander or malicious falsehood) simply to seek a declaration to the effect that a story was defamatory/false or to gain injunctive relief against publication or republication.[25] From a policy perspective, these ambiguities might best be resolved in the following ways.

Lord Keith's oblique reference to 'an action for damages' might best be regarded as a slip of the pen. Restricting the nature of the libel remedy to a non-pecuniary form might reduce, perhaps substantially, the chilling effect of libel laws for newspapers wishing to criticise local authorities. It should be recalled, however, that of the £32,000 awarded against Mr Campion for libelling Bognor UDC in 1972, only £2,000 was damages. In that case at least, it would be the costs, rather than the damages, that might be thought most significantly to deter future criticism of the council. One might therefore assume that Lord Keith intended to bar the libel action *in toto*, rather than to sever it into different remedial parts.

The question whether *Derbyshire*'s ratio reached only to libel actions is rather more important. As suggested in Chapter 2, *Chicago* offered a very dangerous legal principle to accept. That judgment essentially incites an opposition party or the opposition press knowingly to publish the most flagrant lies in an attempt—by deceit—to persuade voters not to support the governing party.[26] It might therefore be sensible to conclude that the House of Lords did leave open the possibility of actions in slander or malicious falsehood to a defamed authority. Read in this way, *Derbyshire* is a less unsatisfactory decision than *Chicago*. That reading does not, however, cure the judgment of one substantial defect. Since malicious falsehood requires the plaintiff to demonstrate quantifiable economic loss caused by the speech (as does, in most instances, the remedy in slander), it is of little use in respect of attacks on a government body's competence or political integrity. In that respect, therefore, *Derbyshire* (in the House of Lords and Court of Appeal) was much too indulgent of free-speech interests.

In another respect however, Lord Keith's opinion was too insensitive to those interests, as were the judgments offered in the Court of Appeal. Despite having invoked *Sullivan* at some length as a source of guiding principle, Lord Keith stated quite clearly (as had Balcombe, Ralph Gibson and Butler-Sloss LJJ) that he was not prepared to approve its actual holding. He was quite content to

[25] As noted in Ch. 5, *Sullivan* contained just the same ambiguity.

[26] Or, equally, might tempt the governing party and its supporters deliberately to circulate lies about their opponents.

engage in the 'legal alchemy' which William Brennan had rejected in *Sullivan*.[27] Lord Keith confirmed that an individual councillor was free to sue in libel as if she were a private individual.[28] Their Lordships did not appear to have realised that *Chicago* built (albeit inadvisably and over-enthusiastically) upon the existing Illinois common law rule formulated in *Ambrosious* v. *O'Farrell*,[29] a rule which echoed the conclusion by then reached in several other American states. One is rather left with the impression that the House of Lords, just like the Court of Appeal, plucked parts of Thompson CJ's judgment out of the comparative constitutional ether, without having any firm understanding of either its political or jurisprudential roots.

That the House of Lords and Court of Appeal were so receptive to arguments drawn from other jurisdictions, and that both courts accepted as beyond argument the assertion that the case raised a matter of constitutional significance, represents a great advance on the judicial method employed in such relatively modern cases as *Campion* and *Blackshaw*. Nonetheless, the House of Lords' rather cavalier use of American legal principle affords a third reason—in addition to the imprecision of Lord Keith's text and the unsophisticated nature of the balance he struck between the suppression of truth and the indulgence of deceit—for regarding *Derbyshire* as one of the most unsatisfactory of the courts' recent public law innovations.[30]

EXTENDING THE *DERBYSHIRE* PRINCIPLE—POLITICAL PARTIES

Lord Keith did not explicitly confirm whether the Labour Party (whether national or local) could have pursued a libel action against the *Sunday Times*. He did however suggest that trade unions or charities could be distinguished from elected government bodies, on the basis that an attack on their reputations could lead to a loss of members, a diminution of public support or difficulties in attracting employees.

These considerations could readily be applied to a political party. It might thus be thought that Lord Keith was accepting that a political party could proceed in its own right, under existing common law rules, in just the same way as the individuals who held office within it. That supposition was put to the test in the High Court several years later in *Goldsmith* v. *Bhoyrul*.[31]

The plaintiffs in *Bhoyrul* were the late Sir James Goldsmith and the Referendum Party. The alleged libel appeared in the weekly newspaper *Sunday*

---

[27] See 68 above.

[28] As a consequence, Bookbinder's action against the *Sunday Times* was rapidly settled, evidently for a very substantial sum of damages. *Sunday Times* readers, Derbyshire's voters and the public at large were thus denied the opportunity of finding out either whether the allegations were true or, if they were false, how careful the paper had been to check the accuracy of its claims.

[29] (1905) 199 Ill. App. 265.

[30] For a less critical analysis see Barendt, E., 'Libel and Freedom of Speech in English Law' [1993] *Public Law* 449.

[31] [1997] 4 All ER 268.

Business. The story, published shortly before the May 1997 general election, suggested that the Referendum Party was so unpopular that it was preparing to withdraw many of its candidates to avoid humiliation. At trial, with Buckley J presiding, two issues arose. The first was whether the Referendum Party *per se* could be a plaintiff. The second was whether the story could bear a defamatory meaning.

Buckley J's conclusion on the second issue seemed eminently sensible. He reasoned that assertions that a party had 'bitten off more than it could chew' or was 'not prepared to risk electoral humiliation' were not capable of bearing a defamatory meaning. They conveyed a change of mind, or at most political misjudgement, rather than, as the plaintiffs contended, an intention to deceive the electorate. Imputations of that sort were not *per se* libellous.

Buckley J's answer to the first question, however, was far less satisfactory. In essence, his judgment uncritically followed and extended the flawed reasoning that the House of Lords had approved in *Derbyshire*. Unsurprisingly, he rejected the absurd contention advanced by counsel for the Referendum Party that, since the party was only seeking governmental power it had no power to abuse, and there was thus no need to prevent it launching libel actions. Buckley's J's conclusion on this point is surely right. Obviously, parties *per se* do not possess governmental power, but since the *sine qua non* of their existence is to acquire such power or influence the exercise of it by others, there is no justification for shielding them from criticism. It is perhaps unfortunate that Lord Keith did not make this point clear in *Derbyshire*.

However, having conditioned his understanding of the common law to recognise this obvious political reality, Buckley J then buttressed his conclusion with the same fallacious reasoning that had informed *Derbyshire*. He suggested that the primary justification for imposing a total bar on libel actions by political parties was that 'any individual candidate, official or other person connected with the party who was sufficiently identified could sue'.[32] By this indirect means, it appeared, the defamed party might vindicate its own reputation and thereby regain such electoral support as it enjoyed before the libel was published. The reasoning has two flaws, both flowing from the judge's failure to take full account of the informed consent interests of the electorate.

The first is a failure to recognise that it is wholly possible for a party's opponents to circulate the most egregious untruths about another party without identifying an individual with sufficient clarity to enable a libel action to proceed. In these circumstances, the electorate's interest in not being misled by political information known to be false by its publishers is wholly sacrificed.

The second flaw is the assumption that—from an electoral perspective—a meaningful distinction can always be drawn between a party and its leaders. *Sullivan* recognised that to draw such a distinction between a government body and the politicians who controlled it was a nonsense. The whole point of facili-

---

[32] [1997] 4 All ER 268 at 271.

tating press discussion of political issues was to allow voters to reach informed decisions about the *people* they elected to office. It was, after all, the politicians who determined what those government bodies would do with their power. Parties do not govern—people do. There could perhaps be no clearer illustration of the coalescence of identity between a politician and a political party than that offered by Goldsmith and the Referendum Party. By allowing Goldsmith to proceed as if he were a private individual, *Bhoyrul* would obviously have enabled him—had he not died in the interim—to chill criticism of his party by threatening to sue in his 'private' capacity.

This creates an apparently absurd situation, namely that the 'public interest' to be served by the common law—in respect of exactly the same political information which would have exactly the same impact on voters' behaviour—evidently forbids a party to sue in libel at all, while enabling an individual who exercises substantial influence within the party to proceed with no significant obstacles placed in her/his way. The only way to explain this extraordinary position is to assume that the judgment had not properly appreciated the audience/electorate interest in the dissemination of the information. The case thus stands as a paradigmatic example of the common law elevating matters of form over issues of substance.

Perhaps paradoxically, these 'reforms' to libel laws focusing on the identity of the plaintiff were introduced at same time as the Court of Appeal was steering another facet of libel law in a direction which, in formal terms, drew no distinction between types of plaintiff, but which in a substantive sense might much reduce a politician's capacity to chill press discussion of her behaviour.

THE HEADS AND QUANTUM OF DAMAGES

Parliament made an ostensibly modest incursion into the field of the quantum of damages in tort actions in the Courts and Legal Services Act 1990 section 8(1). This empowers the Court of Appeal to order a new trial in cases where it considers an award of damages 'excessive'. Under section 8(2) and Rules of the Supreme Court, Order 59 rule 11(4), the Court of Appeal may in such circumstances substitute a different damages award rather than order a new trial. The Act's text does not however make it clear whether the concept of 'excessive' in section 8(1) bears the 'divorced from reality' meaning it had previously been accorded at common law,[33] or whether it indicated Parliament's preference for more rigorous Appeal Court policing of large awards.[34] This was one of the issues before the Court of Appeal in *Rantzen* v. *Mirror Group Newspapers*.[35]

---

[33] See 87–92 above.
[34] It may be recalled that the US Supreme Court in *Gertz* had characterised 'excessive', a formula used in many State jurisdictions, as a 'gentle' guideline.
[35] [1993] 4 All ER 975.

Rantzen v. Mirror Group Newspapers

At trial, the jury had awarded £250,000 damages to Rantzen over a story in the *Sunday People*. The jury concluded that the story falsely implied Rantzen had exposed children to the danger of sexual abuse by not divulging to a school that she knew a teacher it employed was a paedophile. The main issue before the Court of Appeal was whether the award was excessive.

Neill LJ gave the leading judgment. His interpretation of 'excessive' in section 8(1) was driven by various factors. He assumed that section 8(1) raised a literal ambiguity which the court might seek to resolve by referring to Hansard. In Neill LJ's opinion, the sponsoring minister's explanation of the bill's intended purpose did not in itself support adoption of a more intrusive concept of 'excessive'. Neill LJ then asserted that section 8(1)'s meaning had to be found by viewing the statutory formula 'in the light of pronouncements made by the House of Lords in the context of the right of freedom of expression'.[36] These 'pronouncements' were derived from three cases. Brief allusion was made to *Derbyshire*[37] and *Brind*[38] to support the contention that English law on freedom of expression was consistent with the Convention. The demands posed by those requirements were then extracted from *Spycatcher (No. 2)*,[39] in which Lord Goff had held that English law permitted restrictions on free expression only if the end served by such restrictions amounted to a 'pressing social need', and that end was pursued through 'proportionate means'.

In *Rantzen*, Neill LJ viewed Lord Goff's formula as of general application to all free-expression issues. In the context of defamation, the 'pressing social need' was to protect an individual's reputation against false accusations. When conjoined with the proportionality test, this demanded that the question the Court of Appeal should ask itself when exercising its powers under section 8(1) was, 'could a reasonable jury have thought that this award was necessary to *compensate* the plaintiff and to re-establish his reputation?'.[40]

Before answering this question, Neill LJ turned to the distinct issue of whether the mechanism through which the quantum of damages in libel cases was assessed was 'prescribed by law' *per* Article 10. Neill LJ returned to the ECHR's formula in the *Sunday Times* v. *UK*[41] case for the meaning of this term—'[a] norm cannot be regarded as a "law" unless it is formulated with sufficient precision to enable the citizen to regulate his conduct'.[42] He suggested that juries could be given sufficiently precise guidance to meet this requirement

---

[36] [1993] 4 All ER 975 at 988.
[37] [1993] 1 All ER 1011.
[38] [1991] 1 All ER 720.
[39] *A-G* v. *Guardian Newspapers Ltd (No. 2)* [1988] 3 All ER 545.
[40] [1993] 4 All ER 975 at 994, emphasis added. The Court did not regard this as a case where punitive damages were appropriate.
[41] See n. 61 at 103 above.
[42] 2 EHRR 245 at 271.

in any of three ways: first, by being referred to other jury awards; secondly, by looking at personal injury awards; and thirdly, by being referred to Court of Appeal judgments under section 8.

Neill LJ discerned reasons of principle for rejecting the first two options. Since past jury awards had themselves been made without the benefit of clear guiding principles, they could not provide a rational framework for the future exercise of discretion. Although the Court saw some force in the second contention,[43] it ultimately (and very briefly) found such comparators unhelpful, primarily because it assumed that defamation damages contained a vindicatory element that did not feature in personal injury awards.

The third option was unsuitable for practical reasons. While Neill LJ regarded reference to Court of Appeal decisions as the most satisfactory guide to structure jury discretion, this mechanism was not yet available, and it might be some years before a sufficient body of appellate awards emerged. Until then, the courts would have to follow a fourth strategy:

> [T]he jury should be invited to consider the purchasing power of any award which they may make. In addition, they should be asked to ensure that any award that they make is proportionate to the damage which the plaintiff has suffered and is a sum which it is necessary to award him to provide adequate compensation and to re-establish his reputation.[44]

This fourth 'solution' to the 'prescribed by law' requirement couples a repetition of the proportionality test used in respect of Article 10's necessity requirement with a very vague 'purchasing power' yardstick. Using the same test twice to evaluate what are ostensibly discrete issues (namely the actual substance of an award and the criteria intended to guide juries in reaching that decision) might be thought to perpetuate an unfortunate degree of confusion in the law. It may however be defended simply because the 'best' solution does not yet exist.

What was less defensible was the way in which Neill LJ then proceeded to offer a first contribution to the body of Appeal Court awards which he envisaged would eventually satisfy the prescribed-by-law test. In concluding his judgment, Neill LJ returned to his previously posed but unanswered question about the reasonable man's assessment of a 'necessary' or 'proportionate' award in this case. The conclusion reached was brusque, the reasoning behind it cursory.

Neill LJ considered that a substantial award was justified on these facts. However the initial award of £250,000—'judged by any objective standards of reasonable compensation or necessity or proportionality'[45]—was excessive because it was disproportionate to the damage inflicted on the plaintiff. Rantzen's career had evidently not suffered as a result of the libel made against her. Nor was the Court of Appeal satisfied that her reputation had been

---

[43] It may be recalled that Diplock LJ had seen the merit some 30 years earlier: see 89–90 above.
[44] [1993] 4 All ER 975 at 997.
[45] *Ibid.*

irreparably undermined. In the light of those factors, an award £110,000 would be sufficient.

One might be forgiven for thinking that this sum was rather plucked from the air, its main virtue being that it was much less than £250,000. Neill LJ offered no clues about which particular 'objective standard of reasonable compensation' he was deploying, nor indeed as to which such standards he was rejecting.[46]

The *Rantzen* judgment appeared to be driven in large part by the Court of Appeal's wish to pull English law into line with Article 10 before the ECtHR itself took the opportunity to identify any of its deficiencies. In that methodological sense, it reinforced the impression given by both the Court of Appeal and House of Lords in *Derbyshire* that Article 10 had become a 'normal' part of English libel law. Perhaps surprisingly, when the ECtHR shortly afterwards addressed the issue of damages directly, it suggested that *Rantzen* may have gone appreciably further than was necessary to satisfy Article 10's requirements.

Tolstoy v. United Kingdom

In *Tolstoy*,[47] the ECtHR quashed an award of £1.5 million made to Lord Aldington (prior to *Rantzen* being decided) in respect of a defamatory pamphlet accusing him of war crimes. This amount was three times larger than the sum awarded in any previous libel judgment. The ECtHR characterised the award as disproportionate, in a judgment which also suggested that the step taken by the Court of Appeal in *Rantzen* more than satisfied some of Article 10's requirements. Tolstoy attacked the award on two grounds. The first was that the absence of precise guidance for libel juries on quantum meant that awards were not 'prescribed by law'. The second was that the award actually made in his case was so large that it was not 'necessary in a democratic society'.

The ECtHR placed very loose constraints on the 'prescribed by law' formula in respect of defamation cases. It held that laws on this point may have great flexibility, given the variety of libels that may occur. 'Prescribed by law' cannot therefore require that a defendant be able to predict the quantum of damages likely to be awarded against him with any degree of certainty. The ECtHR implied that even the pre-*Rantzen* system would have satisfied the 'prescribed by law' test. That juries were to be instructed about the various factors relevant to assessing damages, coupled with the power of the Court of Appeal to set aside grossly excessive awards (on *McCarey*'s 'divorced from reality' grounds) was in

---

[46] There may be circumstances in which purely 'intuitive' or 'common sense' judicial conclusions have much to commend them. It is thus rather unfortunate that—if that was indeed the motivation for the non-existent empirical grounding of the £110,000 conclusion—that it was not openly acknowledged. Cf Pearson LJ in *McCarey* [1964] 3 All ER 947 at 958 when deciding that the award in that case was excessive, '[i]t is in the end a matter of impression, and I cannot resist the impression that the sum is much, much too large'.

[47] (1995) 20 EHRR 442.

itself a sufficient legal safeguard to comply with the Convention's requirements. The Court of Appeal's assumption of closer control in *Rantzen* was not required to bring English law into line with the Convention on this point. With respect to the necessity issue, the ECtHR concluded that, prior to *Rantzen*, the guidance judges offered to juries was inadequate to ensure that sums eventually awarded bore 'a reasonable relationship of proportionality to the harm suffered'.[48]

The ECtHR was however extraordinarily opaque in its evaluation of *Rantzen*. Like the Court of Appeal, it indicated that a framework of Court of Appeal awards would be the best way to satisfy this test. It offered no opinion, however, on whether the stop-gap solution at which *Rantzen* had arrived was itself acceptable. The ECtHR also hinted that punitive damages could not be awarded at all in civil defamation cases, but offered no reasoned discussion on this point. The inference would seem to be that the 'pressing social need' served by defamation damages is simply and solely to compensate the defamed plaintiff.

Lord Lester, Tolstoy's counsel, also suggested that English law breached Article 10 because it failed to distinguish between 'political' and 'private' libels. Lord Lester argued that Tolstoy's libel concerned the intensely political activities of a man who at the relevant time held an important government office; as such, it should be afforded greater protection than information about the private lives of private citizens. This proposition seems to be clearly supported by dicta in *Lingens* and *Castells*, but the ECtHR refused to confirm it explicitly.

The judgment therefore made no discernable difference to the chilling effect that existing English libel laws might have on the dissemination of political stories. It also confirmed that—at least in respect of damages—domestic courts were not under any obligation to reform English law in a fashion which provided greater protection to publishers of (any kind of) libellous material. But the Court of Appeal had apparently by then been seized with an enthusiasm for damages reform, for in *Elton John* v. *Mirror Group Newspapers*[49] it took just such an 'unnecessary' step.

Elton John v. *Mirror Group Newspapers Ltd*

The ECtHR's decision in *Tolstoy* was one factor which led the Court of Appeal in *John* v. *MGN Ltd* to revisit *Rantzen* and reconsider the desirability of tying defamation awards to those made in personal injury cases.[50] *John* arose over a *Sunday Mirror* story alleging that Elton John was suffering from a bizarre eating disorder, which led him to chew his food but spit it out rather than swallow it. The story was written by a freelance reporter, based on interviews with two

---

[48] *Ibid.*, at para. 49.

[49] [1996] 2 All ER 35 (CA).

[50] The three other reasons were that: first, a coherent body of appeal court libel awards to which juries might be referred has yet to emerge; secondly, large awards which have been substantially reduced on appeal continue to be made; and thirdly the Australian High Court had recently produced an innovative judgment (discussed in Ch. 8 below) on this question.

women who claimed to have seen John doing this at a party. The jury awarded John £75,000 compensatory damages and £275,000 exemplary damages.[51] MGN's appeal contended that both awards were excessive, relying both on *Rantzen* and Article 10.

Lord Bingham MR's sole judgment began by considering the question of how a jury should assess compensatory damages. Lord Bingham identified various factors which contributed to decisions on quantum. The gravity of the libel was the most important issue; how adversely has it affected the plaintiff's integrity and/or professional reputation? The breadth of publication was also a relevant factor. The court did not consider these matters susceptible to precise, arithmetic calculation. However, it considered that the retention of the jury trial has prevented the emergence of a coherent body of judicial awards to which new cases might be compared. Lord Bingham observed that public concern had been raised by huge awards which seemed unrelated to any damage inflicted upon the plaintiff, and suggested that the public interest was not well served if a libel action could be seen, 'risky though the process undoubtedly is, as a road to untaxed riches'.[52]

Lord Bingham accepted that the types of damage inflicted by defamation and personal injury were not identical. Personal injury awards could however serve as approximate comparators and act as; 'a check on the reasonableness of a proposed award of damages for defamation'.[53] Lord Bingham—arriving at the destination that Diplock LJ had reached in *McCarey* thirty years previously—then concluded that it was:

> offensive to public opinion and rightly so, that a defamation plaintiff should recover damages for injury to reputation greater, perhaps by a significant factor, than if that same plaintiff had been rendered a helpless cripple or an insensate vegetable. The time has in our view come when judges, and counsel, should be free to draw the attention of juries to these comparisons.[54]

Lord Bingham was ostensibly unmoved by the ECtHR's hint in *Tolstoy* that punitive damages were not an acceptable element of civil defamation laws. Yet while accepting that punitive damages might be awarded in defamation cases, the court subjected them to a regime that was to be even more restrictive than the existing *Rookes* v. *Barnard* test. Rather than accept the ECJ's intimation in *Tolstoy* that the legitimate policy objective served by libel damages was solely concerned with *compensating* the plaintiff (i.e. that punitive damages were *per se* impermissible), Lord Bingham observed that an award of punitive damages in defamation cases would be 'exceptional', presumably because exemplary damages are in essence a criminal sanction, intended not to compensate the plaintiff but to punish the defendant and to deter others from acting in a similar

---

[51] Having evidently accepted that the *Mirror's* conduct fell within the rule in *Rookes* v. *Barnard*.
[52] [1996] 2 All ER 35 at 51.
[53] *Ibid.*, at 53.
[54] *Ibid.*, at 54.

fashion. Because punitive damages were 'exceptional', Lord Bingham held that their availability and quantum must not exceed that which is 'strictly necessary for the protection of reputation'.[55]

The Court concluded that this objective could best be achieved by requiring the plaintiff to satisfy three criteria:

1. She must prove the defendant knowingly or recklessly[56] published a falsehood;
2. she must prove the defendant was motivated by mercenary considerations specific to the story itself;
3. the plaintiff must prove 1 and 2 to a 'quite inescapable' degree, a standard which sits between the usual criminal and civil law standards.

Points 1 and 2 reiterate *Rookes* v. *Barnard*, while point 3 has obvious echoes of the 'convincing clarity' burden of proof used in *Sullivan*. In an overall sense, this test is virtually identical to the formula adopted by the US Supreme Court in *Gertz*.[57] *Gertz* was not however cited in the judgment, nor raised in argument by counsel. Lord Bingham stressed that the judgment had been formulated purely as a matter of common law: it was not either a pre-emptive or reactive attempt to meet the demands of Article 10. As such, it echoes the House of Lords' judgment in *Derbyshire*, which was also purportedly rooted in purely domestically driven perceptions of public policy.

On the facts, Lord Bingham felt that the plaintiff had proved beyond doubt that the *Sunday Mirror* had been reckless in not checking the truth of its story. It was also evident that the paper had made a cynical economic calculation in running the story, having concluded (obviously erroneously) that it was unlikely that John would sue at all.

It is therefore difficult to understand why the Court of Appeal reduced John's damages substantially. He was awarded £25,000 in compensatory damages and £50,000 in exemplary damages. These sums would apparently 'ensure that justice is done to both sides, and will also fully secure the public interest involved'.[58] That contention does not really withstand close scrutiny. By setting plaintiffs so severe a test if they are to recover *any* punitive damages, *John* obviously envisages that such damages will be available only in respect of the most disreputable press behaviour. It seems illogical for the Court of Appeal to have set a test which requires such extreme malfeasance, and then to 'punish' that malfeasance with such insignificant damages.[59] It is unlikely that the *Sunday*

---

[55] [1996] 2 All ER 35 at 58.

[56] Reckless in this context meant that: '[t]he publisher must have suspected the words were untrue and have deliberately refrained from taking obvious steps which, if taken, would have turned suspicion into certainty': *ibid.*, at 58. This would seem to be a subjective rather than objective understanding of recklessness: see the discussion at 78–80 above.

[57] See 81–3 above.

[58] [1996] 2 All ER 35 at 64.

[59] Although the *Mirror* would also have had to pay Elton John's presumably very substantial costs.

Mirror would feel chastised for its past behaviour, and resolve to reform itself in future, by the mere stigma of having been found to have acted in so disreputable a way.

CONCLUSION—MAKING A MESS OF LIBEL LAW REFORM?

Since *John* applies to *all* libel actions, the restrictive regime it seems to establish for awards of punitive damages may reduce the deterrent effect that libel laws allegedly exercise on potential publishers of unprovable political libels.[60] The result may be reinforced if, as one assumes the Court of Appeal expected in *John*, referring libel juries to sums awarded in personal injuries cases exerts a downward pressure on the quantum of compensatory damages.

This would seem however to be a matter of accident rather than design. It is difficult to avoid the conclusion that the appellate judgments in *Derbyshire* and *John* seem rather unsophisticated when compared to the jurisprudence produced by the US Supreme Court in *Sullivan* and subsequent political libel cases. From a methodological perspective, one might also wonder why, if the courts were willing to draw on *Sullivan* as a persuasive guiding principle, they did not take the opportunity both to search for its doctrinal roots and to explore the way in which its rationale had been developed in later years. What had also become apparent by the mid-1990s was that similarly unfavourable conclusions might be drawn if one compared the decisions of the Court of Appeal and House of Lords to those of the High Court of Australia.

---

[60] For a practitioner's perspective on the likely impact of the case see Tench, D., and McDermott, J., 'The Radical Change in Assessment of Libel Awards by Juries: *Elton John* v. *MGN Ltd*' [1996] *Communications Law* 17.

8

Sullivan *v.* The New York Times
in Australia

An argument sometimes invoked against importing *Sullivan*—or indeed any American constitutional principle—into English law is that the USA's political culture is simply too 'different' from Britain's to permit any helpful transplantation.[1] This perspective is unduly defensive. Much of the jurisprudential reasoning which informed the American colonists' approach to free expression issues in the immediately pre- and post-revolutionary periods was English in origin, deriving from a radical Whig tradition which challenged then dominant British constitutional orthodoxies.[2] Many of the USA's emergent constitutional principles, both at the federal and state level, did not entail rejection of English common law values, but were rather intended to safeguard their substance against factionally motivated legislatures.[3] Less abstractly, as *Coleman* indicates, American courts paid great attention to contemporaneous English common law development into the early years of the twentieth century; *Sullivan's* English lineage is easily traced, even if it is sometimes obscured behind the textual cloak of the First Amendment.

There is nonetheless some merit in offering Ameri-sceptic constitutional lawyers a less 'foreign' example of First Amendment jurisprudence being invoked as a judicial tool with which to redefine contemporary political culture. In respect of *Sullivan*, Australia offers the most illuminating site for comparative legal analysis. The Australian Constitution is in some respects more 'American' than British. It was created in 1901, by a UK Act of Parliament which merged the existing British colonies in Australian into a single legal entity, organised federally, with specific powers reserved to the national and state governments. Its highest court—the High Court—exercises the power of judicial review over national and state legislation and common law rules which breach

---

[1] See e.g. Barendt, E., 'The Importation of United States Free Speech Jurisprudence' in Loveland (ed) 'A Special Relationship' (Oxford: Clarendon Press, 1995): Feldman, D., 'Content Neutrality' and Sedley, S., 'The First Amendment: a Case for Import Controls', both in Loveland, I. (ed) *Importing the First Amendment* (Oxford: Hart Publishing, 1998).

[2] Rabban, D., 'The Original Meaning of the Free Speech Clause of the First Amendment' in Simmons, R. (ed.), *The US Constitution—the First Two Hundred Years* (Manchester: Manchester UP 1988).

[3] See especially Bailyn, B., *The Ideological Roots of the American Revolution* (1967) 199–227: Levy, L., 'Introduction', in Levy, L. (ed.), *The Making of the Constitution* (Cambridge, Mass: Harvard UP, 1987).

constitutional requirements.[4] However, that power has traditionally been exercised sparingly, and largely on the basis that the legal rule under challenge clearly contravenes the Constitution's text. In the 1990s, that tradition lost its hold on several High Court judges. The case for a more activist judicial agenda had been put by the then Chief Justice, Anthony Mason, in a 1988 law review article.[5] It was the High Court's duty, he urged, to protect 'fundamental rights where Parliament fails to do so'.[6] And in so doing, Mason argued, the Court would be safeguarding, not subverting, Australian democracy. The legal community did not have to wait long before the Chief Justice began to turn these academic sentiments into legally enforceable principles.

REDUCING THE CHILLING EFFECT

When *Rantzen* was before the English Court of Appeal, the Australian High Court faced a similar question in *Carson* v. *John Fairfax & Sons Ltd*.[7] Fairfax was the parent company of the *Sydney Morning Herald*, which accused Carson, a prominent lawyer, of attempting to pervert the course of justice. Carson's libel action was launched under New South Wales' Defamation Act 1974. This legislation allowed plaintiffs to recover aggravated damages, but it did not allow a trial court to award punitive damages. The Act could in itself be seen as a modest attempt to reduce the chilling effect of all libel suits, as punitive damages in particular could be the most substantial element of any award. However the Act did not limit the amount of general damages that might be awarded. Nor did it offer a jury close guidance on how damages should be assessed. These lacunae obviously raised the possibility that a 'deserving' plaintiff, represented by a skilful lawyer, could persuade a jury surreptitiously to subsume an element of punitive damages under the general heading. That suspicion was raised at trial in *Carson* v. *Fairfax*. On winning his case, Carson was awarded $200,000 for the first article, and $400,000 for the second—the largest amount of general damages ever awarded in a New South Wales defamation action.

The NSW Court of Appeal subsequently quashed both awards. The Court considered that the $600,000 figure must have contained an element—and probably a substantial one—of punitive damages. The Court inferred this from the size of the award, which it regarded as 'excessive'. This conclusion was in turn arrived at by comparing the award with that made in a recent (unreported) personal injury case when a trial court had awarded $250,000 to a plaintiff who suffered total blindness. This award had been set aside by the NSW Court of Appeal as being excessive. In *Carson*, the NSW Court of Appeal saw little justi-

---

[4] See Kennet, G., 'Individual Rights, the High Court and the Constitution' (1994) 19 *Melbourne LR* 581: Williams, G., '*Engineers* Is Dead: Long Live the Engineers' (1991) 17 *Sydney LR* 62.

[5] 'The Australian Constitution 1901–1988' (1988) 62 *Australian LJ* 256.

[6] *Ibid.*, at 261.

[7] (1992) 178 CLR 44.

fication for assuming that Mr Carson had suffered damages 2.4 times greater than this plaintiff. The Court also considered that Carson's damages were excessive (and so presumptively punitive) because they were the highest ever awarded in New South Wales.

The main ground of appeal before the Australian High Court was on the permissibility of any comparison being drawn by a trial and/or appellate court in a libel action to awards in personal injury cases. A majority (Mason CJ, Deane, Dawson, Gaudron JJ) joined an opinion authored by the Chief Justice. Mason CJ and Deane J had suggested (dissenting) in an earlier case, *Coyne v. Citizen Finance Ltd*,[8] that appellate courts should not be 'indifferent' to comparisons with personal injury cases when considering libel awards. In *Carson*, that view prevailed. The majority concluded that it should henceforth be permissible for appeal courts, trial judges and counsel to make such comparisons. It also held that there must be 'a rational relationship' between awards in the two types of cases. Mason CJ justified this conclusion by referring to arguments he had used in *Coyne*. These operated at two levels.

The first had a distinctly constitutional law dimension.[9] He suggested that existing libel law had created in Australia:

> a common perception that the stop writ and . . . extravagant verdicts have combined to constitute an increasing threat to adequate and informed public discussion of matters of legitimate concern . . . and . . . has even led to the suggestion that extraction of money by a public figure by way of settlement of a defamation action could constitute a sophisticated form of corruption.[10]

Mason CJ seemed to assume that alerting juries in defamation cases to the size of awards made for severe personal injuries would cut the level of damages, thereby reducing the 'chilling' effect that libel law worked on freedom of expression on 'matters of legitimate public concern'.

The second attacked the long-held assumption in both English and Australian common law (reiterated by Neill LJ in *Rantzen*) that physical injuries and injuries to reputation were qualitatively so 'different' that no meaningful comparison could be drawn between them. In an unconvincing passage, Mason CJ argued that severe personal injuries in themselves exposed their victims to a change in their reputation 'at least comparable to that caused by an untrue allegation about lack of physical or mental capability or control'.[11] The inadequacy of the reasoning suggests that this essentially private-law argument was deployed merely to buttress the earlier public-law point—namely that libel damages are *per se* too large to be reconciled with the public interest in promoting debate on issues of public concern. Mason CJ's judgment in *Carson* made further inroads into the potentially chilling effect of libel damages by

---

[8] (1991) 172 CLR 211.
[9] See Thomson, J., 'Slouching Towards Tenterfield: the Constitutionalization of Tort Law in Australia' [1995] *Tort Law Review* 81.
[10] (1991) 172 CLR 211 at 218–19.
[11] *Ibid.*, at 220.

classifying aggravated damages for the defendant's failure to apologise as punitive rather than compensatory. As such, they were not permitted under the NSW statute. As noted in Chapter 5, the ECtHR in *Tolstoy* had hinted that Article 10 precluded the award of punitive damages in defamation cases, but declined to reach the question whether aggravated damages for failure to apologise were acceptable. If, however, one accepts Mason CJ's classification of such damages as punitive, it is difficult to see what 'pressing social need' they might serve in a modern democratic society.

It seems impossible to quantify what effect—if any—the *Carson* principle had on the propensity of defamed plaintiffs to begin libel actions in Australia, or if it substantially altered the way in which the media researched and presented their news coverage. Nor does it seem likely that the 'common perception' to which the Chief Justice alluded had any demonstrable empirical base. His reasoning appeared to be driven by a desire to make libel law responsive to his understanding of the requirements of Australian political culture—that the law should not unduly hinder political news reporting. *Carson* was not an explicitly 'constitutional' decision: but it was soon followed by just such a judgment.

A CONSTITUTIONAL OBSTACLE TO POLITICAL LIBEL ACTIONS

Mason's final years as Chief Justice were marked by several substantial jurisprudential innovations, driven in large part by a distinctly 'American' view of the role that constitutional law should play in regulating legislative and common law constraints on freedom of political expression. The High Court provoked controversy in 1991 by its judgments in *Nationwide News* v. *Wills*[12] and *Australian Capital Television* v. *The Commonwealth of Australia*.[13] In both cases, a majority deployed inventive techniques of constitutional interpretation to invalidate national legislation on the ground that it infringed constitutional guarantees of freedom of political expression.

Nationwide News concerned the constitutionality of section 299(1) of the Commonwealth's Industrial Relations Act 1988. Section 299(1) made it a criminal offence for any person intentionally to bring into disrepute Australia's Industrial Relations Commission[14] or its members. In November 1989, *The Australian* newspaper ran a story accusing Commission members of corruption: its parent company (Nationwide News) was subsequently prosecuted under section 299, and raised the constitutionality of the provision as a defence, maintaining that the Constitution implicitly guaranteed that citizens could not be restrained from voicing reasonable criticism of governmental institutions.

---

[12] (1991–2) 177 CLR 1.
[13] (1991–2) 177 CLR 106.
[14] A quasi-judicial body, created by the Commonwealth Parliament, with responsibility to try to settle inter-state industrial disputes.

Mason CJ, McHugh J and Gaudron J avoided this broad question. They concluded that section 299(1) was a disproportionate exercise of Parliament's powers under section 51(xxxv) of the Constitution, as it placed greater restraints on criticism of the Commission than the common law imposed on criticism of the courts. Since disproportionality is an accepted ground for judicial review of legislative action in Australia, the provision was invalid.

In contrast, Deane and Toohey JJ concluded that Australia's Constitution did indeed contain an implied principle—which they termed 'freedom of communication'—that placed limits on the extent to which legislative and governmental bodies could impinge upon freedom of political speech. There was no explicit textual basis in the Constitution for this conclusion. However Deane and Toohey JJ argued that the Constitution was not to be interpreted literally, but should be construed in the context of 'the fundamental implications of the doctrines of government upon which the Constitution as a whole is structured and which form part of its fabric'.[15] The 'doctrine' raised here was that of 'representative government', which Deane and Toohey derived from the Constitution's requirements that both national and state legislators be elected on the basis of an extensive franchise, and that the Constitution itself could be amended only with the approval of a super-majority (a majority overall and a majority in more than half the states) of the electorate in a referendum. The representative basis of Australia's government in turn required that the Constitution protect 'freedom of communication' for 'well founded and relevant criticism of the legislative, executive or judicial organs of government or of the official conduct or fitness for office of those who constitute or staff them'.[16] Since section 299(1) suppressed all criticism of the Commission, even if 'well founded and relevant', it could not be reconciled with the freedom of communication principle.

Brennan J also recognised that the doctrine of representative government impliedly constrained all grants of legislative authority which the Constitution gave to the national legislature. Representative government could not be effective if the legislature could curb discussion of political matters in a manner 'which substantially impairs the capacity of, or opportunity for, the Australian people to form the political judgments required for the exercise of their constitutional functions'.[17] He rested his analysis on the premise that the Constitution placed a negative constraint on the powers of the national Parliament; it did not endow citizens with positive rights.

The Court's judgment in *Australian Capital Television* v. *Commonwealth of Australia* addressed the Political Broadcasts and Political Disclosures Act 1991. The Act was purportedly intended to reduce the impact of a candidate's wealth on the outcome of the electoral process. It sought to do so in several ways. Section 95B-D forbade television and radio stations from broadcasting 'political

---

[15] (1991–2) 177 CLR 1 at 69.
[16] *Ibid*., at 79.
[17] *Ibid*., at 51.

advertisements'[18] during the run-up to state and federal elections and constitutional referendums respectively. Section 95F-R required broadcasters to offer 'free time' for straightforward 'talking head' advertisements by established political parties. The Court did not produce a unanimous answer to ACT's challenge to the Act, but a majority invalidated both the ban on advertisements and the requirement that broadcasters offer free time.

Mason CJ's majority judgment approved Deane and Toohey JJ's methodology in *Nationwide News*. 'Freedom of communication'—'at least in relation to public affairs and political discussion'[19]—was essential if the legislature was to be properly accountable to the people:

> Absent such a freedom of communication, representative government would fail to achieve its purpose, namely government by the people through their elected representatives; government would cease to be responsive to the needs and wishes of the people and, in that sense, would cease to be truly representative.[20]

Drawing heavily on US First Amendment jurisprudence, Mason CJ acknowledged that 'freedom of communication' did not offer absolute protection to political speech, any more than the First Amendment granted such entitlements in the USA.[21] He accepted that Parliament's wish to 'safeguard the integrity of the political process' might provide a defensible reason for restricting politicians' access to paid advertisements on the broadcast media. However, he invalidated section 95 on the basis that it was on its face both sweeping in scope and discriminatory in nature.[22]

The majority's reasoning was clearly much influenced by First Amendment jurisprudence. This obviously triggered speculation that Australian libel law might shortly be subjected to constitutional scrutiny along *Sullivan* lines. If the Chief Justice was indeed waiting for such an opportunity, he did not have to do so for long.

Theophanous v. *The Herald and Weekly Times*

In 1992, Andrew Theophanous chaired Australia's House of Representatives' Standing Committee on Migration Regulations. In November, the *Herald* newspaper published a letter which accused Mr Theophanous of adopting a pro-Greek racial bias over immigration policy, of planning to undermine the status of English as Australia's main language, and—in general terms—of being a fool.

---

[18] Defined as any matter likely to affect voting behaviour.

[19] (1991–2) 177 CLR 106 at 138.

[20] *Ibid*. at 139.

[21] On the wholly erroneous claim that the First Amendment places the press 'above the law' see Loveland, I., 'A Free Trade in Ideas—and Outcomes', in Loveland (ed.), *Importing the First Amendment* (Oxford: Hart Publishing 1998).

[22] For critical comment on the majority's reasoning see Ewing, K., 'New Constitutional Constraints in Australia' [1993] *Public Law* 256: Sedley, S., 'Human Rights: A Twenty-First Century Agenda' [1995] *Public Law* 386.

Mr Theophanous, evidently a sensitive political soul, was sufficiently outraged to institute a libel action in the Victoria courts.

The *Herald* offered a multi-part defence. Victoria law recognised truth as a complete defence. However the *Herald* additionally submitted that the *Nationwide News/Capital Television* 'freedom of communication' principle offered a defence in libel actions even in respect of some false information. The newspaper couched its argument very cautiously. It suggested that the as yet unrecognised constitutional defence would apply in very narrowly defined circumstances. First, it would reach only to speech concerning an MP's suitability for office. Secondly, the disseminator would have honestly believed in the story's truth and would not have any strong grounds for doubting its truth. And thirdly, the libel had to be published in the run-up to a federal election. In the event, the court's judgment[23] gave the defence substantially greater scope.

Mason CJ produced a plurality opinion joined by two [24] of the Court's seven members which extended the 'freedom of communication' principle. He concluded that Australian constitutional law now required that a disseminator of false information about politicians' behaviour in and suitability for public office would have a complete defence to a defamation claim brought by the politician in respect of factually inaccurate reporting if she could convince the trial court of three factors: that she did not know the information was false; that she had not displayed reckless indifference to the question whether the information was false; and that publication was 'reasonable in the circumstances'.

From a jurisprudential perspective, Mason CJ's conclusion in *Theophanous* had rather amorphous foundations. His reasoning suggests he was concerned to rebut accusations that the Court was usurping powers that it was not granted by the Constitution. He stressed that the freedom of communication principle was not a judicial *creation*. Rather the Court had in *ACT* *uncovered* a constituent legal principle. He had no doubt that constitutional principles should reflect rather than defy contemporary political realities. His opinion made little reference to the 'original intent' of the framers of the Australian Constitution. He presumed they had concluded that common law defamation rules did not adversely affect Australian democracy as then understood. But this historical legacy was irrelevant. His method bore strong echoes of the technique used in relation to the English common law by Cockburn CJ in *Wason* v. *Walter*:

> What the framers of the Constitution thought . . . 100 years ago is hardly a sure guide in the very different circumstances which prevail today. . . . The beliefs of the founders . . . cannot limit the content of an implication to be drawn from the Constitution.

The Court was instead obliged to seek the contemporary purpose that the Constitution should serve, a search which yielded a readily discoverable principle:

> [I]t is incontrovertible that an implication of freedom of communication, the purpose of which is to ensure the efficacy of representative democracy, must extend to protect

---

[23] (1994) 182 CLR 104, (1994) 68 AJLR 713.
[24] Toohey and Gaudron JJ.

political discussion from exposure to onerous criminal and civil liability if the implication is to be effective in achieving its purpose.[25]

Mason CJ regarded this 'implication' as all-pervasive. 'Freedom of communication' did not entail simply a negative constraint on legislative power—whether state or national. It created positive entitlements which fastened directly on individual citizens. The principle had to be respected by all governmental agencies, a classification which included the courts when applying common law rules or interpreting statues:

> [T]he implied freedom is one that shapes and controls the common law. At the very least, development in the common law must accord with its content. And, though it may not have been apparent in 1901 . . . if the content of the freedom so required, the common law must be taken to have adapted to it in 1901.[26]

Mason CJ acknowledged that his judgment was strongly influenced by the reasoning of Thompson CJ in *Chicago* and William Brennan in *Sullivan*. But he was less forthcoming about its factual base. He assumed without discussing any empirical evidence that libel law chilled political speech in modern Australia. The reliance on theory rather than practice is also apparent in the plurality's rejection of previous Australian state legislation dealing with defamation. Mason CJ held that such law could no longer be regarded as authoritative. This was not because it had been shown to be ineffective in practice, but because state legislators had not struck (and obviously could not have struck) a balance between protecting individual reputations and safeguarding freedom of speech which took into account the freedom of communication principle. Similarly, the common law defences of fair comment and qualified privilege, even if available, had not been developed to accommodate that broader consideration, and so could not withstand constitutional scrutiny.

Mason CJ did however emphasise that the judgment would have limited scope. The new defence was a constitutionalised variant of qualified privilege. Its 'reach' would extend to 'political discussion'. Mason CJ had no difficulty in concluding that attacks on an MP's political views or activities would amount to 'political discussion'.[27] But he offered contradictory guidance on the full extent of this concept. He indicated at one point that the substance of the speech was the important factor:

> The concept also includes discussion of the political views and public conduct of persons who are engaged in activities that have become the subject of political debate, e.g. trade union leaders, Aboriginal political leaders, political and economic commentators.[28]

In contrast, a subsequent passage criticised the US Supreme Court's extension of *Sullivan* to candidates for political office, public administrators and 'public fig-

---

[25] (1994) 68 AJLR 713 at 721.
[26] *Ibid*. at 719.
[27] *Ibid*., at 717.
[28] *Ibid*., at 718.

ures'; 'these [post-*Sullivan*] extensions, other than the extension to cover candidates for public office, should not form part of our law'.[29]

The two tests seem incompatible. The first has a greater reach than the second. It recognises that individuals or organisations which do not hold public office may nevertheless wield appreciable political power. Australia's Governor-General is presumably a 'politician' for these purposes, whichever test one adopts, even though the office is appointive and supposedly non-partisan. But the second test would not catch figures such as the media tycoons Rupert Murdoch and Kerry Packer. They are not 'politicians' in the formal, elective sense. Yet they obviously exercise considerable influence over the diet of political news which Australians consume. It would seem odd, given the highly functionalist nature of Mason CJ's reasoning, that such powerful political figures should be treated as 'ordinary citizens' if they launched defamation actions concerning criticism of their efforts to influence government or public opinion on political questions.

While adopting ambiguous language to describe the reach of the new defence, Mason CJ was more lucid in respect of its effect. He firmly rejected the solution advocated by Black, Douglas and Goldberg JJ in *Sullivan*:

> [T]he efficacious working of representative democracy . . . [does not require] that a person . . . be protected from the consequences of a statement which is knowingly false. Nor does that concept require protection of a publication made with reckless disregard for the truth. . . . The public interest to be served does not warrant protecting statements made irresponsibly.[30]

Mason CJ's judgment also adopted a less expansive effect rule than the *Sullivan* majority. He seemed rather to dilute *Sullivan* by concluding that liability could arise if a false story had been published knowingly, recklessly or negligently. He also departed from *Sullivan* in deciding to place the burden of proof on the defendant to demonstrate her integrity and competence rather than on the plaintiff to establish intentional, reckless or negligent dishonesty on the defendant's part. This modification to *Sullivan* would, he suggested, swing the balance within Australian constitutional law more firmly in favour of protecting individual reputation than was the case in the USA. No empirical justification was advanced for this conclusion. It is not obviously apparent that this modification of *Sullivan* would have a major impact in practice. It would not be difficult for a reputable media organisation to leap this no-negligence hurdle. For such actors on the political stage, *Theophanous* was likely wholly to remove the chilling effect of libel law. It should still however serve to deter media organisations or political activists who regarded a concern with the truth of what they publish as an unnecessary encumbrance.

A fourth judge, Deane J, concurred in the result the plurality reached. Deane's preferred reasoning went rather further, however. His view, like that of

---

[29] *Ibid.*, at 724.
[30] *Ibid*,. at 723.

Goldberg *et al.* in *Sullivan*, was that the constitution required a complete prohibition on political libel actions.

In Dissent

Brennan J offered a forceful dissent. He denied that the freedom of communication principle established in *ACT* and *Nationwide News* had any relevance to the *Theophanous* situation. He construed the two earlier cases as concerned solely with imposing negative constraints upon governmental power, and saw no scope for fashioning positive individual rights from the Constitution's guarantee of representative government. Brennan J argued that such rights could have only two sources. The first would be an explicit textual base in the Constitution. Since the text makes no allusion to individual rights of any nature, that source was not available. The second involves a process of implication both from the text itself and its historical context. Brennan J assumed that the relevant historical context is not that of 1995, but that of 1901, when the Constitution was created.[31] Brennan J's analysis of this context was that libel law had developed in England and Australia to strike a balance between free speech and the protection of personal reputation. Since the framers had not evinced any clear wish—whether in the Constitution's text or their discussion of its meaning—to reject the balance which existed in 1901, the Court must assume they left that question as one to be regulated via common law or legislation. There was thus no barrier to state legislatures reforming their defamation laws in accordance with the principle advocated by Mason CJ in *Theophanous*. Similarly, the High Court could reform the common law to achieve a similar result. But no lawmaking process other than amendment to the Constitution's text could imbue that principle with fundamental legal status.

Brennan J saw no scope for arguing that the Constitution's express reference to a system of 'representative government' supported the plurality's reasoning. He observed that libel law, as it existed in 1901, 'was developed both in England and in this country under a representative system of government, albeit universal suffrage arrived late in the history of the development of defamation law'.[32] The balance then struck must therefore be assumed consistent with the notion of 'representative government' which the Constitution guarantees its citizens.

This is a very large 'albeit'. The suggestion that the government of even late nineteenth-century 'England' was 'representative' as we would now use the term is absurd. No adult women, and barely 80 per cent of adult men then possessed the right to vote; the House of Lords remained in legal terms a co-equal partner with the Commons; and the Monarch still held to the view that he was not bound to act upon the advice of his Prime Minister.[33]

---

[31] The date would presumably change in respect of any subsequent amendments to the text.

[32] (1994) 68 ALJ 713 at 734.

[33] See Loveland *Constitutional Law* (London: Butterworths, 1996) chs. 5–7.

Brennan J also rejected the argument that the Court might legitimately fill 'gaps' in the Constitution by inserting legal principles drawn from other western democracies. He suggested that the plurality's invocation of *Sullivan* had little merit:

> [I]n truth, the assistance which cases decided under other Constitutions or Conventions can give in determining the scope of the freedom [of communication] is extremely limited.[34]

His opinions in the freedom of communication cases betray a rather selective view of the 'limitations' of foreign constitutional law. While doubting the relevance of the European Convention on Human Rights, Brennan J sought support for his preferred analytical paradigm in the Canadian principle that Charter Rights did not extend to 'government' in the sense of judicial interpretation.[35]

He also seemed to fall into the same error as did Butler-Sloss LJ in *Derbyshire* of assuming that the First Amendment affords complete legal immunity to those it shields from the full rigour of the common law. He rejected *Sullivan* as a model for Australia because:

> In this country, following the long tradition of the common law, we have accepted that personal reputation is a proper subject of protection, no less for those in public office as for private citizens.[36]

The inference seems to be that under *Sullivan* occupants of public office lose all protection of their right to reputation. Brennan's brief discussion of the political purpose served by *Sullivan* again misconstrued its impact, by suggesting that it permits '*unfettered* expressions of view on public issues'.[37]

If *Sullivan* had promulgated so draconian a principle, any court would be well advised to reject it. But the rationale Brennan J is attacking is the Goldberg, Douglas and Black JJ concurrence in *Sullivan*, rather than William Brennan's majority opinion.

It seems likely that Brennan's judgment was much less concerned with political libel *per se* than with the Court's proper role in determining the scope of constitutional guarantees. He suggested that to accept the plurality view would legitimise 'the introduction of judicial policy into constitutional interpretation'.[38] The question raised here is an important one, no less in Australia than in Britain and the USA. But Brennan has phrased it in rather a misleading way. His inference seems to be that 'judicial policy' arises only when a court makes innovative decisions. But it is equally plausible that a court which refuses to innovate is promoting a 'policy': rigid judicial deference to the values of past generations—whether those values are expressed in constitutional texts, statute or common law—is no less a 'policy' than an actively reformist jurisprudence.

---

[34] (1994) 68 ALJ 713 at 736.
[35] *Ibid.*, at 738–9.
[36] *Ibid.*, at 737.
[37] *Ibid.*, emphasis added.
[38] *Ibid.*, at 735.

The Australian Constitution, like that of the United States, contains no explicit instructions to the courts on how they should structure their interpretative role. Judges must therefore inevitably make 'policy' choices, in terms both of broad interpretative techniques and the application of those techniques to particular controversies. Opinions will differ on whether Mason CJ or Brennan J chose the more defensible judicial policy in *Theophanous*. Yet Mason CJ's position seemed appreciably more candid, a state of affairs quite the reverse of that arising in *ACT*.

Stephens v. West Australia Newspapers Ltd

The *Stephens* litigation was joined with *Theophanous* before the High Court. Stephens was one of six members (Liberal and Labour) of the Western Australia legislature. The defendant's *West Australian* newspaper ran a story quoting the comments of a senior Liberal MP, Phil Lockyer, on an overseas 'fact-finding tour' the six members had undertaken. The six maintained the trip was part of their legislative duties. Mr Lockyer took a different view. According to the *West Australian*:

> Phil Lockyer said the six members . . . had gone without the knowledge of Parliament. 'It is a junket of mammoth proportions' Mr Lockyer said yesterday. 'They've gone in secret hoping no-one would find out about it and this is nothing but a rort [39] which is costing the taxpayers thousands of dollars'.[40]

The report was presumably defamatory in two senses. First, in accusing the six of wasting taxpayers' money on what was essentially a subsidised vacation; and secondly in suggesting that funds had been appropriated without parliamentary approval.

The *West Australian* subsequently acknowledged that the latter accusation was untrue. It nevertheless offered two defences. The first defence maintained that both the Commonwealth and the Western Australian constitution contained an implied freedom of communication principle. Consequently speech concerning legislators' suitability for office disseminated predominantly to electors could not be the subject of either criminal or civil liability if the publication was reasonable in the prevailing circumstances. The second defence argued in the alternative that the publication attracted qualified privilege, on the basis that newspapers had a duty to communicate information on such matters to the relevant electorate, who had a reciprocal interest in receiving it.

As in *Theophanous*, the High Court divided on the issue. The plurality opinion (in the result of which Deane J again concurred) of Mason CJ, Toohey and Gaudron JJ observed that *Nationwide News* and *ACT* had regarded the free-

---

[39] A 'rort' can be an activity involving fraud or deceit as well as simply having a good time. That inference seemed to be the more serious element of the alleged libel.

[40] (1994) 68 ALJ 713 at 766.

dom of communication principle as applicable to all political discussion; it reached as readily to state as to national issues. However, the plurality also found an analogous implication in the Constitution of Western Australia. The substance of the obstacle placed in the way of state legislators was precisely that imposed upon members of the Commonwealth Parliament by *Theophanous*: the *Western Australian* had a defence to the plaintiffs' claim if it could prove that it neither knew the stories were false, or could demonstrate that it had no shown a reckless disregard for their truth. The *Stephens* plurality shed no further light on the ambiguity concerning the reach of the *Theophanous* defence; uncertainty remained about whether it was the political content of the speech, rather than the political identity of the plaintiff, that triggered the constitutional protection.

The three other members of the Court again rejected the *Theophanous* rationale, but offered rather different solutions to the problem before them. Although Brennan J accepted that 'freedom of communication' was a principle as applicable to state as to the national government, he reiterated his view in *Theophanous* that the principle did not reach to the common law. However, he then held that a modified version of the qualified privilege defence at common law should be extended to grant extensive protection to newspaper coverage of political issues.

Brennan J concluded that the reach of the new defence should be quite broad, encompassing stories which assisted voters to exercise their civic right and duty to discuss and evaluate information to 'government, government institutions and political matters'.[41] At first sight, the effect of the defence seemed to be quite limited. Brennan drew a rather curious distinction between two types of false factual allegation. The first involved assertions '[w]here a newspaper publishes a defamatory fact as its own statement of the fact'.[42] The second concerned stories in which the false statement was attributed to a third party or contained in a letter from a reader. Brennan saw no scope to extend privilege to the first type of story. Any such innovation would, he felt, be 'a charter for scandal-mongering'.[43] Privilege would however arise in the second type of case if three conditions were satisfied: first that the third party's claims were accurately reported; secondly that the defamed individual(s) were given an immediate right to rebut the allegations; and thirdly that the newspaper had reasonable grounds for believing the third party's assertions to be true because the third party could reasonably be assumed to have 'particular knowledge' of the issue in question. In effect, Brennan seemed to be offering a 'negligence plus right to reply' test for reports of third-party allegations. He indicated that that the *Western Australian* could satisfy these tests on the facts of this case.

The dichotomy that Brennan offered is curious because it would seem extremely easy for most newspapers to bring every factual assertion they make

[41] *Ibid.*, at 779.
[42] *Ibid.*, at 775.
[43] *Ibid.*, at 776.

within the second category. Brennan did not appear to place any limits on the nature of the third-party source. In *Stephens* itself, the source was presumptively authoritative, since he was a senior member of the legislature. But there is nothing in the opinion to indicate that a newspaper could not reasonably rely on, for example, the assertion of a convicted drug dealer in a story suggesting that a politician was involved in illegal narcotics use. The newspaper would presumably have to demonstrate it had taken reasonable steps to corroborate assertions from such a source, but in a case of this sort a convicted drug dealer is likely to be ideally placed to have 'particular knowledge' of the matter in question.

Indeed, it is difficult to conceive of situations in which any responsible newspaper would make factual claims without having drawn on external sources. Closer consideration of Brennan's defence would thus suggest that it would be ineffective only for those newspapers which were grossly negligent or reckless in failing to check their sources, or which—in order to protect the identity of those sources—were not willing to adduce any evidence demonstrating the reasonableness of their reliance.

The reasoning which led Brennan to this conclusion was shared by McHugh J.[44] He considered that while the Court should not create new rules of *constitutional law*, it faced no such impediment in creating new rules of *common law*. His methodology closely echoed that used by Cockburn CJ in *Wason* v. *Walter* and the Kansan Supreme Court in *Coleman* v. *Maclennan*, and adopted *Toogood* v. *Spyring* as its starting point:

> [I]t is now appropriate for the common law to declare that it is for the 'common convenience and welfare' of Australian society that the existing categories of qualified privilege be extended to protect communications made to the general public by persons with special knowledge concerning the exercise of public functions or the performance of their duties by public representatives or their officials. . . . The defence . . . will be available even if the information is subsequently proved to be incorrect.[45]

He was led to this viewpoint by the belief that the social, economic and political elements of modern Australian culture were so closely integrated that all legislators and government officials had a duty to communicate political facts to the electorate, and the electorate had a corresponding duty to receive them.

However, McHugh saw no reason to apply that new principle to this case. He found little fact in the newspaper's story: it was almost entirely comment. Fair comment was thus the appropriate defence. Dawson J concurred in this reasoning. Neither judge offered any indication whether such a defence might succeed. Nor did either suggest that the fair comment defence might, like that of qualified privilege, be ripe for rigorous overhaul.

---

[44] And Dawson J.
[45] (1994) 68 ALJ 713 at 787.

FROM CONSTITUTIONAL TO COMMON LAW PROTECTION—*LANGE V. ABC*[46]

Mason's term as Chief Justice expired shortly after *Theophanous* was decided. He was succeeded by Brennan. At the same time, Deane J, a trenchant advocate of the freedom of communication principle, also retired. Two new appellate judges, Gummow and Kirby JJ, had joined the bench. The *Theophanous/ Stephens* majority had thus disappeared. This change in the Court's personnel gave obvious grounds for wondering whether Mason CJ's opinion would soon be reversed. Kirby J presumably had little sympathy with *Theophanous*. Writing in 1988, he had warned the High Court against adopting a more activist jurisprudence. Constitutional reform should be conducted through legislatures and referendums, not by unelected judges.[46]

The opportunity for the new Court to reconsider *Theophanous* was quite promptly offered by David Lange, a former Prime Minister of New Zealand. Lange had taken exception to an ABC broadcast questioning his commitment while Prime Minister to his official duties. That he subsequently began a libel action against ABC made it clear that the *Theophanous* rule had not in fact deterred all political plaintiffs from beginning such litigation, even if it had had—although there was no way of gauging this—the desired result of reducing the chilling effect of that threat in Australia's media culture. A central tenet of Lange's case, however, was that *Theophanous* was wrongly decided. An alternative pleading was that even if *Theophanous* correctly stated the law in relation to Australian politicians and political issues, it could not extend to defamatory reporting in the Australian press of overseas political affairs.

The Judgment

The new High Court's decision in *Lange* v. *ABC*[47] was in some senses rather curious. Brennan CJ wrote the sole opinion for a unanimous Court. The judgment appeared to reverse *Theophanous* and *Stephens de facto*, but not *de jure*. Brennan's opinion led the Court back to his dissent in *Theophanous/ Stephens*. The judgment concluded that political libels attracted no constitutional protection, but that their disseminators could invoke a variant of the common law defence of qualified privilege.

Brennan CJ began by announcing that it was settled doctrine that the High Court was not bound by its previous decisions. It would however revisit judgments if they appeared 'manifestly wrong' and raised 'vital constitutional questions'.[48] This might have been thought to set the scene for reversing

---

[46] 'The Role of the Judge in Advancing Human Rights by Reference to International Human Rights Norms' [1988] *The Australian LJ* 514.

[47] (1997) 71 ALJR 818.

[48] (1997) 71 ALJR 818 at 822.

Theophanous/Stephens. But Brennan then argued that there was no need for that to happen, since those cases were not actually an authority for the proposition that the freedom of communication principle extended to political libels. In a passage that rather elevated form over substance, Brennan observed that only three members of the seven-person *Theophanous/Stephens* bench had supported Mason CJ's reasoning.[49] Deane J had concurred only in the result. Thus since Mason CJ's opinion did not have majority support, it was not *stricto sensu* a precedent at all, and the question whether freedom of communication reached to the law of libel remained open.

This reasoning seems rather disingenuous. Deane J obviously provided a fourth vote in *Theophanous* for the proposition that the Constitution itself contained an implied defence to political libels that was at least as extensive as qualified privilege. It is something of an exercise in sophistry to claim that because Deane J went far beyond the point reached by the plurality he cannot be assumed to have approved their destination.

Having adopted this somewhat unconvincing technique to avoid the presumable embarrassment of overturning a Court decision that was barely a few years old, Brennan J then suggested that Mason CJ's methodology in *Theophanous* was misconceived. Rather than fashioning a new defence for political libels from the Constitution itself, Brennan CJ held that his predecessor should first have determined whether the common law had developed to a point which matched the protection that the Constitution required for the dissemination of political information. If that development had indeed taken place, there would be no need for a new 'constitutional' principle.

As he had indicated in *Stephens*, Brennan believed that such a shift in common law understandings had already occurred. He noted that it was undoubtedly the case that Australian common law did not extend the qualified privilege defence to political libels in 1901. However, much had changed since then:

> The expansion of the franchise, the increase in literacy, the growth of modern political structures operating at both federal and State levels and the modern developments in mass communication, especially the electronic media, now demand the striking of a different balance from that which was struck in 1901.[50]

Brennan J then turned—as had the Kansan Supreme Court ninety years earlier in *Coleman*—to Cockburn CJ's opinion in *Wason* v. *Walter*[51] as an authority for the proposition that the common law of libel should be regularly reviewed to ensure that it served the 'wants and usages' of contemporary society. In Brennan's view, the 'wants and usages' of modern Australian society, in which the Constitution afforded fundamental status to the principle of representative government, required that 'political libels' attract a modified version of the qualified privilege defence. In the late twentieth century:

---

[49] Two of whom, Gaudron and Toohey, remained on the bench.
[50] (1997) 71 ALJR 818 at 828–9.
[51] (1868) LR 4 QB 73.

each member of the Australian community has an interest in disseminating and receiving information, opinions and arguments concerning government and political matters that affect the people of Australia.[52]

Significantly, Brennan CJ suggested that the defence was triggered by the substance of the story rather than the identity of the plaintiff. Its 'reach' was thus to be very expansive. In this sense he followed the wider rather than narrower understanding of the ambit of the constitutional defence offered by Mason in *Theophanous*. Brennan confirmed this point by indicating that the substantive issues he had in mind as falling within the new defence were broadly defined. The defence would apply not just to matters affecting voters' choice of candidate at federal elections, or the administration of the national government, or referendums concerning constitutional amendment. It would also extend to local and state government issues, as well as—unfortunately for the plaintiff in *Lange*—Australian discussion of political events in other countries or foreign fora such as the UN—which might 'affect or throw light on government or political matters in Australia'.[53] It thus seems likely that government employees, trades union leaders and members of political pressure groups will find themselves facing the new defence in respect of defamatory reporting of their political beliefs and activities.

The extensive (i.e. beyond *Sullivan*) reach of the defence was however to be coupled with a more narrowly defined 'effect'. Brennan appeared to have appreciated the superfluity of the dichotomous analysis he applied to this issue in *Stephens*. In *Lange*, he discarded any suggestion of a distinction between a publisher's own assertions and those which reported a third party's allegations. What he offered instead was a straightforward 'negligence plus right to reply' test with the burden of proof on the defendant:

> [A]s a general rule, a defendant's conduct in publishing material giving rise to a defamatory imputation will not be reasonable unless the defendant had reasonable grounds for believing the imputation to be true, took proper steps, so far as they were reasonably open, to verify the accuracy of the material and did not believe the imputation to be untrue.[54]

Brennan additionally held that even a 'reasonable' publication could found liability if the plaintiff proved (presumably to the ordinary balance of probabilities standard) that the publisher was motivated by 'spite or ill-will'.[55] This seems a very odd test, since Brennan went on to hold that the publisher's desire to cause 'political damage' to the plaintiff could not amount to spite in a political libel case. It is difficult to conceive of any ill-will which could not be brought within that 'political damage' heading when a political libel is in issue; an all-consuming desire to ruin a politician's career and subject her to such

[52] (1997) 71 AJLR 818 at 833.
[53] *Ibid*., at 835.
[54] *Ibid*., at 835.
[55] *Ibid*., at 834.

opprobrium that she could never again expect to occupy political office would presumably come within the notion of 'political damage', and so not found liability.[56] One is rather left with the impression that Brennan CJ was so concerned to distance his new rule from the constitutional foundations of the *Theophanous* rule that he seized on a common law label as part of his formula without fully considering the label's practical insignificance.

Even if one accepts that the issue of 'spite' is *de facto* redundant in political libel cases, Brennan's test is somewhat less accommodating to the defendant than the *Sullivan* 'actual malice' formula and the principle offered by Mason CJ in *Theophanous*.[57] Nonetheless, it offers perfectly adequate protection to serious, investigative journalism. There is no obvious public interest to be served—whether here, in the USA or in Australia—in the law encouraging the mass media to be negligent in establishing the trustworthiness of their sources and the accuracy of their stories. Brennan CJ clearly felt that his judgment did no disservice to the constitutional requirement of freedom of communication, observing that:

> It may be that in some respects, the common law defence as so extended goes beyond what is required for the common law of defamation to be compatible with the freedom of communication required by the Constitution.[58]

CONCLUSION

There is perhaps little practical difference between the pre- and post-*Lange* situations in Australia: the obstacles facing defamed politicians remain broadly the same. This may explain why Toohey and Gaudron JJ concurred in *Lange* rather than reiterating their position in *Theophanous*. Superficially, *Lange* appears to have changed the way in which those obstacles might be removed. The Commonwealth Parliament may now reverse *Lange* by simple majority legislation. *Theophanous*, in contrast, could have been reversed only by constitutional amendment. It is however clear that Australia's Parliament cannot simply reverse *Lange* and restore the orthodox common law position. Brennan's judgment in *Lange* confirms that any such legislation would contravene the freedom of communication principle, and would thus have to be invalidated by the Court. His suggestion that the qualified privilege defence may go beyond what the freedom of communication principle requires may afford Parliament some room for legislative manœuvre if it should wish to take an initiative in this area—but it could hardly do so in the belief that it has been offered a precise indication of what the Constitution allows it to do. One might suggest that the

---

[56] I am grateful to Paul Mitchell (1999 *op. cit.* at fn. 50) for alerting me to my previous failure to address this point.

[57] The 'right to reply' provision would fall foul of the First Amendment in the USA: see *Miami Herald* v. *Tornillo* (1974) 418 US 241.

[58] (1997) 71 AJLR 818 at 833.

judgment has—to adopt a familiar term—'chilled' legislative innovation in this area, while at the same time enabling the new Court to claim that it has retreated from the controversially activist jurisprudence favoured by the Mason Court. In so doing, it has offered a lead for the English courts to follow in respect of our political libel laws which is not tainted with what many English judges appear (erroneously) to perceive as the supra-legislative basis of *Sullivan* v. *The New York Times*.

And just as a foreign ex-Prime Minister with an allegedly injured reputation presented the Australian courts with the chance to revisit *Theophanous*, so the English courts in 1997 were afforded the opportunity to reconsider English law. The plaintiff was Albert Reynolds, Ireland's former Taoiseach. The defendant was—as in *Derbyshire*—*The Sunday Times*. The alleged libel was that Reynolds *qua* politician had been a liar.

9

English Law—The Second Phase of Reform?

Lange's impact on English law is considered later in this chapter. That the English Court of Appeal was so persuaded in *Elton John* by Australian reasoning on libel damages in *Carson* might be thought to lend *Lange* a particularly forceful character in English law, given that *Carson* was an early response to the essentially public-law concerns that eventually manifested themselves as a rule of constitutional law in *Theophanous* and then of common law in *Lange* itself. Before returning to developments in English common law however, it is helpful to consider two further sources of legal innovation that appeared in the mid-1990s. The first derived from the case law of the European Court on Human Rights (ECtHR), the second from an initiative taken by the UK Parliament.

FURTHER DEVELOPMENTS BEFORE THE ECtHR

As noted in Chapter 7, the ECtHR had not accepted the invitation made by Anthony Lester QC in *Tolstoy* to confirm unambiguously that Article 10 demanded that civil libel laws distinguished between political and non-political suits. In two further criminal libel suits decided in 1997 however, it again offered clear indications that such a distinction would be required.

The applicants in *De Haes and Gisjels* v. *Belgium*[1] were journalists who had written a vigorously abusive attack on several members of the Antwerp Court of Appeal for awarding custody of a child to a father suspected of having committed incest and child abuse. As well as castigating the judges' decision, the journalists accused them of bias in favour of the father, who was also a member of the legal profession. The judges themselves initiated criminal libel proceedings against the journalists under Articles 275–276 of the Belgian Penal Code, which make it a crime to 'insult' members of the judiciary, even if the insults are premised on factual criticisms proven to be true. The journalists were convicted.

The ECtHR declared the convictions invalid perhaps surprisingly, given that it had upheld a similar conviction under Danish law in *Barfod* in 1989.[2] The ECtHR's reasoning in *De Haes* indicated that it now embraced a more rigorous

---

[1] (1997) 25 EHRR 1.
[2] See 110–11 above.

defence of freedom of political expression. The ratio of the judgment is not immediately apparent, but can readily be teased out.

The central issue was whether the degree of interference with press freedom imposed by the Belgian Penal Code was necessary to safeguard the reputation of the judiciary. The ECtHR afforded that Article 10(2) consideration substantial importance:

> The courts—the guarantors of justice, whose role is fundamental in a State based on the rule of law—must enjoy public confidence. They must accordingly be protected from destructive atttacks that are unfounded.[3]

The key question then became whether the attacks were 'unfounded'. The ECtHR seemed to apply a negligence test on this point. It stressed that the journalists had investigated the case carefully before writing their articles. In such circumstances:

> it is incumbent on the press to impart information and ideas of public interest. Not only does the press have the task of imparting such information and ideas; the public also has a right to receive them.[4]

The obvious implication is that a critical attack is unfounded only if its publishers have not exercised a reasonable level of journalistic care and scruple in satisfying themselves as to the truth of the underlying claim.

The ECtHR also stressed that if a journalist had met that level of investigative responsibility, she was not obliged to render her criticism in polite terms; 'Article 10 protects not only the substance of the ideas and information expressed, but also the form in which they are conveyed'.[5] Insult and invective consequently merited protection under Article 10, as did 'a degree of exaggeration, or even provocation'.[6]

What is perhaps most significant about *De Haes* is that it confirms the evident extension of Article 10's 'public–private' defamation divide that the ECtHR introduced[7] in *Thorgeirson* from matters affecting just politicians to all information raising a legitimate matter of public interest. In terms of reach, the European Convention on Human Rights defence to libel actions would thus seem to go beyond *Sullivan* and cover the same, more expansive ground as *Coleman*. The most apposite English comparator would be the discredited (in *Blackshaw*) 'fair information on a matter of public interest' formula offered by Pearson J in *Webb*.[8]

---

[3] (1997) 25 EHRR 1 at para. 37.

[4] *Ibid.*, at para. 39.

[5] *Ibid.*, at para. 48.

[6] *Ibid.*, at para. 46.

[7] Even though it denied it had done so.

[8] It should be noted that having extended the reach of the *Lingens* defence(s), the ECtHR also seemed rather to narrow its (their) effect. In *Lingens*, the ECtHR had suggested that the publication of 'opinions' could not be punished at all, since opinions could not be proven true or false. *De Haes* qualified that ostensibly absolutist 'fair or unfair comment' defence rule by indicating that opinions could be punished if they were 'excessive, in particular in the absence of any factual basis' (at para. 47).

The judgment seems impossible to reconcile with *Barfod* v. *Denmark*, but the ECtHR did not even mention—still less overrule—the earlier case. This lack of judicial candour is perhaps regrettable, but it does not detract from the force of the assertion that Article 10 now seems to require that the publishers of libels on matters of legitimate public interest must be afforded substantially more effective defences than those available to purveyors of 'private' information.

Shortly after *De Haes*, the ECtHR issued judgment in *Oberschlick* v. *Austria (No. 2)*.[9] The case arose from an article in *Forum* which labelled Jorg Haider, leader of Austria's neo-Nazi Freedom Party as a 'Trottel' when commenting on an inflammatory speech Haider had made. The closest English translation of the term is 'idiot', although 'Trottel' evidently bears a much more insulting meaning to Austrians than its English counterpart would to English readers. Oberschlik was convicted under Article 115 of the Criminal Code, a provision of apparently extraordinary width:

> Anyone who, in public or in the presence of several others, insults, mocks, mistreats or threatens to mistreat a third person, shall be liable to imprisonment not exceeding three months or a fine.

The conviction was premised on the ground that the use of 'Trottel' did not even amount to the expression of an opinion; 'it was nothing but an insult used to denigrate and disparage an individual in public'.[10]

The conviction was declared invalid on the basis of reasoning drawn virtually verbatim from *Oberschlick (No. 1)*, which had itself borrowed the words of *Lingens*. Thus:

> the limits of acceptable criticism are wider with regard to a politician in his public capacity than in relation to a private individual. A politician knowingly and inevitably lays himself open to close scrutiny of his every word and deed . . . and must display a greater degree of tolerance.[11]

In *Oberschlick (No. 2)*, the ECtHR added a further clause to this analysis, 'since exceptions to freedom of expression must be interpreted narrowly'.[12] This additional clause should perhaps not be taken as an indication that the ECtHR is about to afford much more expansive and effective protection to all forms of speech. In almost contemporaneous judgments on obscenity and blasphemy the court has evinced a clear willingness to uphold national laws which would certainly not survive judicial scrutiny under the First Amendment.[13] It may however signify a stiffening of judicial resolve to protect speech that has a demonstrably 'political' content.

---

[9] (1997) 25 EHRR 357.

[10] *Ibid.*, at para. 28.

[11] *Lingens*, para.42; *Oberschlick (No. 1)*, para. 59; *Oberschlick (No. 2)*, para. 29.

[12] (1997) 25 EHRR 357 at para. 29.

[13] *Otto-Preminger Institut* v. *Austria* (1995) 23 EHRR 34; *Wingrove* v. *United Kingdom* (1996) 24 EHRR 1. For comment see Loveland, I., 'A Free Trade in Ideas—and Outcomes', in Loveland, I. (ed.), *Importing the First Amendment?* (1998); Warbrick, C., 'Federalism and Free Speech', in *ibid.*

This supposition is perhaps reinforced by the ECtHR's ostensibly curious emphasis in *Oberschlick (No. 2)* on Haider's identity as a 'politician', rather than as a player within a drama that fell within the broader notion of 'public interest' used in *De Haes*. This technique is strongly reminiscent of the US Supreme Court's strategy following *Sullivan*. Even though it had extended the 'actual malice' defence to 'newsworthy events' in *Hill*, the Supreme Court still preferred to justify the use of the defence in subsequent cases in terms of the more narrowly defined status of the plaintiff/story.[14] The ECtHR's method raises the inference that Article 10 now requires a fourfold rather than tripartite approach to defamation laws, distinguishing between government bodies, politicians, public-interest stories and private matters, in respect of the severity of the obstacles that the plaintiff or prosecution must surmount to succeed. If this is indeed the case, it raises the spectre of the same kind of unwelcome complexity in defamation law that initially attended post-*Sullivan* developments in the USA. These would however seem to be conceptual complexities that escaped the attention of British legislators.

THE DEFAMATION ACT 1996

The libel action begun by Neil Hamilton MP, a former minister in the Major government, against *The Guardian* was prompted by stories accusing Hamilton of receiving large sums of money, not declared in the Commons' Register of Members' Interests, from various commercial sources. Hamilton resigned as a minister before beginning proceedings 'to clear his name'. *The Guardian* pleaded justification. It did not seek to raise the issue of qualified privilege, nor a *Lingens* defence. At the trial, in July 1995, May J ordered a stay of the proceedings. He considered himself bound to do so by a recent Privy Council decision, *Prebble* v. *Television New Zealand Ltd*.[15]

Prebble was a libel action brought by a government minister in New Zealand. The defendant wished to refer to statements made by the plaintiff in the New Zealand legislature as part of its defence. At first instance, NZTV's defence to Prebble's action was simply justification. Prebble applied to have those parts of the defence relating to his speeches in the legislature struck out. He succeeded at first instance. The court considered that any such reference was precluded by provisions of New Zealand's Legislature Act 1908, which were textually identical to Article 9 of the English Bill of Rights.[16]

As noted in the previous discussions of *Stockdale* v. *Hansard* and *Dillon* v. *Balfour*,[17] English law has long provided that Article 9 affords absolute immu-

---

[14] Cf. the 'public figure' in *Butts*; the 'vortex of political controversy' in *Walker*; and the candidate for office in *Monitor Patriot*. See 73–8 above.

[15] [1994] 3 NZLR 1. See Marshall, G., 'Impugning Parliamentary Impunity' [1994] *Public Law* 509; Leopold, P., 'Free Speech in Parliament and the Courts' (1994) 15 *Legal Studies* 204.

[16] See 12 above.

[17] See 21–4 and 36 above.

nity from defamation actions for any oral statement or written publication that forms part of a 'debate or proceeding in Parliament'. The question whether Article 9 prevents such statements being invoked as *evidence* in a legal action, even if the statements concerned are not themselves the subject of the suit in issue, is less clear.[18] Section 3 of the Parliamentary Papers Act 1840 obviously allows a court to refer to such statements to decide whether an allegedly accurate report thereof really was accurate. As noted in Chapter 2, this was done in *Wason*. In *Dingle* v. *Associated Newspapers*[19] in 1960, Pearson J had indicated that Article 9 precluded a court from questioning the validity of a parliamentary proceeding, but accepted (though without reference to section 3) that its text could be admitted as a simple fact. Browne J had reached a similar conclusion in *Church of Scientology* v. *Johnson-Smith*[20] in 1972. The text of a parliamentary proceeding was admissible for the purpose of establishing what was said by whom and when. But it could not be used—as the plaintiff wished—as a subject for analysis to support the accusation that speeches the defendant made elsewhere were made with malice. The trial court in *Prebble* applied this rationale to the case before it. NZTV was not permitted to invoke parliamentary proceedings as evidence in the way it wished, and therefore faced considerable difficulty in proving its defence.

The New Zealand Court of Appeal[21] agreed that the evidence was not admissible. However, it then reasoned that if such evidence was inadmissible, NZTV could not mount an effective defence to the claim. Consequently, the 'interests of justice' demanded that the action be stayed. On further appeal,[22] the Judicial Committee of the Privy Council approved the New Zealand Court of Appeal's interpretation of Article 9 in so far as it affected New Zealand. In *Hamilton*, May J held that Article 9 required the same result in England. Mr Hamilton chose not to appeal against this ruling, but instead took advantage of his position as a government party MP to try to reverse the judgment by securing the amendment of a bill then before Parliament.

The Terms of the Act

The Defamation Bill 1996 began its life as an essentially technical piece of law reform. It was designed to enact recommendations made by a committee, chaired by Neill LJ, charged with formulating proposals to streamline the resolution of libel suits.[23] The bill proposed some modest changes to existing law. A

[18] *Dingle* v. *Foot* [1960] 1 All ER 294; *Church of Scientology of California* v. *Johnson-Smith* [1972] 1 All ER 378.
[19] [1960] 1 All ER 294.
[20] [1972] 1 All ER 379.
[21] [1993] 3 NZLR 513.
[22] [1994] 3 NZLR 1.
[23] Supreme Court Procedure Committee Report on Practice and Procedure in Defamation (HMSO, London, 1991).

defence of 'offer to make amends' would be made available; the limitation period for defamation actions would be reduced to one year; and the defence of innocent dissemination would be slightly extended. Initially, the bill's most controversial provision was that the courts should be empowered to dispose of cases summarily where they considered either the plaintiff or defendant's claim manifestly ill-founded. Damages awards in summary judgment cases would be limited to £10,000. These initiatives promised slightly to reduce the chilling effect of libel actions in all cases, although the report did not couch its recommendations in those terms. As such, the bill would have been expected to excite discussion among libel lawyers, but it was hardly a measure of constitutional significance. May J's decision to stay proceedings in Hamilton's case changed that picture entirely. What is now section 13 of the Act surfaced as a proposed amendment to the bill submitted by Lord Hoffmann. The nub of the proposal was that an individual MP should be empowered to permit House proceedings to be used as evidence in any libel litigation in which she was involved. Lord Hoffmann suggested that it was 'unjust that [Mr Hamilton] should not be able to put the matter before a judge and jury, like any other citizen who feels that his integrity has been publicly defamed'.[24] He rejected as 'deceptive' the suggestion that *Prebble* merely created a 'symmetry' between the MP and the citizen—namely that if Article 9 gave MPs absolute immunity for defamatory statements made in either House about companies or private individuals, it should also prevent MPs suing such companies or individuals for defamation in circumstances where parliamentary proceedings formed part of the defence. Lord Hoffmann saw a profound public interest in the first limb of this equation, and none in the second.

The amendment attracted some opposition in the Lords. Lord Ewing of Kirkford observed that his experience in the Commons had led him to conclude that MPs themselves readily abused their protection from defamation suits by making unsupportable accusations in the House. He suggested that to leave the victims of such defamation without a remedy, while enhancing the remedies available to MPs, was not an appropriate course for Parliament to follow. Lord (Anthony) Lester QC was the only member of the House to dwell on the implications the amendment would have for the freedom of the press, and thence on the electorate's access to critical information about MPs and ministers. He observed that press uncertainty about whether an MP would waive privilege might 'chill' the dissemination of critical news stories.

Lord Lester's concerns failed to sway the majority of his colleagues. The government had maintained that Lord Hoffmann's amendment, while introduced into a government bill, would not be whipped. Members could vote on it as they wished. Yet over 200 peers voted on the amendment at third reading—an extraordinarily high number. The vote was 157 in favour and fifty-seven against.

The suspicion that a *de facto* if not *de jure* whip was operating was reinforced by events in the Commons.[25] The amendment was bundled through at second

[24] Hansard (HL), 7 May 1996, col. 22.
[25] See Paul Boateng MP, Hansard (HC), 21 May 1996, col. 134.

reading. The prevailing mood on the Conservative benches was best illustrated by Sir Peter Tapsell, who described the amendment as saving MPs from 'persecution . . . from what many people regard as an over-mighty press that is owned, for the most part, by foreigners'.[26] The Hoffmann amendment was approved, and the bill received the Royal Assent in the autumn.

Rupert Allason was the first MP to take advantage of section 13, waiving the House's privilege in order to continue a libel action against the Mirror Group. Hamilton followed by recommencing his action against *The Guardian.* He then decided not to proceed with the litigation when it appeared that he and his co-plaintiff, the lobbyist Ian Greer, would offer the court contradictory accounts of their financial relationship. The obvious suspicion was that Hamilton—like Jonathon Aitken—had been prepared to take action even though he knew *The Guardian*'s coverage to be accurate and was relying on the onerous burden the paper would face to prove justification as sufficient to enable him to 'vindicate' his reputation and presumably recover substantial damages. The plan only failed when his co-plaintiff decided not to support Hamilton's version of the facts.

What the Defamation Act 1996 had of course not done was to introduce a *Sullivan*-type defence for political libels. The suggestion had briefly been raised by Lord Williams of Mostyn, a Labour peer and leading libel barrister. The government was wholly unreceptive to the claim. The then Lord Chancellor, Lord Mackay, suggested that any such change was a matter for the courts. That it might be required by the ECHR was not a consideration to which the government attached any weight. Perhaps ironically however, that consideration was shortly to prove of great significance to the members of the New Zealand Court of Appeal when they found themselves caught up in former Prime Minister David Lange's continuing attempts to extract libel damages from critics of his political behaviour.

LANGE IN NEW ZEALAND

As noted in Chapter 4, New Zealand common law—in *Truth (NZ) Ltd* v. *Hollway*—had in 1960 set itself firmly against recognition of an expansive, *Webb*-type extension of qualified privilege to all matters of legitimate public interest. In the intervening years, the New Zealand courts had not indicated that they were ready to accept that the defence could be extended much more narrowly to cover political libels. While the Court of Appeal in *Templeton* v. *Jones* had given substantial consideration to *Sullivan*, and had indicated it was attracted to the introduction of a negligence-based defence in political libel actions, it considered any such initiative a matter for the legislature rather than the courts to introduce. In *Lange* v. *Atkinson*, however, the New Zealand High

---

[26] Hansard (HC), 24 June 1996, col. 58.

Court suddenly took a very substantial step in the *Sullivan* direction, in a judgment subsequently supported by Court of Appeal.[27]

The High Court

The only issue before the High Court was whether the publication attracted qualified privilege or could be protected by a new defence which defendant's counsel styled as 'political expression'. The two claimed defences were subsumed into one at the trial, which took place before judgment was delivered by the Australian High Court in *Lange* v. *ABC*, with Elias J presiding.

Elias J's judgment raises several important issues of both substantive law and legal methodology. It could plausibly be characterised as a late-twentieth century restatement of *Wason* v. *Walter*; the court's starting point for analysis was acceptance of the political principle that common law regulation of freedom of expression should enhance public awareness of governmental behaviour along with a recognition that the detailed rules which the principle produced would have to reflect more pervasive contemporary societal understandings of the relationship between the citizenry and those who governed them.

Elias J accepted (and quoted at length) Cockburn CJ's characterisation in *Campbell* of the balance that the law had to strike between the dissemination of information raising matters of 'public interest' and the protection of the reputations of 'public men'.[28] She also couched her inquiry in terms of the pursuit of a rule which would, *per Toogood* v. *Spyring*, serve the 'common convenience and welfare of society'. In seeking to identify society's current needs, Elias J swept (as had Mason CJ in *Theophanous*) over a wide range of jurisprudential sources, with *Sullivan* and its progeny receiving detailed attention. However her conclusion, while obviously informed by nominally 'foreign' legal authorities, was driven in large part by indigenous factors.

As noted in Chapter 2, it is difficult to resist the inference that the common law innovation introduced in *Wason* was an immediate response to the passage of Disraeli's 1867 Reform Act, even though Cockburn CJ did not acknowledge that linkage explicitly. In *Lange*, Elias J reasoned that a shift in the common law was not simply desirable but also necessary in the light of recent statutory innovations which had substantially redefined the basis of New Zealand's democratic settlement. She pointed in particular to the enactment of the New Zealand Bill of Rights Act 1990, which had elevated various civil liberties including freedom of expression to—if only in symbolic terms—the status of fundamental constitutional rights. She also concluded that the introduction of a new electoral system based on a form of proportional representation by the Electoral Act 1993 indicated that the concept of representative government also possessed enhanced significance in modern New Zealand society. This innovation had in

[27] [1997] 2 NZLR 22 (HC), [1998] 3 NZLR 424 (CA).
[28] See 24–5 above.

particular destroyed any suggestion (a suggestion accepted in *Braddock* v. *Bevins* and *Templeton* v. *Jones*) that a citizen's interest in receiving information about politicians was constrained within constituency boundaries. A national electoral list system necessarily lent all political matters a national dimension.

In this changed statutory context, the common law was bound to accept that the dissemination of political information had acquired much greater importance than it enjoyed in the past. Elias J indicated that New Zealand had now reached a stage of political maturity in which the reciprocal duty/right to disseminate/receive information that was needed to trigger the qualified privilege defence now existed between the press and the electorate in respect of what she termed 'political discussion', namely, 'discussion which bears upon the function of electors in a representative democracy by developing and encouraging views upon government'.[29] This formula has a potentially very broad reach, going far beyond *Sullivan*, and embracing not just elected politicians and candidates for office, but also public officials and nominally 'private' citizens who have involved themselves in governmental issues.

The question which then arose was just how substantial the protection that was afforded to such political discussion should be. Elias J did not consider it desirable markedly to dilute the traditional effect of the qualified privilege defence. As in the American common law decisions discussed in Chapter 3, Elias J removed the notion of 'overbroad publication' from the malice stage of the inquiry. Political information was legitimately disseminated to the electorate at large; it could not therefore be published too broadly. She also seemed to follow American principle by confining the 'malice' investigation to the question of the publisher's belief in the truth of her story, dispensing with any concern for the publisher's motives. However, on the most important element of the defence, Elias J adhered to the orthodox position. She considered that introducing a negligent falsity test would not afford sufficient protection to the press, and accepted instead that the *Horrocks* v. *Lowe* test of 'honest belief' was the appropriate standard to apply.

In a rather curious passage, Elias J suggested that the new defence would apply only in respect of claims for damages.[30] A plaintiff who merely sought a declaration that a story was libellous would not have to surmount the qualified privilege burden. Such a distinction has unwelcome echoes of the abstract complexities introduced into US law by *Gertz*. It also seems problematic on a practical basis; in so far as the chilling effect may owe as much to a publisher's fear of having to pay a defamed politician's costs as to having to pay damages,[31] a

---

[29] [1997] 2 NZLR 22 at 46. Elias J did not regard *Truth (NZ) Ltd* v. *Holloway* as a barrier to this conclusion. She construed that case as rejecting the claim that qualified privilege should attend all discussion of matters of public, rather than just political, interest. The claim advanced in *Lange* was tailored much more narrowly, to an appreciably less extensive range of information.

[30] It appears that this was a conscious and careful choice, unlike the ambiguous comments to the same effect made by William Brennan in *Sullivan* (68 above) and Lord Keith in *Derbyshire* (122 above).

[31] See the discussion of *Campion*, at 93–4 above.

'damages-only' defence might do little to encourage greater dissemination of political news.

This point aside, in terms of both its reach and effect Elias J's rule represented a marked departure from previous common law understandings, and extended a very high degree of protection to a very wide range of political information. From a methodological perspective, the Court of Appeal approved Elias J's judgment; although on matters of substance, it offered a rather different set of innovations.

The Court of Appeal

The court unanimously endorsed Elias J's methodology of altering the common law of political defamation in response to a changing statutory framework concerning the relationship between the citizenry and the government in New Zealand. In addition to the Bill of Rights Act 1990 and the Electoral Act 1993, the Court made specific mention of section 4 of the Official Information Act 1982, the explicit purpose of which was to enable citizens to participate more effectively in the government process.

The Court of Appeal also concluded that New Zealand's common law was being pushed in a similar direction by libel law developments in other western democracies. The Court's opinion swept widely across a range of comparative jurisdictions. *Sullivan* received extensive and approving attention, as did the Australian decisions discussed in Chapter 8. The Court also dwelt upon the ECtHR's case law, and attached considerable importance to the *Lingens/ Oberschlick (No. 1)/Oberschlick (No. 2)* distinction between politicians and private individuals. It attached especial significance to the ECtHR's addition to the *Lingens* formula in *Oberschlick (No.2)*—namely that 'exceptions to freedom of expression must be interpreted narrowly'.[32] Although these authorities were extra-territorial in a formal sense, the Court of Appeal seemed to be assuming that they should no longer be regarded as 'foreign' when it came to assessing the moral principles which they served.

In addition, the court made substantial resort to English authority, and extracted from it an argument in favour of extending the qualified privilege defence to political libels. As in *Coleman*, Cockburn CJ's judgment in *Wason* v. *Walter* was quoted extensively as both a methodological and substantive authority: the common law should be flexible in its terms, and those terms should be geared to enhancing electors' ability to give informed consent to the governmental process.[33] The Court of Appeal also drew extensively on Lord Greene MR's opinion and reasoning in *Braddock* v. *Bevins*—a case which the

---

[32] The phrase is italicised for additional emphasis in the Court of Appeal's judgment: [1998] 3 NZLR 424 at 459.

[33] Neither *Coleman* itself nor any other American common law decisions were cited in the judgment.

Court noted had not been overruled by New Zealand legislation and which could therefore be considered a sound exposition of New Zealand common law. What then needed to be done was to update the rule in conformity with post-1948 shifts in the democratic basis of New Zealand's constitutional structure.

The Court of Appeal restricted the new reach of the defence rather more narrowly than Elias J had done. Although it held out the prospect the defence might in future extend to 'statements which directly concern the functioning of representative and responsible government', it explicitly limited its holding to:

> statements made about the actions and qualities of those currently or formerly elected to Parliament and those with immediate aspirations to such office, so far as those actions and qualities directly affect or affected their capacity (including their personal ability and willingness) to meet their public responsibilities.[34]

In the same way as Brennan's judgment in *Sullivan*, this formula recognised that politicians retained a private identity which they could defend against defamatory attack on the same basis as all other citizens.

In considering the effect of the defence, the majority observed (apparently overlooking *Campbell* v. *Spottiswoode*, Cooke J's suggestion in *Templeton* and the ECtHR's reasoning in *De Haes*) that negligence had no role to play in defamation law. Like Elias J, it concluded that the *Horrocks* v. *Lowe* test of 'honest belief' was the appropriate formula to apply.[35] The plaintiff would have to prove knowledge of falsity or indifference to truth on the defendant's part if he were to succeed. The Court also indicated that the new remedy would be as readily applicable to actions seeking simply a declaration as to those involving a claim for damages.

REYNOLDS V. *TIMES NEWSPAPERS*

The decisions in *Lange* (Australia) and *Lange* (New Zealand) present interesting parallels with the turn of the twentieth-century judgments produced by American state courts that were discussed in Chapter 3. Those judgments also proceeded from the same moral base, namely an acceptance that in a representative democracy common law rules of libel had to be modified in order to prevent politicians unduly stifling public examination and discussion of their behaviour. The precise reach and effect that were accorded to the qualified privilege defence in these jurisdictions varied from state to state; but those variations were all clearly distinguishable from the rule applied by English common law.

This is a hallmark of the way one would expect laws to operate within a federal system of government. The legal rules adopted in response to particular political problems can differ (perhaps quite noticeably) in their detailed

---

[34] [1998] 3 NZLR 424 at 468.
[35] Although Tipping J concurred in this conclusion, he indicated that he considered that a negligence test would be a better solution.

substantive content between jurisdictions, while simultaneously sharing a clear fidelity to the principle from which they emerged. In this context, the US Supreme Court's subsequent decision in *Sullivan* can be seen as an attempt to prevent renegade state jurisdictions from abandoning or ignoring that common moral base rather than as the imposition of a centralised legal rule.

The *Lange* judgments offer, one might suggest, an interesting example of the 'federalist' potential of the common law within the broader community of democratic nations at the end of the twentieth century. *Lange* (Australia) has created a defence for political speech which has a very expansive reach, but a fairly limited effect. *Lange* (New Zealand) offers a defence with a limited reach, but a very expansive effect. Both decisions represent a clear departure from their respective jurisdictions' previous treatment at common law of political libels. Both rest on the respective courts' assumptions that the common law rules on this issue no longer respected the principle from which they emerged; they were no longer serving the common convenience and welfare of countries which had grown into mature, democratic societies.

As the *Lange* cases were proceeding through the New Zealand and Australian courts, the English judiciary was also presented with the opportunity to re-examine the English common law. It did so in a style, and with an outcome, that seemed to compare rather poorly to the efforts of its commonwealth brethren.

The High Court

The story at issue in *Reynolds* was one of some considerable factual complexity. Reynolds, the former Taoiseach of Ireland, resigned from that post in November 1994. He did so in the wake of a controversy in which—in his version of events—he had unwittingly misled the Dail on a matter of great political significance. The affair was thoroughly—and in Mr Reynolds' view accurately—covered in a long article published in the Irish edition of the *Sunday Times* of 20 November 1994. The suit arose in respect of a shortened version of the article in the British edition of the paper. This story, Reynolds maintained, falsely accused him of having deliberately lied to the Dàil, an accusation which was highly defamatory. Reynolds had won a pyrrhic victory at first instance in a jury trial presided over by French J. An award of 1p damages left him facing a costs bill estimated at close to £1,000,000, as the paper had taken the tactical precaution of paying some £5,000 into court.[36] He appealed against the judgment on the basis of inadequacies in the judge's summing up. The defendant cross-appealed on the question whether or not it should be able to invoke the defence of qualified privilege in any retrial. The Court of Appeal[37] allowed Reynolds' appeal and ordered a new trial. However, it rejected the cross-appeal by the defendant.

[36] *The Guardian*, 20 Nov. 1996.
[37] [1998] 3 All ER 961 (Lord Bingham MR and Hirst and Robert Walker LJJ).

The Court of Appeal

Anthony Lester QC led for the defendant. His brief offered the court a wide-ranging survey of the various ways in which assorted English, Commonwealth, American and European jurisdictions had recognised that defendants in political libel cases should be able to invoke the qualified privilege defence. His argument, following American, Australian and New Zealand precedent, adopted both a 'reach' and 'contents' approach to the application of qualified privilege to political libels. On the issue of reach, he urged the court to adopt the *Lange* (Australia) test, namely, 'information, opinions and arguments concerning government and political matters that affect the people of the United Kingdom'.[38] On the effect of the defence, Lord Lester advocated that the Court adopted the orthodox meaning of qualified privilege—i.e. *Lange* (New Zealand)—rather than a modified version such as the more expansive one adopted in *Sullivan* or the less substantial one adopted in *Lange* (Australia).[39]

The Court's judgment acknowledged and discussed most of the 'foreign' innovations to which Lord Lester had referred, clearly indicating that the court was willing to accord persuasive influence to a wide array of pertinent comparative material. In what may however have been a crucial omission, Lord Bingham made no reference to the American common law decisions. His visit to US jurisprudence was limited to *Sullivan*. And like Lord Keith and Butler-Sloss LJ in *Derbyshire*, Lord Bingham appeared to perpetuate the evidently well-established tradition among the English judiciary substantially to misunderstand that case. He noted that *Sullivan* was 'not directly in point here' as it 'was essentially based on the First Amendment to the US Constitution'.[40] As indicated in earlier chapters, that conclusion is quite erroneous. The *Sullivan* test was actually 'essentially based' on long-established principles of American common law. The First Amendment served simply as the tool with which the Supreme Court was able to give that common law tradition national and supra-legislative effect. And had the Court of Appeal in *Reynolds* visited some of the relevant American case law—and particularly *Coleman*—in any detail, it would have found much of it to be explicitly inspired by English jurisprudence—which perhaps makes *Sullivan* more 'directly in point' than any other authority to which Lord Lester referred.

This was not the only instance when the Court's of Appeal's assessment of whether or not an authority was 'in point' seemed to go sadly awry. In explaining the policy which underpinned the law, Lord Bingham placed substantial

---

[38] *Ibid.*, at 989. Cf Lord Lester's skeleton argument: 'the privilege is not derived merely from the identity of the Plaintiff as an elected politician . . . if that were so it would include defamatory publications about his private life': at para. 4. My thanks go to Lord Lester for making the argument available to me.

[39] Although he suggested that most juries would regard gross negligence on a newspaper's part as *prima facie* evidence of malice.

[40] [1998] 3 All ER 961 at 1003.

reliance on what he described as Diplock J's 'classic statement' in *Silkin* v. *Beaverbrook Newspapers* of the way in which the English constitutional tradition balanced the individual politician's interest in the protection of her reputation with the public's interest in receiving information pertinent to her suitability for office. As suggested in Chapter 4,[41] Diplock J's analysis in *Silkin* can readily be seen as deeply flawed. For the Court of Appeal in *Reynolds*, however, it was evidently beyond reproach. Lord Bingham MR's judgment seemed to proceed from just the same ill-conceived 'first place' as the opinion offered by Diplock J in *Silkin* and precisely echoed the European Commission on Human Rights' subsequently discarded views in *Lingens (No.1)* and *X* v. *Germany*[42]:

> While those who engage in public life must expect and accept that their public conduct will be the subject of close scrutiny and robust criticism, they should not in our view be taken to expect or accept that their conduct should be the subject of false and defamatory statements.[43]

Once again, an English court has approached this question by assigning primary importance to the protection of reputation, thereby necessarily assigning a secondary, subsidiary role to the dissemination of political information. Just the opposite approach was taken in *Sullivan* and the American common law judgments which preceded it, by the ECtHR in *Lingens*, and by the New Zealand and Australian courts in the *Lange* cases. To portray the dichotomy in a different but no less apposite way, one might suggest that while the ECtHR and the courts in the USA, Australia and New Zealand now categorise political libels as a facet of constitutional law, the English Court of Appeal continues to approach them as a part of the law of torts. Lord Bingham's Court of Appeal may have acknowledged the jurisprudence of other nations—and in that respect its judgment is a considerable advance on its predecessor's efforts in *Blackshaw*—but it did not really seem properly to have understood the principles underpinning the laws concerned.

Having laid these unstable constitutional and public policy foundations for his judgment, Lord Bingham then proceeded to erect upon them a peculiarly inelegant superstructure. As noted above, the Australian, New Zealand and American common laws offer a two-part ('reach' and 'contents') test for the qualified privilege defence: was the libel 'political information', and, if so, was it published with 'malice'? Rather than adopt this approach, as Lord Lester had advocated, the Court of Appeal in *Reynolds* advanced a *four*-part test:

1. Was the publisher under a legal, moral or social duty to those to whom the material was published . . . to publish the material in question? (We call this the duty test).
2. Did those to whom the material was published . . . have an interest to receive that material ? (We call this the interest test).
3. Were the nature, status and source of the material, and the circumstances of the

publication, such that the publication should in the public interest be protected in the absence of proof of express malice? (We call this the circumstantial test).[44]

[4. If all these points could be answered in the defendant's favour, was the publication was made with malice?[45]]

Lord Bingham's conclusions on parts one and two of his test were broadly comparable to part one of *Lange* (Australia). He afforded the concept of 'political libel' a wide reach, including 'the conduct of government and political life, elections . . . and public administration' and also 'matters such as (for instance) the governance of public bodies, institutions and companies which give rise to a public interest in disclosure'.[46] From this point onwards, however, *Reynolds*' parity with *Lange* (Australia)—and the clarity of its reasoning—largely disappeared.

The problems—both conceptual and empirical—are caused by Lord Bingham's so-called 'circumstantial' test. The way in which this test was explained was rather unclear, but it seems to require that the source of the information on which the defamatory story relied could be regarded as authoritative. This is perhaps best illustrated by a melodramatic passage towards the end of the judgment. Stories relying on the first trio of sources would apparently pass the circumstantial test, while the second trio would not:

[I]t is one thing to publish a statement taken from a government press release, or the report of a public company chairman, or the speech of a university vice-chancellor, and quite another to publish the statement of a political opponent, or a business competitor or a disgruntled ex-employee.[47]

The couplings are presumably intended as an illustration of principle rather than an exhaustive exposition of rules. Nonetheless, a dichotomous test of this nature rather seems to 'depoliticise' political information by refusing to acknowledge that politics is an adversarial, partisan and often disreputable business. In Lord Bingham's strange political fantasy world there is presumably no such thing as a government cover-up, or a government press release designed to discredit opposition parties and politicians, or a public company taking part in an illegal cartel. And, by the same token, a politician's opponents can never expose her hitherto hidden failings, Freddie Laker in the 1980s and Richard Branson in the 1990s were hallucinating when they accused British Airways of predatory pricing, and no government employee has ever resigned or been dismissed because she has uncovered corruption or illegality in the administration of public services. The dichotomy is simply a nonsense.

Nonsensical or no, the consequences of Lord Bingham's reasoning are severe. If information is not drawn from a *prima facie* authoritative source, a privileged

---

[44] [1998] 3 All ER 961 at 994–5.

[45] *Ibid.*, at 995. Lord Bingham considered 'malice' to have been authoritatively defined by Lord Diplock in *Horrocks* v. *Lowe*: see 95–6 above.

[46] N. 44 above, at 1004.

[47] *Ibid.*, at 1004.

occasion does not arise. If that is so, there is no need to move on to the question of malice. The publisher is liable for the dissemination of false and defamatory material even if he/she not only believed it to be true but took every reasonable precaution to establish its truth. The defence would thus have been of no use at all to *The Guardian* in the *Aitken* or *Hamilton* cases, as its primary sources in those stories were the manifestly non-authoritative assertions of assorted shady arms dealing middlemen (*Aitken*) and Mohammed Al-Fayed (*Hamilton*), a man evidently so lacking in moral scruple that the present Home Secretary considers him unworthy of British citizenship. That the paper may have done all it possibly could to corroborate these claims is apparently of no relevance in Lord Bingham's test.[48]

The court also asserted that '[w]e question whether in practice this is a test very different from the test of reasonableness upheld in Australia [in *Lange*]'.[49] This is a curious statement, as the two tests are obviously quite different. *Lange* gives no indication that the issue of reasonableness goes predominantly to the ostensible reliability of the source of political information. As noted in Chapter 8, there is some suggestion that Brennan J had such a test in mind in his dissenting judgment in *Stephens*, but those tentative intimations had altogether disappeared in *Lange*. Nor is such reasoning evident in those few American common law decisions which imposed a negligence test. All these authorities approach 'reasonable' as a facet of malice—reliance on a source of even the most dubious repute does not *per se* negate the reciprocal interest/duty between the publisher and the audience to disseminate and consume the political information. Similarly, the most pertinent ECtHR judgment—*Lingens*—draws no distinction between 'authoritative' and 'non-authoritative' sources in its definition of political information.

This may be because such a distinction is so nebulous and elusive that it could never be articulated in a form that satisfied Article 10's provision that any restraints on freedom of expression be 'prescribed by law'. But it is equally possible that the ECtHR accepted—as have the Australian and American courts—that the distinction makes no sense when applied to the practicalities of political life in a modern, multi-party democratic nation, in which political information is likely to come from all manner of sources. This point was made quite forcefully by the New Zealand Court of Appeal in *Lange* when it approved Elias J's rejection of the 'authoritative source' rule at first instance; 'in the marketplace of ideas it seems to me invidious and dangerous to make judgments that free speech is not served except by those with special knowledge'.[50]

What is even more peculiar is that Lord Bingham does not actually apply his own test to the facts of *Reynolds*. At the end of the judgment, he suggests that

---

[48] Lord Bingham's evident antipathy to the idea that the press should be encouraged to investigate the integrity of politicians is perhaps best summarised by a comment at 1005, when he suggested that allegations that a businessman had corrupted a serving politician were part of 'the small change of political controversy'.

[49] *Ibid.*, at 1005.

[50] [1998] 3 NZLR 424 at 434.

the story failed the 'circumstantial test' because the accusation that Reynolds lied came from a junior member of Dick Spring's entourage, rather than from the former Foreign Minister himself. The obvious inference is that Mr Spring would have been an authoritative source. Yet he was by the relevant time, having withdrawn from the coalition government, one of Mr Reynolds' 'political opponents'—a group whose comments Lord Bingham had said cannot be relied upon.

If Lord Bingham had adopted this 'authoritative source' rule as simply one potentially relevant component part of a wider, multi-faceted negligent falsity test, it would have been an unobjectionable, albeit novel, attempt to pull English common law into line with with contemporary notions of democratic constitutionalism. A test of that sort would also have enjoyed a (limited) common law pedigree, ranging from Cockburn CJ's dicta in *Campbell* v. *Spottiswoode*, through dissenting judgments in *Briggs* v. *Garrett*,[51] to Cooke J's evident but unindulged preferences in *Templeton* and to Brennan J's formula in *Lange*. But as it stands, the test makes little sense. In one (narrow) respect it is too protective of false speech, for it seems to absolve the defendant from any substantial responsibility to consider whether the 'authoritative source' is telling lies. Yet by denying most sources of information 'authoritative' status, it has little discernible impact on the chilling effect of libel law.

If one looks very hard, the Court of Appeal's judgment *Reynolds* did produce a (very) modest reform to our defamation laws in the direction of hindering recovery in political libel actions. It offered a hitherto unavailable defence to the non-malicious publisher of false but authoritatively sourced factual assertions. What it most certainly did not do was extend the protection granted by the English common law to political libels to a level comparable with that available in Australia, New Zealand and the USA.

REYNOLDS IN THE HOUSE OF LORDS

In the House of Lords, a 3–2 majority broadly upheld the Court of Appeal's decision. The leading judgment was written by Lord Nicholls of Birkenhead.[52] Unusually in the English context, Lord Nicholls claimed to take as his analytical starting point the need for the common law to assist electors in making informed choices about who should govern their country:

> [F]reedom to disseminate and receive information on political matters is essential to the proper functioning of the system of parliamentary democracy cherished in this

---

[51] The leading Pennsylvanian case on the issue: see 43–5 above.

[52] Lord Nicholls' judgment was supported by Lords Cooke and Hobhouse. Lords Hope and Steyn dissented, but on narrow grounds sepcific to the facts of *Reynolds* itself. They were supportive of the broad thrust of the majority opinion. For a more detailed treatment of the judgment than is offered here see Loveland I. (2000) *Reynolds* v. *Times Newspapers* in the House of Lords' *Public Law* (forthcoming).

country. This freedom enables those who elect representatives to Parliament [sic] to make an informed choice. . . .[53]

Such sentiments might suggest that the Court was about to subject English libel law to the type of innovative, constitutionally driven reform already established in the USA, Canada, or New Zealand. But while aspects of the way in which Lord Nicholls presented his judgment seemed to break radically with English orthodoxies, the result he eventually produced and the details of his reasoning were altogether more modest affairs. Lord Nicholls' judgment focused on two questions. The first was whether 'political information' should attract a generic claim to qualified privilege. The second, if the first were answered in the negative, was whether publishers of individual stories covering political issues might be able to invoke the defence, and if so under what conditions would the defence be available?

Lord Nicholls was clearly unimpressed by the Court of Appeal's 'circumstantial test', and concluded that such a device had no role to play in modern libel law. This did not mean however that he accepted that all political information would therefore come within the reach of the qualified privilege defence. While rejecting the circumstantial test, Lord Nicholls advanced a much more restrictive, ad hoc notion of 'political information'. Lord Nicholls was not persuaded to accept that political information—in the broad sense (borrowed from the Australian High Court in *Lange*) adopted by the Court of Appeal—should be regarded as a 'category' or 'generic class' of presumptively protected material. Rather, he concluded that political information would only fall within the reach of the defence; 'if the public was entitled to know the information'.[54] This was, he acknowledged, an 'elastic test', which required case by case scrutiny of each story for which privilege was claimed. While this might inject an element of uncertainty into the law, Lord Nicholls felt this was—if intrinsically undesirable—then a lesser evil than adopting the generic test. That would, he suggested, lead to too much false information being published. The electorate (and the courts) could not rely upon the press to take sufficient care in checking the factual accuracy its stories; 'the sad reality is that the overall handling of these matters by the national press, with its own commercial interests to serve, does not always command general confidence'.[55]

His Lordship had no confidence in the *Sunday Times'* handling of the Reynolds story. He concluded that the Court of Appeal had been correct in holding that the claim for privilege should not be made at the new trial. The primary jusitification for this conclusion seemed to be that the paper had not presented its readers with a balanced view of the episode, since it had not alluded to Mr Reynolds' explanation for his conduct; 'these serious allegations by the newspaper, presented as statements of fact but shorn of all mention of Mr

---

[53] [1999] 4 All ER 609 at 621.
[54] *Ibid.*, at 622.
[55] *Ibid.*, at 623.

Reynolds' considered explanation, were not information the public had a right to know'.[56]

That Lord Nicholls abolished the Court of Appeal's circumstantial test but nonetheless supported the result it had reached might suggest that this sentiment was an innovation more of form than of substance. His approach is obviously problematic, in so far as it demands that the publisher's motive and level of awareness as to truth be considered at the 'reach' stage of the trial court's inquiry. Lord Nicholls listed ten illustrative factors relevant to deciding if an occasion of privilege has arisen. Several of these criteria directly address the issue of how much care the publisher has taken to establish if factual claims are true—for example;

3. The source of the information
4. The steps taken to verify the information
7. Whether comment was sought from the defendant.[57]

In the USA, Australia and New Zealand such questions are not part of the 'reach' inquiry at all, but are considered when assessing if the publisher has demonstrated 'malice' in the various senses that those countries use that term. Lord Nicholls suggests that where and one one ask these questions is of no particular importance:

> there seems to be no significant practical difference between looking at all the circumstances to decide if a publication attracts privilege, and looking at all the circumstances to see if an acknowledged privilege is defeated.[58]

But it might be argued that the issue of the location of these factors has two important consequences. The first arises because, under English law, determining if an occasion of privilege arises is a matter for the judge; assessing malice is a question for the jury. Put simply, where one puts the test determines who would answer it. More significantly, if such factors fall within the second ('contents/effect') stage of the inquiry, they are being applied in a situation where the presumptive importance of the information has already been established. The *Reynolds* test, by assigning them to the reach question of the importance of the information itself necessarily devalues the substance of that information.

It would be inaccurate to suggest that all Lord Nicholls has done is relocate the Court of Appeal's circumstantial test into an earlier part of the court's decision-making equation. He did stress—importantly—that the presumptive lack of 'authority' of the defendant's sources is not in itself a reason for holding that an occasion of privilege has not arisen. Nor should a defendant's refusal to divulge its sources necessarily play even a contributory role in establishing that publication was not reasonable. These are significant modifications. But they

---

[56] *Ibid.*, at 627.
[57] *Ibid.*, at 626.
[58] *Ibid.*, at 624.

ameliorate rather than remove the problems inherent in the Court of Appeals's judgment.

Lord Nicholls' conclusion on the facts would suggest that those parts of his judgment which seemed—in rhetorical terms—to assign an enhanced importance to the dissemination of political information should be taken with more than a pinch of salt. Lord Nicholls urged that, having considered all the factors relevant to determining if publication should be protected, a trial court:

> should have particular regard to the importance of freedom of expression. The press discharges vital functions as a bloodhound as well as a watchdog. The court should be slow to conclude that a publication was not in the public interest and, therefore, the public had no right to know, especially when the information is in the field of political discussion. Any lingering doubts should be resolved in favour of publication.[59]

Lord Nicholls' evident wish to retain the motive of personal spite as a sufficient basis on which to conclude that information was published maliciously is also difficult to reconcile with his professed concern to ehance the electorate's capacity to make informed decisions on political issues.[60] Spite would apparently suffice even if the defendant honestly and reasonably believed the asserted factual claims to be true. Most, perhaps all, partisan political information is intended to 'damage' particular politicians either by influencing electors to vote against them or to vote in favour of other candidates. From the audience's interest, spite is an irrelevance; it has no necessary bearing on the likelihood that the disseminated information is true. As noted above, this point was recognised by the Australian High Court in *Lange*, and has long been accepted in the USA. A publisher known to be involved in a political feud with a particular politician would be ill-advised to rely on the *Reynolds* formulation of qualified privilege, as the jury would be offered copious evidence that the publisher's desire to inform the electorate was but a subsidiary motive for dissemination.

A further unfortunate feature of Lord Nicholl's judgment was his refusal to accept that the 'effect' or 'contents' element of the orthodox qualified privilege test could sensibly be altered. Lord Nicholls is obviously correct in asserting that; 'Malice is notoriously difficult to prove'.[61] But the correctness of this assertion might readily be thought to prompt the suggestion that we should therefore, in political libel cases, make malice less difficult to prove. As noted in earlier chapters, this was a step taken by many American state jurisdictions around the turn of the century, and—more obviously and recently—by the Australian High Court in *Lange*.

There is no compelling reason for the House of Lords not to have followed this lead. Lord Lester QC, for the paper, had offered as one fallback position if his primary contention was rejected, the suggestion that the effect of qualified

---

[59] *Ibid.*, at 626.

[60] 'Freedom of speech does not embrace the freedom to make defamatory statements out of personal spite'; *ibid.*, at 622. His Lordship presumably meant false defamatory statements, since truth can of course be defamatory.

[61] *Ibid.*

privilege in political libel cases might be diluted by placing the burden of proof as to malice on the defendant. Lord Nicholls rejected this idea; 'if this shift of the onus were acepted generally, it would turn the law of qualified privilege upside down'.[62] Quite why Lord Nicholls felt it necessary to portray Lord Lester's argument as one of general rather than particular application is something of a mystery. There is no obvious reason why such a change could not readily be confined to political libel questions, leaving all other applications of the defence—to information which has no political dimension—unchanged.

That Lord Nicholls reached all these rather conservative conclusions seems largely attributable to his methodology. The judgment creates the impression that Lord Nicholls' rhetoric about the importance of informed electoral consent to governance was not firmly connected to his detailed reasoning; that his analysis had slipped back into the traditional format evident in most English political libel judgments—namely balancing the politican's right to reputation against the press' right to publish. There is no doubt that the House of Lords—and indeed the Court of Appeal—in *Reynolds* accepted that the electorate's interest in consuming political information should *inform* the way the balance was struck. But neither court accepted—as have their counterparts in the USA, Australia and New Zealand—that this concern should *determine* the balance.

This point is perhaps best illustrated by the way in which Lord Nicholls used some of the classic nineteenth century English cases on political libels. As suggested in earlier chapters, the ratios of *Wason* and *Purcell* were narrow.[63] But the judgments can readily be seen as extremely radical assertions of the informed consent principle, given the very primitive understanding of democratic governance which then prevailed in British society. A contemporary judgment that was faithful to the principles underlying those two cases would have to extend their ratios considerably, simply to keep pace with the much more sophisticated understanding of democracy to which our society now adheres.

But in *Reynolds*, Lord Nicholls treated *Wason* and *Purcell* in much the same way as had the Court of Appeal in *Blackshaw* v. *Lord*; the narrow ratio of each case was plucked from the judgment without any consideration being given to the political context in which that ratio was formed. Lord Nicholls' use of *Webb* was similarly selective. He made no mention at all of Pearson J.'s innovative obiter suggestion that the common law should recognise a defence of 'fair information on a matter of public interest', but simply represented the case as one which rejected the contention that fair and accurate reportage of any foreign court proceedings should attract qualifed privilege.

As one might expect, Lord Nicholls also upheld the long-established English judicial tradition of misrepresenting *Sullivan*. While he avoided the myth that *Sullivan* provides complete protection for the press, Lord Nicholls did tell us— quite incorrectly—that it produced a rule applicable to all 'public figures' generally. Similarly, Lord Nicholls maintained that *Sullivan's* 'actual malice' rule

---

[62] *Ibid.*, at 624.
[63] On *Wason*, see 26–30 above. On *Purcell*, see 30–2 above.

was derived from the First and Fourteenth Amendments to the constitution. That the rule is actually derived—via *Coleman*—from *Wason* v. *Walter* is a point of legal history which has yet to impress itself upon the British judiciary. Both misrepresentations undermine *Sullivan*'s cogency as a source for influencing the development of English common law: the first by suggesting the case goes to impractical extremes; the second by assuming the actual malice formula is a supra-legislative concept, and therefore alien to the English constitutional tradition.

Lord Nicholls also offered a peculiar interpretation of *Lingens*. As suggested in Chapter 6, the ECtHR's primary concern in that case was to draw a clear distinction between the way in which domestic legal systems treated political and non-political libels. As well as stressing that dichotomy, the Court had added— almost as an afterthought—that a distinction also had to be drawn between assertions of fact and expressions of opinion. In *Reynolds*, Lord Nicholls appeared to elevate this marginal fact/opinion dichotomy to be the key holding of *Lingens*, while downplaying the political/non-political distinction.

CONCLUSION

In the immediate aftermath of the House of Lords' *Reynolds* judgment, a solicitor for the *Sunday Times* was perhaps putting a brave face on events by commenting that the paper had won a 'significant victory'. Geoffrey Robinson's comment in *The Guardian*, to the effect that the Lords were 'tiptoeing towards free speech' was nearer the mark,[64] as was the 'cautious welcome' extended to the decision by Alan Rusbridger, the editor of *The Guardian*.[65]

The unfortunate irony of the House of Lords majority opinions in *Reynolds* is that the result that they have reached on the particular facts of the case— namely that the *Sunday Times* should not be protected by qualified privilege— is surely correct. But that result has been reached through a route almost as conceptually and (thus constitutionally) unsatisfactory as that followed in the Court of Appeal. The *Sunday Times'* behaviour in respect of the story was reprehensible, in that its Irish and English editions offered their readers two quite different versions of events: in the Irish edition Mr Reynolds was the hapless victim of circumstance; to readers in Britain he was portrayed as a wilful liar. In those circumstances, the paper's claim that it did not know the London story was false, or was not recklessly indifferent to its truth, has no credibility. Mr Reynolds could plausibly expect to win his case even if he had to surmount—as in New Zealand—the orthodox qualified privilege defence. He certainly would have recovered under the Australian test. And it is even arguable that he would win under the *Sullivan* rule.

---

[64] October 29 1999.
[65] *Ibid.*

But in all three of those jurisdictions he would win on the basis of a legal test which is much more securely and sensibly founded than the one applied in this country. In the final chapter of this book, some suggestions are offered that might lead to a more conceptually coherent common law approach to the problem of political libels; an approach which—while sensitive to the freedom of the press and the reputations of politicians—takes as its beginning, middle and end the quintessentially constitutional law point that the courts' dominant priority when faced with litigation initiated to restrict public dissemination of political material is to protect the principle that electors be afforded the maximum opportunity to exercise informed consent to the process of governance.

10

Conclusion

Any suggestion that English courts should develop the English common law of libel along American, Australian or New Zealand lines is one that derives from notions of political desirability rather than legal necessity. In opposing any such reform, it might perhaps be argued that English common law has arrived at the correct solution, while courts in many other parts of the English speaking world have been unknowingly seduced by the beguiling rhetoric of free speech extremism. That argument does however seem rather fanciful, and it is by no means a radical proposal to suggest that the time has now come for English courts to give a much more measured and sophisticated consideration to the importation of a variation of the *Sullivan* defence than they have done thus far.

Arguments as to political desirability have however been rather overtaken by considerations of legal necessity flowing from the enactment of the Human Rights Act 1998, which, after a fashion, 'incorporates' much of the European Convention into domestic law.[1] When it comes into force, the Act will essentially oblige domestic courts to ensure that the common law on all freedom of speech issues is compatible with Article 10. As noted in chapter 6, the margin of appreciation which Article 10 extends to signatory States is generally substantial. There is no obvious indication in the ECHR's case law that those margins would be narrowly drawn in respect of the the political libel issue. Nonetheless, it seems scarcely credible to suggest that the barely discernible distinction between political and private libels drawn by the Court of Appeal in *Reynolds* would meet the Convention's requirements, and little more credible that the House of Lords' subsequent tinkering with that distinction will achieve the necessary result. In order to comply with Article 10, the common law will presumably have to recognise a significant substantive distinction in the legal regimes regulating the two types of defamatory material. That innovation will have to address two questions. What *reach* should be accorded to any new defence? And what should be its *effect*?

THE QUESTION OF REACH—DEFINING 'POLITICAL' INFORMATION

It was suggested in chapter five that the decision produced by the majority of the US Supreme Court in *Hill* v. *Time Inc*[2] offered an absurd, indefensible position

---

[1] See Tierney, S. (1998) 'The Human Rights Bill' *European Public Law* 299: Ewing, K. (1999) 'The Human Rights Act and Parliamentary Democracy *Modern Law Review* 79: N. Bamforth (1998) 'Parliamentary Sovereignty and the Human Rights Act 1998' *Public Law* 572.
[2] (1967) 385 US 374.

for the law of defamation[3] to adopt. The judgment cast aside any concern with political accountability as a justification for defending freedom of expression, and—in what seems to have been a state of post-*Sullivan*[4] free speech euphoria—settled on the unhappy notion of 'newsworthiness' as the trigger for granting extensive legal protection to mendacious journalism. *Hill* has perhaps done much to discredit *Sullivan* in other parts of the English speaking world, and the alacrity which the US Supreme backtracked from the *Hill* position is itself a good indication of the judgment's untenable conclusion.

Sullivan itself had a very narrow reach. It is far less expansive than *Coleman*, and in concentrating on the political capabilities and qualifications of elected politicans seems to be in quite close correspondence with *Lingens*[5]. It would thus seem to offer an attractive solution for English law to adopt; any new defence could be imposed only on occupants[6] of elected political office—in either central, devolved, or local government—and could accept that even individuals in that position retained an inner core of 'private identity'. An extension of the defence (*per Monitor Patriot*) to candidates for such office would also presumably be unproblematic.[7]

Yet it is readily apparent that an elected office test makes little sense in a constitutional context in which some of the most powerful political offices are gained through appointment rather than election. Almost half of the members of Parliament and several members of the Cabinet (namely all those sitting in the House of Lords) would not fall *strictu sensu* within the *Sullivan* test. They would however obviously be political figures in the *Lingens* sense, and so would have to be drawn within the new defence.

This points towards a presumption that any individual who exercises lawmaking authority should be recognised as a 'politician' for these purposes. Adoption of this criteria would (per *Salinger* v. *Cowes*[8] and *Garrison* v. *Lousiana*[9] but contra *Barfod*[10]) indicate that holders of judicial office would caught by the new provisions, notwithstanding that many such offices are presumed to filled by occupants who have foresworn any party political affiliation.

That a party political identity might be unnecessary for a person to be a 'politician' for defamation law purposes leads us towards a more problematic element of the reach question—namely the status of appointed officials. It is evident that many such individuals exercise significant political power, be they high ranking members of the police or armed services, senior civil servants within government departments, chief executives of next steps agencies or local authorities, or directors of less overtly party political bodies in areas such as sport and the arts. There

---

[3] Although, as noted in chapter 5, *Hill* was strictu sensu not a libel action.
[4] *Sullivan* v. *New York Times* (1964) 376 US 374.
[5] *Lingens* v. *Austria* [1986] 8 EHRR 407.
[6] And one assumes to former occupants.
[7] Although this would apply only after candidacy had been declared.
[8] (1992) 191 NW 167.
[9] (1964) 379 US 64.
[10] *Barford* v. *Denmark* (1989) 11 EHHR 493.

is no obvious functional reason why public appointees who control substantial programmes of governmental activity, or dispense substantial sums of government money, should enjoy some 'talismanic immunity' from the political figure test.[11] The oft-aired hypothesis that exposure to media scrutiny would deter well-qualified candidates from seeking such office—to the general detriment of society as a whole—is just a hypothesis, and one that could only be evaluated in the domestic context by introducing reform and then observing the results.

This type of 'substantial governmental responsibility' test offers a dividing line with blurred edges, although one would not expect the courts to experience any difficulty in concluding that the plaintiff in *Blackshaw* v. *Lord*[12] occupied such a position.[13] But domestic courts are now well versed in the intricacies of drawing a public/private dichotomy in several areas of law, and will be asked to do so again when the Human Rights Act comes into force.[14] To introduce an additional, similar distinction into defamation law is unlikely to create significant difficulties for the administration of justice.

Any new defence premised on notions of 'political' accountability would also have to pay heed to the fact that in recent years many traditionally 'governmental' activities have been handed over to nominally private sector bodies. The privatisation of the power, water and rail industries have placed formerly political responsibilites wholly in commercial hands, while the growth in the contracting-out of formerly public sector activities to commercial organisations has created a situation in which citizens can claim a legitimate interest in being informed of the integrity and competence of such organisations' activities. This would suggest that in so far as businessmen and women choose to pursue profit by providing public services they should expect to be subject to vigorous (and well-protected) media scrutiny. Owen Oyston's involvement with Derbyshire County Council's pension funds should surely have made embroiled him in a 'political' issue for libel law purposes. The argument would seem similarly plausible in respect of the action brought by Guy Snowden, the businessman employed by Camelot to run the national lottery, against Richard Branson over the latter's allegations that Snowden had offered him a bribe to withdraw his bid to win the lottery franchise.[15]

---

[11] See for example my discussion of the action initiated by Tim Brighouse, Birmingham Director of Eduction against John Patten, then Secretary of State for Education, over Patten's allegations that Brighouse was utterly unfit to hold such a post. Patten paid substantial damages to settle the case; Loveland, I. (1997) 'An agenda for the constitutionalisation of political libels', in Birks, P. (ed.), *Privacy and loyalty* (Oxford: Clarendon Press). The plaintiff in *Blackshaw* v. *Lord* would seem to have been a sufficiently senior civil servant to come within this category.

[12] [1984] 1 QB 9.

[13] A perhaps more difficult example is posed by Dr Frank Skuse's case against Granada TV. Skuse, fromerly a senior forsensic scientist at the Home Office, was accused in a tv programme of gross incompetence in his work during the Birmingham Six trial, incompetence which played a major part in the defendants' conviction. See *The Guardian*, 10 January 1996.

[14] As the Act will apply only to the actions of 'public authorities', a concept which is not further defined in the legislation itself.

[15] On the background to the case see *The Times* 13 December 1995. In the ensuing trial, Branson successfully pleaded justification for his claims.

The 'vortex of public controversy' plaintiff would seem similarly unproblematic. Mohammed Al-Fayed's alleged bribery of assorted Conservative MPs was an intensely political activity. A less acute example of such a situation would be provided by Victoria Gillick's libel action against the BBC over comments linking the suicides of several pregnant teenagers with her campaign against providing contraception to young women. Gillick did not hold either elected or appointed government office. She was in almost all respects a private figure. This particular case arose however because she voluntarily thrust herself firmly into the vortex of a major public controversy. She did not limit her activities to the pursuit of court action, nor did she make any attempt to shun the media publicity that her campaign attracted. It would surely be an exercise in 'legal alchemy' to depoliticise political campaigns for defamation law purposes simply because their proponents do not occupy public office.

There would however seem to be little defensible scope for extending the reach of any new defence beyond 'political' matters to embrace merely newsworthy issues, even if the protagonists have become involved in such events voluntarily. The dietary habits of rock stars have no bearing on the formation and implementation of government policy or the husbandry of public money. It might be thought a profoundly undesirable use of the legal system's resources to have a judge and jury occupied for many days with the question of whether former England cricketers Ian Botham and Alan Lamb had falsely accused Imran Khan of cheating.[16] It might seem still more absurd that the Court of Appeal should find itself hearing an action brought by the actor/director Steven Berkoff against the journalist Julie Burchill over her suggestion that he was 'hideously ugly'.[17] A *Sullivan* defence for defamers of celebrities might have the welcome effect of freeing our judges to spend their time on less trivial matters, but it could hardly be thought to contribute to the health and dynamicism of our political culture.

This line of argument appears to have led us to the reach test adopted in *Lange* (Australia). That test goes substantially beyond *Sullivan*, and offers a definition of 'political' driven by the substance of the story rather than by the identity of the plaintiff. It should thus be stressed that even elected politicians can expect to retain a limited zone of 'private life' if a reform of this nature were adopted. And as the identity of the plaintiff changes from elected politican to appointed official to political activist to businesswomen so the proportion of her life in respect of which she has surrendered her privacy to the demands of public scrutiny will decline. A realignment of libel law principles in a way that affords

---

[16] The case ran for more than a week in July 1996. See *The Observer* 21 July 1996.

[17] [1996] 4 All ER 1008. The case had reached the Court of Appeal on the *preliminary* issue of whether or not calling someone 'hideously ugly' could bear a defamatory meaning. At first instance, Sir Maurice Drake concluded that it could. In the Court of Appeal, the majority agreed with this decision. Millet LJ evidently took a more sensible view; 'If I have treated Mr Berkoff's claim with unjudicial levity it is because I find it impossible to take seriously . . . [T]he proceedings are as frivolous as Miss Burchill's article. The time of the court ought not to be taken up with either of them'; *ibid*., at 1020.

greater protection to the dissemination of political information need not place all aspects of any individual's life permanently in a goldfish bowl subject to unrelenting and unscrupulous media scrutiny.

Determining the effect that should be accorded to a new defence for political libels is perhaps a less difficult matter than settling on its reach. The most extreme solution—and the one with nothing to commend it—is the position adopted in *Chicago*[18], by Goldberg/Black and Douglas JJ in *Sullivan* and by Deane J in *Theophanous*; namely a complete bar on any 'defamation'[19] action. The allegations levelled against Michael Foot by *The Sunday Times* in 1995 illustrate the undesirable practical consequences—that would flow from adopting this solution. A front page lead story maintained that Foot had been a Soviet spy. In Foot's view, the article was objectionable not simply because of the slur it cast on his own reputation, but because it was also likely to undermine the Labour party's electoral fortunes by implying that its senior ranks were infiltrated by communist sympathisers. As such, it damaged Foot, members of his party, and all Labour supporters. The only 'evidence' the paper had for its story was an allegation by Oleg Gordievsky, a former Soviet agent who has been regaling the British media with evermore outlandish stories since his defection to this country.

Foot commenced proceedings immediately. *The Sunday Times* moved with similar speed in offering a settlement, evidently accepting that its story lacked any plausible foundation (and so by implication that it regarded Gordievsky as a thoroughly unreliable source). The paper's position is difficult to fathom. The interesting question—to which Mr Foot would have had no opportunity to get a court to gve us an answer if the *Goldberg* rationale were adopted—was whether its editorial team knew the accusations were a lie and published regardless, calculating that Foot would not sue; or whether they were simply reckless or negligent in failing to given any serious consideration to the accuracy of Gordievsky's claims.

One might intuitively regard *The Sunday Times*' behaviour in this episode as thoroughly reprehensible. One might also initially assume that it was just such outrageous falsehoods that Brennan J in *Sullivan* and Mason CJ in *Theophanous* had in mind when they declined to fashion an absolute bar to political libel actions. But it is by no means clear that Michael Foot would have succeeded in his libel action had these events occurred in the USA or (post-*Lange*) in New Zealand. We might assume for the moment that the paper did not know that the Gordievsky's claims were a lie. The answer to the question of whether publication nevertheless amounted to reckless falsity as *Sullivan* used

---

[18] (1923) 139 NE 87.
[19] The term is used loosely to include malicious falsehood.

that term or to a lack of honest belief within *Lange* is obscure, as a matter both of law and fact.

It should of course be recalled that a plaintiff who sues and wins under *Sullivan* or *Lange* (New Zealand) will not just vindicate her own reputation. Equally importantly, she will substantially undermine the reputation of the defendant, thereby—if it is a newspaper or broadcaster—alerting its customers and the general public to its cavalier disregard for the truth of its stories and perhaps lessening the likelihood that people will trust its reporting in future.[20]

These are valuable public interest considerations, but they can only be well served if speech tort laws are not so heavily stacked against the falsely impugned plaintiff that she is not unduly—to use familiar terminology in an unusual sense—'chilled' from beginning proceedings at all. *Sullivan* and *Lange* set the test too high. A plaintiff facing these obstacles who considers she could demonstrate negligence (perhaps even gross negligence) on the publisher's part knows she would lose. She is unlikely to regard the substantial inconvenience and financial costs that such a defeat would entail as being adequately compensated by the fact that a court has publicly confirmed that a publisher was careless in assessing the reliability of his allegations.

For these reasons, the *Derbyshire*[21] principle of restricting political plaintiffs to actions in malicious falsehood also seems unduly indulgent of mendacious speech. Allowing recovery only for economic loss ignores the fact that voters' interests are damaged by the dissemination of information which falsely traduces a politician's political reputation.[22]

This book has offered a pervasive argument which has been critical of the general failure of English judges and legislators to recognise that a political libel should more properly be seen as raising an issue of constitutional rather than tort law. It is therefore perhaps something of a paradox to suggest that the most propitious way to 'constitutionalise' defamation laws would be to bring them rather more closely into line with the more 'ordinary' causes of action available in tort.

This re-alignment would be rather modest. One might retain the fiction that the plaintiff's loss of reputation flows automatically from the publication of defamatory material. We might also keep the anomolous presumption that it

---

[20] An equally compelling example is offered by a Conservative party political broadcast on television in 1994 which told such outrageous and readily discoverable lies about a Labour-controlled local authority that one cannot possibly conceive that their disseminators though them true: see Birmingham Ire at Tory Travesty' (1994) *Independent on Sunday* 4 April. Under *Derbyshire*, the defamed council could not sue in libel. Nor, under *Bhoyrul*, could the Labour Party do so. No councillors chose to begin an action.

[21] *Derbyshire County Council* v. *Times Newspapers* [1993] 1 All ER 1014.,

[22] It would seem quite plausible to suggest that Michael Foot could not have established a loss of this sort, given that he was retired from the Commons and presumably derives most of his income from journalism for publications which would have considered *The Sunday Times'* allegations quite ludicrous. Whether a reduction in a prospective MP's chances of winning a seat in the Commons could be regarded as a recoverable loss in malicious falsehood is an interesting but unanswered question.

should be for the defendant to prove truth rather than for the plaintiff to establish falsity in respect of the justification defence. The crucial reform would be to reject the current law's insistence that liability in defamation is strict. And this rejection could itself be cast in very modest terms. We might for example not embrace the usual tort law presumption that it is for the plaintiff to prove fault on the defendant's part. All that the common law need do to alert individuals who choose to involve themselves in 'political' activities to the fact that the electorate has a substantial interest in encouraging press investigation of their integrity and competence is to provide that their claims would fail if the defendant proved she was not negligent in investigating the truth of any allegations made.

We thus seem to have arrived once more if not quite at *Lange*[23] (Australia) then in very close proximity to it. The 'right to reply' component of the *Lange* defence would not survive scrutiny under the rigorous standards of the First Amendment.[24] It would however seem to serve a useful political function, in that it enhances the flow of pertinent information to the electorate.

English courts could not of course go much further afield in the geographical sense in search of a detailed guide for the development of English defamation law. It also seems that the route which *Lange* followed to its eventual destination was exotic both in jurisdictional terms—trailing as it did through the USA, Canada and the ECHR—and in a jurisprudential sense—given its preoccupation with identifying the appropriate limits of both common law and supra-legislative legal principle. And like *Sullivan* (or *Coleman*[25], or *Lingens*) before it, *Lange* (Australia) rests on skimpy empirical foundations. There is little empirical evidence as to the precise impact of the 'chilling effect' on political journalism, whether in the USA, the United Kingdom Western Europe, Australia or New Zealand.[26] This may indeed prove to be an empirical phenomenon which defies any attempts at detailed calibration;[27] which means of coure that the current English law is similarly lacking a defensible empirical base.

One would thus seem compelled to return to theoretical surmises as to the relative importance of a 'politician's' entitlement to expect the law to deter attacks

---

[23] *Lange* v. *ABC* (1997) 71 ALJR 818.

[24] A Florida law insisting on a right to reply to defamatory articles was struck down by a unanimous Supreme Court in *Miami Herald* v. *Tornillo* (1974) 418 US 241.

[25] *Coleman* v. *McClennan* (1908) 98 PAC 281.

[26] The most helpful study in the United Kingdom context is offered by Barendt, E., Lustgarten, L., Norrie, K. and Stephenson, H. (1997) *Libel and the Media*; see especially pp 60–70 in which the authors report a considerable amount of qualitative data which suggests that many journalists and editors on national newspapers have slipped into an almost sub-conscious pattern of self-censorship in respect of potentially defamatory stories. See also the more modest study conducted by Weaver, R. and Bennet, G. (1993) 'Is the New York Times "Actual Malice" Standard Really Necessary? A Comparative Perspective' *Louisiana LR* 1154.

[27] Not least because any researchers who reported in any detail why a particular story was 'censored' would themselves be likely to end up libelling the political figure concerned. It would perhaps be foolhardy for such researchers to assume their findings would benefit from the qualified privilege defence.

on her reputation with the electorate's entitlement to be provided with as much accurate information as possible about her fitness to discharge governmental responsibilities. To borrow Pearson LJ's intuitive methodology in *McCarey*;[28] 'It is in the end a matter of impression, and I cannot resist the impression that the present rules interfere much, much too severely with freedom of political expression'.

Whether a new defence was to be labelled as a variant of qualified privilege, or designated as a free standing defence of 'political expression' is an issue of limited significance. What is important is that English courts now take the opportunity to reflect more carefully and informedly on the political purposes that the common law ought to serve in a society whose constitutional structure and democratic culture have evolved to a maturity unthinkable one hundred years ago. To maintain that the 'common convenience and welfare' of that society do not demand that the common law draws a sharp disinction between libels of politicians and private citizens is to laud the values of an archaic political morality—and to deny the presumption that those who govern deserve to do so only if they continue to attract the informed consent of the electorate.

---

[28] *McCarey* v. *Associated Newspapers Ltd.* [1964] 3 All ER 147. See 128 above.

Bibliography

Bailyn, B. (1967) *The Ideological Roots of the American Revolution* (Cambridge, Mass: Harvard University Press)

Bamforth, N. (1998) 'Parliamentary Sovereignty and the Human Rights Act 1998' *Public Law* 572

Barendt, E. (1993) 'Libel and Freedom of Speech in English Law' *Public Law* 449

—— (1998) 'The Importation of United States Free Speech Jurisprudence', in Loveland (ed.) *infra.*

Barendt, E., Lustgarten, L., Norrie, K. and Stephenson, H. (1997) *Libel and the Media: the Chilling Effect* (Oxford: Clarendon Press)

Bass, J. (1993) *Taming the Storm* (New York: Anchor Books)

Brazier, M. (1993 9th ed) *Street on Torts* (London: Butterworths)

Brennan, W. (1965) 'The Supreme Court and the Meiklejohn View of the First Amendment' 79 *Harvard LR* 1

Carter, Ruck P. (1992 4th ed) *Libel and Slander* (London: Butterworths)

Cowling, M. (1967) *1867: Disraeli, Gladstone and Revolution* (Cambridge: CUP)

Dias, R. and Markesinis, B. (1984) *Tort Law* (Oxford: Clarendon Press)

Duncan, C. and Neill, B. (1978) *Defamation* (London: Butterworths)

Ewing, K. (1993) 'New Constitutional Restraints in Australia' *Public Law* 256

—— (1998) 'The Human Rights Act and Parliamentary Democracy' 61 *Modern LR* 79

Ewing, K. and Gearty, C. (1989) *Civil Liberties Under Thatcher* (Oxford: OUP)

Feldman, D. (1998) 'Content Neutrality', in Loveland (ed.) *infra.*

Gatenby, J. (1973) 'More Bother in Bognor' 36 *Modern LR* 307

Ghandi, S. and James, J. (1998) The English Law of Blasphemy and the European Convention on Human Rights' *European Human Rights Review* 430

Harris, D., O'Boyle, M. and Warbrick, C. (1995) *Law of the European Convention on Human Rights* (London: Butterworths)

Hooper, D. (1986) *Public Scandal, Odium and Contempt* (London: Coronet)

Hunt, M. (1997) *Using Human Rights Law in English Courts* (Oxford: Hart Publishing)

Irons, P. (1990) *The Courage of Their Convictions* (Los Angeles: University of California Press)

Janis, M., Kay, R. and Bradley, A. (1995) *European Human Rights Law* (Oxford: Clarendon Press)

Kalven, H. (1964) 'The New York Times Case: a Note on the Central Meaning of the First Amendment' *Supreme Court Review* 191

—— (1967) 'The Reasonable Man and the First Amendment: Hill, Butts and Walker' *Supreme Court Review* 267

Kennet, G. (1994) 'Individual Rights, the High Court and the Constitution' 19 *Melbourne LR* 581

Kirby, J. (1988) 'The Role of the Judge In Advancing Human Rights Norms' *The Australian LJ* 514

Laws, J. (1988) 'Meiklejohn, the First Amendment and Free Speech in English Law', in Loveland (ed.) *infra.*

Leopold, P. (1994) 'Free Speech in Parliament' 15 *Legal Studies* 204

Levy, L. (1985) *Emergence of a Free Press* (Cambridge, Mass: Harvard UP)

—— (1987) 'Introduction', in Levy, L. (ed.), *The Making of the Constitution* (Cambridge, Mass: Harvard UP)

Lewis, A. (1991) *Make No Law* (New York: Vintage Books)

Lloyd, D. (1952) 'Reform of the Law of Libel' *Current Legal Problems* 168

Loveland, I. (ed) (1995) *A Special Relationship ?* (Oxford: Clarendon Press)

—— (1996) *Constitutional Law* (London: Butterworths)

—— (1997) 'An Agenda for the Constitutionalisation of Libel Law', in Birks, P. (ed.), *Privacy and Loyalty* (Oxford: Clarendon Press)

—— (ed.) (1998) *Importing the First Amendment* (Oxford: Hart Publishing)

—— (1998) 'A Free Trade in Ideas—and Outcomes', in Loveland (ed.) *supra.*

—— (1998) '*City of Chicago v Tribune Co*—in Contexts', in Loveland (ed) *supra.*

—— (1999) *By Due Process of Law? Racial Discrimination and the Right to Vote in South Africa 1850–1960* (Oxford: Hart Publishing)

—— (2000) '*Reynolds v Times Newspapers* in the House of Lords' *Public Law* (forthcoming)

Markesinis, B. and Deakin, S. (1994 2nd ed) *Tort Law* (Oxford: Clarendon Press)

Marshall, G. (1994) 'Impugning Parliamentary Impunity' *Public Law* 509

Marston, G. (1993) 'The United Kingdom's Part in the Preparation of the European Convention on Human Rights' 42 *International and Comparative Law Quarterly* 796

Mason, A. (1988) 'The Australian Constitution 1901–1908' 62 *Australian LJ* 256

McEwen, R. and Lewis, P. (1967 6th ed) *Gatley on Libel and Slander* (London: Sweet and Maxwell)

McGregor, H. (1988 15th ed) *McGregor on Damages* (London: Sweet and Maxwell)

Meiklejohn, A. (1961) The First Amendment Is an Absolute' *Supreme Court Review* 245

Nimmer, M. (1969) 'The Right to Speak From *Times* to *Time*' 56 *California LR* 935

Note (1923) 'Torts—Power of a Municipal Corporation to Sue for Libel' 21 *Michigan LR* 915

Note (1923) 'Libel and Slander—Suit by Municipal Corporation' 23 *Columbia LR* 685

Note, (1929) 'Libel and Slander—Municipal Corporations' 28 *Michigan LR* 460.

Rabban, D. (1988) 'The Original Meaning of the Free Speech Clause of the First Amendment', in Simmons, R. (ed.), *The US Constitution: the First Two Hundred Years* (Manchester: Manchester UP)

Rogers, W. (1984 12th ed) *Winfield and Jolowicz on Tort* (London: Sweet and Maxwell)

Rubinstein, D. (1984) *Wicked, Wicked Libels* (Harmondsworth: Penguin)

Sedley, S. (1995) 'Human Rights: a Twenty-First Century Agenda' *Public Law* 386

—— (1998) 'The First Amendment: a Case For Import Controls', in Loveland (ed.) *supra.*

Smolla, R. (1986) *Suing the Press* (Oxford: OUP)

—— (1988) *Jerry Falwell v Larry Flint* (Urbana, Ill: University of Illinois Press)

Spencer, Bower G. (1908) *The Law of Actionable Defamation* (London: Sweet and Maxwell)

Tench, D. and McDermott, J. (1996) 'The Radical Change in Assessment of Libel Awards by Juries: Elton John v MGN Limited' *Communications Law* 17

Thompson, J. (1995) 'Slouching Towards Tenterfield: the Constitutionalisation of Tort Law in Australia' *Tort LR* 81

Tierney, S. (1998) 'Press Freedom and Public Interest' *European Human Rights Review* 419

Todd, E. (1953) 'The Defamation Act (1952) 15 *Modern LR* 198

Tushnett, M. (1995) *Making Civil Rights Law* (Oxford: Clarendon Press)

Van Veeden, Vechter (1903) 'The History and Theory of the Law of Defamation I' 3 *Columbia LR* 546

—— (1904) 'The History and Theory of the Law of Defamation II' 4 *Columbia LR* 33

Warbrick, C. (1998) 'Federalism and Free Speech', in Loveland (ed.) *supra*.

Weaver, R. and Bennet, G. (1993) 'Is the New York Times "Actual Malice" Standard Really Necessary? A Comparative Perspective' *Louisiana LR* 1153

Wechsler, H. (1959) 'Towards Neutral Principles of Constitutional Law' 73 *Harvard LR* 1

Weir, A. (1972) 'Local Authority v Critical Ratepayer—a Suit in Defamation' — *Cambridge LJ* 238

Williams, G. (1991) 'Engineers Is Dead: Long Live the Engineers' 17 *Sydney LR* 62

Index

Absolute privilege:
  basic scope, 11–12
  judicial proceedings, 5–6
  parliamentary proceedings, 5–6, 26–8, 36,
    158–159
'Actual malice' in *Sullivan,* 70–1
  and appointed officials in US, 73–4
  and issues of public interest in US, 74–6,
    82–3
  and political candidates in US, 77–8
  subjective or objective test, 78–82
Aitken, Jonathan, 1
Al-Fayed, Mohammed, 1
Allason, Rupert, 2, 159
Australia:
  constitutional structure, 133–4
  constitutional limits on libel law, 136–46
  common law limits on libel law, 147–50,
    183–4

Bingham, Lord, 130–2, 165–9
Brennan J (American), 67–75, 105, 163
Brennan J (Australian), 142–3, 145–7

Cockburn CJ, 24–33, 52, 61, 97–98
  influence on American common law, 37–9
Chilling effect:
  in *Sullivan,* 69–71
  empirical basis in UK, 183
  empirical basis in US, 85
Common law:
  dynamic understanding, 28, 92–3
  English influence in US law, 37–41, 83–5
  static understanding, 23, 51–2
  in American states, 37–50, 64–5
  in Australia, 136–8, 147–50, 183–1
  in Ceylon, 55–7
  in New Zealand, 61–3, 99–101, 156–7
Criminal libel:
  basic scope, 14
  in USA, 37–8, 70
  under ECHR, 106–14, 153–6

Denman CJ, 20–3
Damages:
  Australian common law, 134–6
  availability of punitive damages, 13–14,
    88–92
  basic scope , 13–14
  guidance on quantum, 88–9, 115–17, 125–32
  and First Amendment, 80–3

impact of ECHR on English law, 88–92

Fair comment
  basic scope, 12–13, 57, 58–9, 146
Faulks Committee, 100–1

Guardian, The, 1, 174
Greene, Lord, 51–4

Hamilton, Neil, 1, 156–7

Judicial proceedings:
  not actionable in libel, 5–6
Justification, 7–8, 57

Keith, Lord, 120–4

Lester, Anthony:
  as counsel in *Derbyshire*, 117–20
  as counsel in *Reynolds*, 165–70
  as counsel in *Tolstoy*, 128–9
  opposes Defamation Bill 1996, 158–9
Libellous publication:
  meaning of, 4
Local authorities:
  capacity to sue in libel in England, 34–5,
    93–4, 117–23
  capacity to sue in libel in USA, 46–8

Malicious falsehood:
  basic scope, 15–16
  as alternative to libel, 121–2
Mason CJ, 134–46

Negligence as standard of fault, 24–6, 44–5,
  100, 146–9, 154, 183–4
Nicholls, Lord, 169–74

Parliamentary proceedings:
  and absolute privilege, 26–8, 36
  and freedom of expression, 19–20, 21–3,
    158–9
  and qualified privilege, 27–30, 92–3
  not actionable in libel, 5–6
Pearson J, 59–61, 64, 157
'Political information':
  nineteenth century English ideas, 23–7, 32–4
  nineteenth century American ideas, 37–50
  twentieth century English ideas, 52–4, 57–8,
    59–61, 94–7, 167–74
  twentieth century American ideas, 66–85

'Political information' (*cont.*):
  under Australian law, 136–7, 148–1
  under ECHR Article 10, 105–14, 153–6
Political parties
  capacity to sue in libel in England, 123–4

Qualified privilege:
  basic scope, 8–10
  and election pamphlets, 52–4, 56–7, 63–4
  and parliamentary proceedings, 27–30, 92–3
  and 'political information', 164–74
  and speeches in council meetings, 95–6
  and trade unions, 54–5
Slander:
  basic scope, 15

distinguished from libel, 15
  speeches in council meetings, 95
Sullivan v *New York Times*, 67–72
  misrepresentation in English law, 116, 118–19, 165, 173–4
  use in Australian law, 134–8
Sunday Times, The
  and *Derbyshire*, 2, 117–23
  and *Reynolds*, 163–174

Times, The
  and *Wason* v *Walter*, 27–30

Wechsler, Herbert, 66–7